LEARNING

LEARNING

A Survey of Psychological Interpretations

Fourth Edition

Winfred F. Hill
Northwestern University

1817

HARPER & ROW, PUBLISHERS, New York
Cambridge, Philadelphia, San Francisco,
London, Mexico City, São Paulo, Singapore, Sydney

Sponsoring Editor: Susan Mackey
Project Editor: B. Pelner
Cover Design: Wanda Lubelska/Wanda Siedlecka
Text Art: Fine Line Illustrations, Inc.
Production: Willie Lane
Compositor: ComCom Division of Haddon Craftsmen, Inc.
Printer and Binder: R. R. Donnelley & Sons Company

Learning: A Survey of Psychological Interpretations, Fourth Edition

  87 9 8 7 6 5 4

Library of Congress Cataloging in Publication Data

Hill, Winfred F.
  Learning: a survey of psychological interpretations.

  Bibliography: p.
  Includes index.
  1. Learning, Psychology of. I. Title.
LB1051.H524 1985   153.1'5   84-15679
ISBN 0-06-042818-X

To my father
a devoted educator

And my mother
whose experience in education
helped her to educate me

Contents

Preface

This edition maintains the same approach as earlier editions, focusing on the development of learning theory and on issues of long-term learning and of motivation rather than of short-term information processing. This approach is enhanced by two additions: (1) Pavlovian conditioning, which has become increasingly prominent in recent years, receives more attention, with new sections on Pavlov's own work and on Wagner and Rescorla's conditioning model. (2) There is a separate chapter on motivation, including a new section on Solomon and Corbit's opponent-process model, an expanded section on cybernetics as a model for purposive behavior at all levels from simple movement to life goal, and previous material on alternative interpretations of reinforcement.

At the same time, the increasing prominence of cognitive models is recognized in a number of ways. The former chapter on cognitive theories is now two chapters, and includes an expanded treatment of computer problem solving. The topic of memory has been expanded to a full chapter, with new treatments of the Atkinson and Shiffrin three-stores model, depth of processing, and memory schemata. The treatment of Bandura, regarded as a link between cognitive theory and more traditional behaviorism, has been expanded. There is an explicit contrast of Lewin's and Skinner's alternative approaches to lawfulness in the single case as they would apply in a counseling situation. The final chapter provides a checklist of issues on which learning theories differ, as a basis for considering what the properties of an ideal theory would be.

Although the additions have been balanced to a small degree by deletion of some details from older theories, there is still somewhat more material than in the previous edition. This fact reflects my conviction that as new theories appear, old ones still maintain their relevance, not only for putting the newer ones in historical perspective but also for providing alternatives ways of analyzing specific learning situations and developing practical interventions. Though the detailed study of learning is a cumulative science, there is still a good deal of art in its application, hence an acquaintance with alternative interpretations is a valuable resource.

As the above suggests, the book is designed for students both of psychology and education. It can be used as the primary text in a course on principles of learning and motivation, as a co-principal text in a general learning course, or as a supplementary reading in a variety of courses, including general experimental, developmental, principles of instruction, or history and systems. However used, the book is designed to offer students both a cognitive understanding of various theoretical approaches to learning and a basis for modifying their behavior in situations relevant to learning.

WINFRED F. HILL

LEARNING

chapter 1

Understanding and Explaining Learning

Theoretical systems for the interpretation of learning have grown up along with the experimental study of learning, and to understand one it is necessary to understand the other. Although the experimental study of learning to a large extent grew out of everyday problems, particularly problems in education, it soon became involved with theoretical issues and with experiments appropriate for dealing with them. This theoretical involvement proceeded to such an extent that the original problems became barely recognizable. It is therefore worthwhile to take a long look at the interrelations among theory, research, and applications in the field of learning before undertaking a detailed survey of different theoretical systems.

The reader should be warned at the outset that psychologists use the term "learning" more broadly than it is used in popular speech. While it is almost impossible to give an exact definition of learning that will be generally acceptable to psychologists, we can at least note certain phenomena to which the term is or is not applied. In psychological usage, what is learned need not be "correct" or adaptive (we learn bad habits as well as good), need not be conscious or deliberate (one of the advantages of coaching in a skill is that it makes us aware of mistakes we have unconsciously learned to make), and need not involve any overt act (attitudes and emotions can be learned as well as knowledge and skills). Reactions as diverse as driving a car, remembering a pleasant vacation, believing in democracy, and disliking one's boss all represent the results of learning.

How does learning take place? What factors determine what we will learn and how rapidly we will learn it? There are innumerable people in situations in which it would be useful to have answers to these questions. We think at once

1

of students looking for better methods of study, of teachers wanting to improve their classroom techniques, and of people in industry seeking better ways of training new workers. We may also consider the mother looking for the best way of raising her children, the counselor trying to improve a client's emotional and social adjustment, the animal trainer preparing seeing-eye dogs for their work, and the advertiser attempting to develop a consumer's preference for a client's product. In all of these cases, knowledge about the learning process represents power.

The above practical needs are not the only reasons for wanting to know more about learning. People have always been curious about themselves, have always wanted to know more about what "makes them tick." Since learning is such an important factor in what we are and do, a greater understanding of the learning process would go far toward increasing self-knowledge. Consequently, people are motivated to study learning, not only by the practical benefits to be gained but also by curiosity about themselves and how they came to be as they are.

LEARNING IN SCHOOL

Our discussion begins by looking at a setting in which learning is the primary focus: the school. Children in school face a bewilderingly complex learning situation. It is complex from their point of view; it is even more so from the point of view of the psychologist who bravely attempts to analyze it. The children are influenced in countless ways by the varied aspects of the classroom situation. They learn much from the teacher, including many things not prescribed in the curriculum and some things of which neither teacher nor pupils are aware. They also learn from books, from fellow students, and from the physical arrangements of the school. Part of what they learn is measurable as specific knowledge and skills, while another part involves changes, some very subtle but a few quite dramatic, in attitudes, emotions, social behavior, and a variety of other reactions. The psychologist's job is to analyze such complex situations into their component parts and to try to understand the principles of learning and motivation involved.

Let us consider some incidents in the school day of a particular sixth-grader, Alex B. We meet Alex first as he is studying a vocabulary list in his reading book. His teacher (a trifle old-fashioned) has instructed the class to learn to spell these words. He is thus confronted with a list of 12 words for which he must learn to give the correct written form when presented with the spoken form. However, in studying from his book he faces a slightly different task, since only the written form is before him and he must provide the spoken version (subvocally) himself. He goes through the list, pronouncing and spelling the words to himself, but finds his attention wandering. He looks out the window and remembers how much he enjoyed the previous weekend. Snapping back to the spelling book, he continues dutifully to the end of the list. Then he tries covering all but the first letter of each word with his hand in an attempt to spell the word to himself. At "r" he proceeds cautiously, trying to remember the rule for "i" and "e." Finally he decides on "receive," moves his hand away, and relaxes a bit as he finds his guess confirmed. At "s" he spells to himself without hesitation, "seperate," then frowns as he sees his mistake. He stares for a moment at the "ar," trying to fix it in his memory, then continues through the list. Halfway through, he finds himself unable to remember a word from the first letter.

Annoyed, he looks at the word and then concentrates heavily on trying to remember it. Two words later, the same thing happens again. He looks at the word, wonders why it should be hard to remember, and begins to feel discouraged. He stares at the picture on the wall of Washington crossing the Delaware, and imagines himself leading such an expedition. Catching the teacher's eye, he returns quickly to his book and finishes the list. He spells the last word confidently, "cematary," only to find "cemetery" staring back at him from the page. Puzzled, he looks back and forth from "separate" to "cemetery" and thinks, "I hate spelling."

We see Alex next at recess running excitedly out to join a softball game. He begins the game in the outfield. As the batter hits a ground ball in his direction, he starts running, his speed and direction adjusted to make his path intercept that of the ball. As he nears the ball he bends over, puts his hands in front of it, and closes them at just the right moment to catch the ball. He then looks up, notes the position of the runner, and throws the ball in the direction of first base, his arm motion just forceful enough to carry the ball to the first baseman. This whole sequence of coordinated, purposeful behavior occurs rapidly, almost automatically, with no evidence of thought or verbal self-instruction. Watching him, the teacher is impressed by how much Alex has improved at softball since she has known him.

During the game, Alex calls frequently, "Wait'll I get to bat!" and "When'm I up?" Finally his turn comes. He pounds the plate and shouts, "Put it over!" When the pitcher throws the ball, Alex takes a mighty swing at it, and misses. He looks chagrined, but shouts, "Let's have another!" Again he swings and misses. This time he frowns and says nothing. He stands more rigidly at the plate, his teeth clenched. His swing at the third pitch is more tense, less free, and again he misses. He throws the bat down and stalks away. At his next turn in the outfield, he does no shouting, and his fielding is less coordinated. When recess ends, he returns quietly to the classroom, ignoring the chatter around him. He seems relieved that recess is over.

Later we see Alex during his math lesson. The class has been learning how to find the areas of rectangles. Now the teacher raises the problem of how to find the area of a triangle. She draws a right triangle with a 4 in. side and a 3 in. side on the blackboard and asks the students what the area is. Alex likes math and enjoys learning how to solve new problems, so he eagerly tries to figure this one out. He tries to apply the rule for rectangles, but cannot see how to do it. Then the teacher draws two more lines, making a rectangle with the hypotenuse of the triangle as its diagonal. Alex stares at this for a moment, then grins and excitedly holds up his hand. "The area is 6. The whole rectangle is 12, and there are two triangles, and each triangle is half of the rectangle!" The teacher smiles. "Very good. The area is half of 4 times 3. Math makes a lot of sense when you figure it out like that." Alex basks in his success, pleased both with the teacher's approval and with his triumph over the impersonal challenge of the problem.

We leave Alex now, happy that a rather frustrating day for him has ended with success. However, the challenge to a psychologist to analyze Alex's experiences lasts long after the incidents are over. In fact, the narrative of Alex's day might be used as a hidden-picture puzzle: "How many aspects of learning can you find illustrated in these incidents?" Consider, for example, the similarities and differences among the three situations in which we saw Alex. All involved learning, motivation, goal-directed behavior, and success or failure. All could be analyzed in terms of the responses that Alex made to various stimuli in his environment, and also in terms of the way he perceived the environment. All occurred in social situations and against a background of norms and values shared (though not completely) by Alex, his teacher, and his fellow students. However, the three situations differed in the principal kinds of learning involved (verbal memorization of the spelling list, motor skill on the softball field, and logical insight in the math problem). The situations also differed in the emotional learning that occurred and in some of the subsidiary principles. In each situation we may ask what factors contributed to Alex's successes and failures. How much did his difficulty in spelling "cemetery," for example, depend on the word itself, on its position in the list, on the fact that "separate" came earlier in the same lesson, on distractions in the room at that moment, or on a variety of other facts about Alex, the lesson, and the general situation? There are endless possibilities for the psychologist to analyze in these three everyday situations.

However, such analysis assumes that we already know a great deal about the principles of learning. In cases where a number of factors might have influenced Alex's behavior, we cannot make worthwhile guesses about how important each was unless we have information about how important each has been in other similar situations. For example, we cannot judge whether the word "cemetery" itself or the situation in which Alex encountered it contributed more to his error unless we know something about the relative importance of words and their context in other cases of memorization. It is to provide such information about the regularities in behavior that we do experimental studies. If we know from such studies that certain situations cause special difficulty in memorizing, we are in a much better position both to explain Alex's errors and to find ways of helping him.

LEARNING IN THE LABORATORY

Let us now look at some typical laboratory learning situations. As compared with Alex's experiences, some of these may appear artificial or trivial. This difference is the price we pay in order to have situations in which we can manipulate certain variables, hold others constant, and measure precisely the resultant changes in behavior. We will see many relations between the complex situations in which Alex learned and these simpler, better controlled, laboratory learning situations.

Two Complex Learning Situations

In the first laboratory situation, as in Alex's math lesson, the learner (commonly called the subject) is presented with a problem for which he must find a solution. A traditional problem for use with college students requires the subject to tie together two strings hanging from the ceiling. The strings are so far apart that when he holds one, he cannot reach the other, which is why this otherwise easy task constitutes a problem. The only equipment available to help him do the job is a pair of pliers. Can he find a way of tying the string together? (There need not be an actual room with two strings; problem and solution can all be given with pencil and paper.)

What commonly happens in this situation is that the subject tries a variety of approaches, all unsuccessful. The pliers might be used as an extension of his arm to reach the second string, but they are too short. It might be possible to cut a piece off one of the strings and tie it to the other, but the two strings could still not be brought together. Finally the thought of swinging the strings occurs to most people. Given this lead, the solution usually comes quickly: tie the pliers to one of the strings, start the string swinging as a pendulum, then run over to the other string, bring it as close as possible to the one that is swinging, and catch the swinging one at the closest point of its arc. Since the subject is now holding both strings, he can easily tie them together.

How does this laboratory problem differ from the geometric problem that Alex solved in the classroom? In principle, there is very little difference. Both have simple solutions drawing on the solver's past experience, but both are difficult because they require the use of this past experience in new ways. The solution in each case usually involves a period of futile search followed by a flash of insight. A hint, such as the two extra lines the teacher drew, or the word "pendulum" in the two-string problem, often results in quick solution of the problem. The ability to tie the strings or compute the area not only appears suddenly but is also very well retained as compared with most other learned material.

The important difference is not between the two problems but between the classroom and the laboratory. In the classroom case, we do not know how soon (if at all) Alex would have solved the problem without the teacher's hint, or why Alex rather than another student solved it first, or how many other students would have found the solution if he had not beaten them to it, or how the presence of other students helped or hindered him. In the laboratory, on the other hand, all of these questions can be systematically studied. The problem can be presented to subjects singly or in groups, with hints at predetermined points, and each person's time to solution (and mistaken "solutions") recorded. This laboratory situation makes it possible to investigate two sets of factors—those in the situation and those in the individual—that contribute to this learning.

Another laboratory example, closer to the popular image of a learning situation, involves rote memorization. The items to be memorized are commonly either words or trigrams (three-letter sequences that do not make a word), but they may be sentences or longer passages of connected material. The task may be to learn a series of them in order (as would be the case in learning a series of instructions), or to remember as many as possible of the items regardless of order (as for remembering a number of jobs that need to be done), or to learn a number of pairs of items with one member of the pair always given as the response to the other (comparable to learning a foreign language vocabulary), or any of various other possibilities. Usually the rate at which the items are presented to the learner is controlled by the experimenter, such as by presenting them on the screen of a computer terminal.

The contrast between such a learning task and Alex's spelling lesson is again largely in the precision of control that the laboratory setup permits. Alex could approach the words to be learned in any order and divide his time among them in any way he chose. Moreover, he had to study from a book, even though the test of his mastery would consist of writing the words in response to oral dictation. This difference forced him to devise techniques of practice that would as nearly as possible match the test procedure. Finally, he was subjected to the distractions of the classroom situations. The laboratory subject, on the other hand, commonly sees the items in a predetermined order and for constant amounts of time in a small room with a minimum of distractions. Often the subject is automatically tested on each item each time through the list, so there is a continuous record of mastery of each item at each stage in the learning. This record makes possible separate analyses of different stages of learning, different parts of the list, and different individual items.

Three Simpler Learning Situations

Both the problem-solving and the rote-learning situations in the laboratory represent refinements of learning situations found in the classroom and elsewhere in everyday life outside the laboratory. However, many psychological experimenters analyze these and other examples of learning (e.g., Alex's learning of the motor skills involved in fielding a softball) into simpler components and then study these components separately. Rather than working with complex patterns of responses such as Alex learned, they study changes in the frequency or magnitude or speed of a single response. Their object is not to study everyday kinds of learning under better-controlled conditions, but to study the underlying components of everyday learning in order to get a better understanding of what learning is. Such understanding, it is hoped, can then be used to predict learning in a great variety of more complex situations. This approach is comparable to that in other sciences, where complex chemical substances are analyzed into their component elements, or where the speed of a falling object is studied as a function of the distance it has fallen, without regard to whether the object is a mailbag, a skydiver before the parachute opens, or a hydrogen bomb.

Since research of this sort attempts to reduce learning to its assumed simplest essentials, animals have often been found more satisfactory subjects than humans. Animals lack the complexities of language and cultural traditions, their background of previous experience is both simpler and (at least if they are reared in the laboratory) less variable than that of humans, and their heredity as well as their rearing can to a considerable extent be controlled. All of these factors make it easier to study one aspect of the animal's learning processes at a time while holding others constant. For example, if we want to study the rate at which a dog learns to flex his leg to avoid an electric shock, we probably do not have to worry about his interpretation of the purpose of the experiment or about his concern with behaving bravely, politely, or rationally, all of which would be factors if we were studying the same behavior in humans. This is not to say that humans cannot usefully be studied in such situations, for they often are; but it points out why for certain purposes animals often are preferred.

The above discussion implies that it does not make much difference what species we study—that the basic laws of learning are the same in rats, dogs, pigeons, monkeys, and humans. Learning theorists have indeed commonly made that assumption. The emphasis here is on the word "basic." No one doubts that there are differences in the way different species learn, but it is often assumed that there are common underlying principles that apply to a wide range of species, principles from which we can deduce the detailed patterns of learning in different species. We will have more to say about this assumption in Chapter 11, but for the present it is enough to note how important the assumption has been in learning theory over the years. We will see many examples of its application in the chapters that follow.

One simple animal response that has been extensively studied is the pecking response in pigeons. A lighted disk is displayed on the side of the box in which the pigeon is confined. The disk is referred to as a key, since like a telegraph key it closes an electrical circuit to record the pigeon's response, and the whole apparatus is known as a Skinner box, in honor of the theorist we will consider in Chapter 4. If a hungry pigeon is occasionally rewarded with food for pecking the key, it will peck it at a high rate. This pecking rate is quite sensitive to changes in level of hunger, frequency of food reward, and other variables. It can thus be used to investigate many of the phenomena of simple learning.

The low rate at which the pigeon pecks before food is introduced is called the *operant* (or *baseline*) *rate.* When food is first presented as soon as the pigeon pecks the key, the rate of pecking rises. In technical terms, this change indicates that the food *reinforces* the pecking, or that it is a *reinforcer.* If some but not all pecks are followed by food, the particular pattern used (e.g., food after every tenth peck, or after one peck each minute) is known as the *schedule of reinforcement.* If pecking is no longer followed by food, the rate drops. This decline in rate resulting from the removal of the reinforcer is known as *extinction.* If after extinction takes place there is an interval of time during which the pigeon does not have access to the key, and then the key is presented again, the pecking rate is likely to be higher than it was at the end of extinction. This increase in rate is called, naturally enough, *spontaneous recovery.* If a key that the pigeon has been reinforced for pecking is replaced by another key of a different color, the pigeon will peck at this key also, though not as much as at the original one. This tendency to respond to stimuli other than the one used in training is known as *general-ization.* If, however, the two keys are presented alternately, with pecking at one reinforced and pecking at the other nonreinforced (extinguished), the pigeon will learn to peck the reinforced key at a high rate and the nonreinforced key very little. We then say that a *discrimination* between the keys has been formed.

Many aspects of the above learning phenomena have been studied experimentally. How does the rate of pecking vary with the amount of food given, the schedule of reinforcement, or the delay between peck and food? How does spontaneous recovery vary with the time interval between extinction and test, or generalization vary with the difference in color between the two keys? Will making a pigeon more hungry increase or decrease his ability to form a discrimination? Questions of this sort may be studied, not only with regard to the rate of key-pecking in pigeons, but with regard to many other forms of behavior in a variety of species.

These learning phenomena, established in experimental studies, can be applied (though often with some modification) to complex learning in everyday life. Though we did not see Alex over a long enough period of time to observe the effects of reinforcement and extinction in his behavior, we can note a number of cases where these processes were probably occurring for him. His statement about the area of the triangle was reinforced by the teacher's praise, his techniques of fielding the softball by the approval of his fellow players, and his correct spellings by seeing his spellings confirmed by the printed words. On the other hand, his incorrect spellings, his batting techniques, and his confident manner with regard to batting were not reinforced and hence presumably underwent some extinction. The disappearance of his confident shouting after he struck out might be taken as evidence of extinction. If the shouting reappeared at his next softball game, this renewal could be interpreted as spontaneous recovery. The problem of spelling "separate" with an "ar" and "cemetery" with an "er" clearly involved making a discrimination between two similar situations, and it might also be interpreted as extinguishing the tendency to spell phonetically.

Not only can we identify these learning processes operating in everyday life; we can also make predictions from learning experiments to everyday learning situations. For example, it is commonly found in experiments that a delay between the response and the reinforcer results in poorer performance of the learned response. From this finding we could make predictions about the efficacy of different teaching methods. If Alex had taken a spelling quiz on one day but had not found out which words he got right until the papers were handed back the next day, he probably would have learned less spelling than he did with his book, because of the delay of reinforcement. However, it is possible that the opposite might be true, either because correctness on a graded test is more reinforcing than correctness on a private self-test, or because writing from dictation is a better way of studying spelling, or for a variety of other reasons. This example thus points up both the usefulness of laboratory study in making suggestions about everyday learning and the danger in taking such suggestions uncritically.

A fourth example of laboratory learning, and one even less like the ordinary picture of a learning situation, occurs in experiments on *classical condition-*

ing. The first of these, and still the most famous, were those in which the Russian physiologist Ivan Pavlov used the procedure to train dogs to salivate. Another version of this procedure (less famous than Pavlov's salivating dogs, but more popular in American labs) is the conditioning of the eye-blink reflex in humans. If a person who is watching a dim light sees the light grow somewhat brighter, he ordinarily does not blink his eyes in response to this stimulus. If, however, he is hit in the eye by a mild puff of air, he does blink. The conditioning procedure consists in pairing these two stimuli, with the brightening of the light coming a fraction of a second before the puff of air. Each time this sequence occurs, the subject blinks in response to the air puff. Presently, however, he begins to blink as soon as the light changes, before the puff comes. Since the changing light now produces a blinking response which it formerly did not produce, learning is said to have taken place. In this setup the puff, which already produced blinking, is called the *unconditioned stimulus,* and blinking to the puff is the *unconditioned response.* The increase in brightness of the light is called the *conditioned stimulus,* and the learned response of blinking to it is the *conditioned response.* The whole learning sequence is known as *conditioning.* The same principles of reinforcement, extinction, spontaneous recovery, generalization, and discrimination that were illustrated by the pigeon pecking a key can also be demonstrated in classical conditioning situations.

The distinctive characteristic of this kind of learning is that the conditioned stimulus elicits a response after the learning experience that only the unconditioned stimulus elicited before. (Because some authorities use the term "conditioning" rather broadly, the adjective "classical" is often added to "conditioning" to make clear that this form of learning is meant.) Since classical conditioning does not involve learning new responses, solving problems, or carrying out goal-directed activity, it seems at first glance to be of little importance compared to the other forms of learning so far discussed. Some theorists have concurred in this judgment, regarding classical conditioning as nothing more than a laboratory curiosity. Others, as we shall see, have regarded it as being of central importance. One viewpoint is that its importance is mainly for understanding the learning of emotional reactions. When Alex experienced failures at spelling and at batting, he reacted with discouragement and anger. These can be considered unconditioned responses to the unconditioned stimulus of failure. When he said, "I hate spelling," this opinion may have indicated that conditioning was taking place, with the spelling lesson as the conditioned stimulus and discouragement and anger as the conditioned response. This interpretation makes classical conditioning of emotional responses crucial to our learning of attitudes toward all the people, objects, and situations we encounter in our lives.

A fifth and final laboratory example of learning is in the *maze.* The principles involved in maze learning are similar to those in the key-pecking experiments already mentioned, but the maze has been used so widely in learning experiments that it deserves separate mention. The original mazes were modeled after the Hampton Court maze in England, where tall hedges formed an intricate pattern of winding pathways through which visitors tried to find their way. Miniature versions of this maze were used to study the ways in which both humans and animals learned to avoid the many blind alleys and find the correct path from the starting point to the goal. Over the years mazes have become simpler and simpler as psychologists tried to find the basic principles involved in learning them. The winding pathways of the Hampton Court maze have been replaced by alleys with a simple series of left and right turns. Even these, however, have been considered too complicated, and have been largely replaced with "mazes" in which there is only a single choice to be made, between a right and a left turn. Because of their shape, these are known as T-mazes. These are too easy to be useful with humans, but are widely used with animals. The learner (typically a well-domesticated white rat) runs along the stem of the T and then enters one of the arms. If he chooses the correct one, he finds food at the end of the arm. If he chooses the incorrect one, there is no food. The rate at which he learns to choose the correct side can be studied in relation to the amount of food he gets, how hungry he is, and other more complex variables. Finally, even the one choice point may be eliminated, leaving only a straight runway. Here one can study only how fast the animal runs and whether he runs at all. Simple as it is, the runway has proved valuable for studying many aspects of reinforcement, extinction, and even discrimination.

Advantages of Laboratory Study

The preceding examples should have helped to indicate the relations between the sorts of learning situations studied in the laboratory and those of most interest to educators and to others directly concerned with the problems of learning in everyday life. However, it may be well to discuss certain aspects of the relationships more explicitly. Two main points need to be considered: (1) what psychologists gain by studying learning under the somewhat artificial conditions of the laboratory, and (2) what difficulties are involved in applying the results to other, nonlaboratory, situations.

There are two main ways in which psychologists gain by taking questions about learning into the laboratory. One of these pertains to *measurement*. The laboratory situation permits experimenters to measure the subject's behavior more adequately than is usually possible outside the laboratory. They can keep an accurate record of how long it takes a subject to memorize certain material or to solve a given problem, of how many and what kind of errors a subject makes, and of the successive stages by which mastery is reached. This improved measurement is valuable for three reasons. First, it gives a more complete picture of the learning process. Details are recorded that otherwise would be overlooked or quickly forgotten. Second, it protects researchers from the mistake of noticing and remembering only what they expect. Thus a teacher who is convinced that a certain new method of teaching long division will work better than the old method may remember clearly striking successes with the new method, while overlooking the failures as unimportant exceptions. It is possible, of course, that in this case the failures *are* unimportant exceptions, but whether or not they are should be decided by careful consideration, not by spur-of-the-moment intuition. If both successes and failures are recorded as they occur, and if extenuating circumstances are noted for the successes as well as for the failures, the effect of teaching with the new method can be more objectively evaluated. Third, apart from such systematic biases as this teacher has, careful measurement also protects researchers against all the unsystematic errors of observation and memory that are likely to occur when research is carried on as part of everyday work. Thus measurement in the laboratory will probably be more thorough, more precise, and more objective than measurement in comparable situations elsewhere. Although in principle it is possible to achieve equally good measurement outside the laboratory, in practice it is usually much harder to do so.

The other gain from studying learning in the lab is in *control.* Essentially, this gain is associated with our ability to study one thing at a time. When we control a variable, we hold it constant so that it will not interfere with our studying another variable. Suppose, for example, that we want to find out whether it is easier to learn spelling when words that are likely to cause confusion with one another (e.g., "separate" and "cemetery") are in the same lesson or in different lessons. We can study this problem by preparing two sets of lessons, one according to each principle, and using them with two sets of students. However, we must see to it that the two sets of students do not differ in intelligence, interest in spelling, previous experience with these words, or motivation to do well in their studies. We must also see that the groups are taught by teachers who do not differ in teaching ability or in enthusiasm. In other words, we must control intelligence, motivation, and all the other above variables except arrangement of the words in the spelling lessons. Only then can we be confident that any difference we find in mastery of the spelling lessons is due to arrangement of the words rather than to some other difference between the two sets of students. Because the practical demands of the classroom make it difficult to obtain such control, or even to know whether one has obtained it, it is valuable to have laboratories specially arranged for doing well-controlled experiments.

Though laboratory studies of learning provide great advantages in measurement and in control, we must not suppose that they provide easy answers to questions about the practical management of learning. Because they typically study single variables out of their usual context, laboratory experiments can seldom give direct answers to questions about how these variables work together in that context. For example, it has been established in a number of experiments that larger reinforcers lead to better performance in a learning situation. Does it follow that the more lavishly a teacher praises students for their successes, the better the students will do their work? Perhaps, but there are various reasons why this result might not follow. The students might become so used to this effusive praise that it would soon be no more reinforcing to them than mild praise would be to other students. Or, perhaps, those who failed to win the praise might be all the more frustrated because the praise they missed was so desirable, which might result in more disappointment and anger becoming conditioned as responses to the stimuli of the whole situation. Moreover, neither the reinforcers nor the learning tasks used in the laboratory are likely to be the same ones used in the classroom (in fact, many of the studies on reinforcement magnitude were done with animals); this kind of difference will probably make the outcomes different in degree, and possibly in kind. Finally, even if the subjects, tasks, and reinforcers are all similar in the laboratory and in the classroom, the difference between working alone in an unfamiliar situation (the laboratory) and working in a familiar group situation (the classroom) may produce considerable differences in behavior. For all of these reasons we would be rash to generalize directly and confidently from the laboratory studies to the classroom application. However, the laboratory studies, in addition to providing basic knowledge about the processes of learning, suggest many possible applications to the classroom and to other applied settings.

VARIABLES, LAWS, AND THE PROCESS OF ABSTRACTION

Researchers in the field of learning, like those in any other branch of science, are concerned with discovering scientific *laws*. All the experimental procedures we have discussed are directed toward such discovery. A law is a statement about the conditions under which certain things occur. Some laws are highly precise and accurate, as in the physicist's statement that the period of a pendulum is proportional to the square root of its length. Other laws are much less precise and much more subject to error, as when the amateur weather prophet maintains, "Red sky at night, sailor's delight; red sky in the morning, sailor take warning." In both cases, however, we are being told that certain events occur under certain conditions. Given those conditions, we can predict that these events will occur. The prediction need not always be correct, so long as it is correct often enough to be useful. If bad weather occurs 75% of the time when the morning sky is red and only 20% of the time when the morning sky is gray, the amateur weather prophet has a useful law, even though not a wholly accurate one, for predicting the weather.

Kinds of Variables and Laws

All laws state a relationship between a *dependent variable* and one or more *independent variables*. A variable is any measurable characteristic, whether of a person, a situation, or anything else. A dependent variable is one about which we make a prediction; an independent variable is one we use to make the prediction. In the above examples, the length of the pendulum and the color of the sky were independent variables while the period of the pendulum (the time it takes to make its complete swing) and the weather were dependent variables. In a study of learning, the dependent variable is some aspect of the learner's performance, while the independent variables may be any characteristics of the learner, the task, or the situation.

In some cases these variables and the laws relating them to one another involve merely the presence or absence of something. This is true with the weather-production law. Red in the evening indicates good weather and red in the morning bad weather; that is all we are told. Does it matter whether the red is pale or deep? Will the bad weather be a drizzle or a hurricane? The law does not tell us. In other words, it deals with *qualitative* information only, information about the *kinds* of events that occur. In other cases, however, degrees of the independent variable are related to degrees of the dependent variable. The physicist's law tells us how much of a change in pendulum length will produce how much of a change in period. This, then, is a *quantitative* law, one that gives information about *amounts* of things, about the degree to which certain events occur. In learning, the statement that removal of a reinforcer produces extinction is a qualitative law, since it refers only to whether or not reinforcement is removed and whether or not extinction occurs. On the other hand, the statement that a larger reward results in a higher level of performance is quantitative, since it deals with different amounts of reward and different levels of performance. Both qualitative and quantitative laws are found in all branches of science, but in general the more highly developed sciences tend to have more quantitative laws, resulting in more precise predictions.

Independent variables also differ in another respect. Some independent variables can be directly varied by an experimenter, who can arrange the independent variable in a certain way and then see what happens to the dependent variable. For example, a physicist can change the length of a pendulum in order to see how this difference affects the rate at which the pendulum swings. Likewise, a psychologist can stop reinforcing a pigeon for pecking a key and watch what happens to the rate of pecking. Such a study, in which the independent variable is manipulated by the researcher, is called an experiment. If the experiment is properly controlled, we can conclude definitely that the changes in the independent variable caused the changes in the dependent variable.

There are other independent variables, however, that cannot be manipulated by an experimenter. The weather prophet cannot make the sky red in order to see what will happen to the weather. One has to wait until the sky gets red by itself and then watch for changes in the weather. This is still a perfectly valid scientific study, but it is not an experiment, for the researcher does not manipulate the independent variable. A similar example in learning would be a study of memorization rate in people of varying IQs. Here IQ would be the independent variable and rate of learning the dependent variable. The researcher could not change a person's IQ; he could only choose subjects who already had different IQs and then compare their learning rates. A difficulty with this kind of nonexperimental study is that we can seldom be sure just what is causing what. We would not be likely to say that red in the evening sky caused good weather; presumably some atmospheric condition caused both. The red sky was merely an indicator of good weather, not its cause. We might say that high IQ caused faster memorizing (if we found such a relation, as we quite likely would not), but perhaps it would be just as reasonable to say that high memorizing ability was responsible, over a lifetime, for the development of a high IQ. These nonexperimental studies still give us laws that are valuable for prediction, but for telling us what causes what, they are definitely inferior. For this and other reasons, experimental studies are preferable wherever it is possible to do them, and the great majority of psychological studies of learning are experiments.

As we have seen, scientific laws may differ in several ways. They may indicate simply that when something happens, something else will happen, or they may relate the amount of something to the amount of something else. They may be based on experiments or on nonexperimental observations. They may be very precise or they may allow for a large amount of error. In all cases, however, they state a relationship between an independent and a dependent variable in such a way as to make possible prediction from the independent to the dependent variable. These laws are the primary focus of science in general and hence of the psychology of learning in particular.

Abstraction

Scientific laws are statements about the way the world operates, and like all statements they involve abstractions. Whenever we apply words to things and events, we ignore a great deal of what is there in order to focus attention on what this particular thing or event has in common with others. For example, when we call something a car, we are ignoring its make, model, year, and color in order to emphasize the features it has in common with other cars. In other words, we are abstracting its "carness" from all the other characteristics of the particular battered, brown, 8-year-old, two-door Ford. The same is true when we use the term "discrimination" to describe the behavior both of a rat learning whether to turn right or left in a T-maze and of a pupil learning whether to use "ar" or "er" in spelling a word. Again, we are dealing with an abstract concept, ignoring most aspects of the two situations in order to concentrate on one thing that they have in common.

Since some degree of abstraction is inescapable, any statement, however concretely "factual," is an abstract formulation that tells only a part of the truth. To say, "Columbus crossed the ocean blue in 1492," is to give only the barest outline of that momentous event. Even to say, "John Doe dropped a copy of *A Tale of Two Cities* from his school desk to the floor in the middle of an arithmetic lesson in Room 6 on the morning of March 17" is to give only a minute fraction of the detail that could have been observed. For all their tremendous value, words are only pale shadows of the things they represent.

This process of abstraction goes on in all description and in all thought. Every intellectual activity involves the organization and simplification of "reality" as it is presented to our senses. This statement is true whether we consider simple perceptions or complex thoughts, and whether we look at science, art, sports, business, or any other area of human interest. Imagine, for example, what the radio broadcast of a football game would sound like if it were presented by a society editor, or by the proud father of one of the players, or by a foreigner studying American customs. The society editor might concentrate on the uniforms and the family backgrounds of the players; the proud father might report only what his own son was doing; and the foreigner might be much more interested in the cheers and card stunts than in the progress of the game. Each of these three descriptions could be perfectly true and valid as far as it went, but what football fan would accept any of them as an adequate report of the game? Each description, including the professional sportscaster's, would deal with only some aspects of the "real game"; each would reflect not only what "really happened" but also the interests and biases and vocabulary of the reporter.

In effect, there is no such thing as pure reality; there is only reality as described and interpreted and reacted to by someone. Some descriptions are more accurate or more detailed than others, but no description is complete. Even if someone were ambitious enough to collect descriptions of a football game from everyone who was there, check them with other kinds of evidence, spend years sifting and combining these accounts, and give a final report of the game many volumes long, there would still be details that were omitted. The report would still be only an abstract, even though a very detailed one, of what happened at the game. In any case, no one would read the report, since each possible reader would be interested in those aspects of the game that the reader considered interesting or important, not in the most detailed account that human patience and ingenuity could devise. Hence, any useful report of the game would involve far more abstraction and organization and simplification than our imaginary multivolume monstrosity of a description.

This process of abstraction is carried even further in scientific laws than in many other kinds of statements. In history, biography, and literature, as well as in everyday speech, we are often concerned with describing an event in as much rich detail as time and the limitations of language permit. Our several imaginary broadcasts of the football game, different as they were, were nevertheless all trying for such completeness within the limits of the reporters' interests. In science, however, we always are concerned with picking out certain aspects of the situation to be related to other aspects. In relating the period of a pendulum to its length, the physicist need not be concerned with what the pendulum is made of or with whether it is a clock pendulum, a plumb bob, or a museum display. Similarly, the psychologist's statement that removal of the reinforcer reduces the frequency of the response applies whether the reinforcer is food or praise and whether the response is pecking a key or studying spelling. The laws connecting independent and dependent variables are not descriptions of any particular event—they are statements about the conditions under which certain kinds of events occur. Scientific laws are not concerned specifically with the red sky in Chicago on June 10 or with the pendulum of Mary Jones's grandfather's clock, but with all red skies or all pendulums. Some laws may be quite narrow in the range of phenomena to which they refer, but even the narrowest always refers to collections of certain kinds of events, never merely to a single unique event.

The Value of Scientific Laws

Scientific laws serve two main purposes. One purpose is practical—to provide the means of predicting and controlling events. Simply being able to predict what will happen and thus take measures to deal with it is of considerable value. Such prediction is what keeps the weather bureau and the various investment advisory services in business. It is even more useful, however, to be able to control events. An independent variable that we can manipulate gives us some degree of control over the dependent variable. This fact is the meaning of the saying that "knowledge is power." Only if we have a law about the conditions under which certain kinds of events happen can we set up the necessary conditions for one such event to happen when we want it to. It is not necessary, of course, for the law to be formally stated; much of our practical knowledge is very casual. However, the more complete and accurate our formulation of the law is, the better able we are to control the world around us.

Scientific laws also have a less utilitarian value. Since earliest times, people have sought to understand the world in which they lived. From the child trying to find out what makes the watch tick to the cosmologist trying to find out what makes the universe tick, people constantly are asking "What is it?" and "How does it work?" and "Why?" No practical benefits are required to justify this curiosity; to gain the knowledge is benefit enough in itself. This benefit is the basis of pure science, the search for fundamental knowledge about the world.

Both of these purposes of science are exemplified in the study of the psychology of learning. The laws of learning are of crucial importance to education, to industrial, military, and other forms of training, to child rearing, to psychotherapy, and to a variety of other practical areas of work. They are also basic to an understanding of how individuals and societies come to be as they are, of how knowledge is obtained, indeed of how people acquire their unique humanness. Hence for both reasons an increase in our knowledge of the laws of learning is much to be desired.

THE NATURE OF THEORIES

Researchers are rarely satisfied, however, merely to collect more and more laws about learning or anything else. To satisfy our desire for understanding, knowledge must be organized. An encyclopedia full of laws relating each of a vast number of independent variables to each of a vast number of dependent variables might give its owner the emotional satisfaction of having a great deal of knowledge available, but it would not give the intellectual satisfaction of understanding the topics involved. Such satisfaction requires more general knowledge than that provided by this imaginary encyclopedia of laws. Even for practical purposes, such an encyclopedia would be cumbersome. It would be more convenient to have general principles from which the specific laws could be deduced. So, although the establishing of laws is in one sense the most basic activity of science, it is not the end of scientific activity. Much of the researcher's effort is dedicated toward establishing more general principles or interpretations. This effort takes one into the realm of scientific theory.

We have already seen that description represents some abstraction and organization and simplification of the events being described, and that the statement of laws represents a higher level of abstraction. With theory we come to a still higher level of abstraction. It differs in degree but not in kind from the lower levels. It is a serious mistake to think of a realm of theory that is separate and different from the realm of fact. When people speak of "facts," they are sometimes referring to descriptions of single events ("It is a fact that John W. Hinckley, Jr. shot President Reagan in 1981") and sometimes to laws ("It is a fact that hydrogen and oxygen will combine with one another to form water"). As we have seen, both descriptions and laws represent organizations and simplifications of what is "really there" according to the language and the biases and the objectives of whoever is describing the event or stating the law. Theory exemplifies the same processes, but in still greater degree. It would be reasonable to say either that facts represent one kind of theory or that theories represent one kind of fact, but most reasonable to say that fact and theory represent different degrees of what is basically a single process.

What is a theory? This is not an easy question to answer, partly because there are a number of different opinions about what a theory should be like and what functions it should serve. It is really only through studying different theories —noting their similarities and differences and the purposes their creators had in mind—that one can get a general understanding of what theories are. In a sense, therefore, the rest of this book is an attempt to answer this question. In this chapter we can hope to get only a rough and general overview.

In the broadest sense, a theory is a systematic interpretation of an area of knowledge. In the psychology of learning, "system" or "systematic interpretation" is probably a better term than "theory," for theory sometimes is used in a narrower sense to refer to a kind of formal logical system. However, in this book we will use *theory, system,* and *systematic interpretation* as synonyms.

Three Functions of Theory

A theory of learning usually consists of three different but closely related functions. First, it is an approach to the area of knowledge, a way of analyzing and talking about and doing research on learning. It represents the researcher's point of view about what aspects of learning are most worth studying, what independent variables should be manipulated and what dependent variables studied, what research techniques employed, and what language used to describe the findings. It focuses the researcher's attention on certain topics and helps the person to decide which of all the possible abstractions will be most useful. Thus theory serves as a guide and a source of stimulation for research and for scientific thought.

Second, a theory of learning is an attempt to summarize a large amount of knowledge about the laws of learning in a fairly small space. In this process of summarization, some exactness and detail are likely to be lost. In such precise and well-developed sciences as physics, theories do quite well in summarizing laws so that the same exact predictions can be made from the theories as from the much more detailed laws. Psychology, to date, has been less successful in finding such theories. Theories of learning, in attempting to summarize large amounts of knowledge, lose a good deal in completeness and precision. They are simplifications or skeletal outlines of the material with which they deal. As such, they represent a gain in breadth, in organization, and in simplicity, but also a loss in accuracy of detail.

Third, a theory of learning is a creative attempt to explain what learning is and why it works as it does. The laws give us the "how" of learning: the theories attempt to give us the "why." Thus they seek to provide that basic understanding which is one of the goals, not alone of science, but of all forms of scholarship. Theories represent people's best efforts to determine the underlying structure of the world in which they live.

Intervening Variables

In most cases, theorists have sought this underlying structure in entities that were not visible to the observer. Theorists in the field of chemistry, for example, assumed the existence of molecules long before anyone had ever seen a molecule under the microscope. They did so because the laws of chemistry formed a simpler and more logical pattern if all substances were assumed to be made up of molecules. The laws of chemistry did not themselves deal with molecules, but with substances that could be seen and touched and weighed. The molecules were in effect invented by the theorists as an explanation for the laws. This invention was a creative guess that has received more and more support from later evidence and that has contributed immensely to the development of chemistry.

Let us consider a corresponding example, though admittedly a less striking one, from the psychology of learning. A person might be deprived of water for a period of time, or be on a daily ration of water below his normal intake, or have a chance to drink only for a limited time once a day, or eat a lot of dry food without water available, or have a hypertonic salt solution intubed directly into his stomach. The extent to which any one of these things happened (e.g., how much the water ration was reduced or how concentrated the salt solution was) would be an independent variable. We would find that each of these independent variables was related in much the same way to each of several dependent variables. As any of these independent variables increased, he would probably become more restless, would drink more water when water was available, would work harder to get to a drinking fountain, and would do more complaining about how thirsty he was. These relationships constitute 20 laws, relating each of the 5 independent variables to each of the 4 dependent variables. We can, however, reduce this amount to 9 laws by saying that each of the 5 independent variables produces a state of thirst and that this thirst in turn produces changes in the 4 dependent variables. By hypothesizing this state of thirst, we have more than cut in half the number of laws required to describe the relationships involved.

So far this act of theoretical simplification is no more than what any layman does. It is so commonplace, indeed, that it is easy to overlook its importance. No one has ever seen or touched or weighed thirst. We have felt it in ourselves, but in anyone else we can only infer it. We have to infer someone else's thirst from what has happened to him (the independent variables) or from what he does (the dependent variables). If he tells us he is thirsty, his statement is only one of the possible dependent variables, and not necessarily the most reliable. When a child gets out of bed for the fourth time and tells his mother he is thirsty, she is understandably more likely to trust other evidence than what the child says. Anyone who thinks it is possible to differentiate sharply between theory and fact should consider how much theory there is in the simple "factual" statement, "He is thirsty."

The psychologist's use of the concept "thirst" differs from the layman's in two respects. One is in precision. The psychologist, not satisfied with saying that certain manipulations will produce thirst and thirst will produce certain behaviors, goes on to determine what degrees of the independent variables are related to what degrees of thirst and what degrees of thirst are related to what increases in the dependent variables. Thus the psychologist's use of the concept "thirst" allows for more complete and accurate detail than the layman's.

The other difference is that the psychologist is likely to go further than the layman in relating this concept to others. Many theorists of learning have been struck with the similarities among hunger, thirst, pain, and a variety of other such hypothetical states (hypothetical because none of them can be directly observed). All of these tend to produce increases in activity and physiological changes characteristic of stress. Moreover, the termination of any of these is reinforcing. They have therefore often been classified together as *drives*. This concept of drive provides a higher level of theoretical integration, bringing together far more laws than the separate concepts of hunger, thirst, pain, and the like.

Theoretical concepts of the sort we have been discussing are often called *intervening variables*. This name reflects their place in the theoretical structure, coming between the independent and the dependent variables, forming a link connecting them together, and serving to explain how the independent variables produce changes in the dependent variables. These intervening variables are states or conditions of the individual that are inferred from observations. *Habits, beliefs,* and *motives* are examples of intervening variables that are important in various theories of learning.

By this time the reader is very likely asking, "Are these intervening variables really there, waiting to be discovered, or are they invented by theorists as a matter of convenience?" In other words, is the theorist more like an explorer, discovering hidden truths, or more like an artist, creating views of the world that suit his own purposes? If the discussion so far has been vague on this question, it is because theorists are by no means agreed on the matter. Undoubtedly both discovery and creation enter into theory, as indeed into all scientific work. A theory must lead to accurate predictions, must be consistent with well-established laws, otherwise it is worthless. This requirement sets limits on the theorist's creative freedom. However, the same laws can be interpreted in different ways, and these interpretations are not waiting around to be discovered—they must be created by an interpreter. Perhaps the theorist is less like either an explorer or an artist than like an architect, limited by materials and by the demands of the job, but still working with originality and imagination to produce a new, useful, and beautiful structure.

This is admittedly not a very adequate answer to the question of whether the intervening variables are "really there." Some theorists talk as though they are really there and others as though it is merely convenient to pretend that they are there. It has been suggested that there should be two different terms, one for those that theorists think they have discovered and the other for those that they think they have invented. Fortunately, we can leave this issue to the philosophers and concern ourselves only with the part that intervening variables play in the various theories we will be studying.

In any case, the element of creativity in theory construction explains why there are many theories of learning. All theorists try to find ways of structuring reality that will be useful and meaningful to themselves. The differences among the resulting theories reflect partly the differences in the topics that various theorists find most interesting to work with, and partly differences in the kinds of systematic structures that different theorists consider worth producing. All, however, reflect the efforts of thoughtful humans to interpret the phenomena of learning in coherent and intellectually satisfying ways.

Kinds of Learning Theories

Theories of learning can be classified in a number of ways. For our purposes, one difference is particularly outstanding, the difference between the *connectionist* and the *cognitive* theories. Connectionist interpretations of learning, however much they may differ among themselves, agree in treating learning as a matter of connections between stimuli and responses. (A response may be any item of behavior, while a stimulus may be any input of energy that tends to affect behavior. Connectionist theorists typically assume that all responses are elicited by stimuli.) These connections which are a simple kind of intervening variable, are called by a variety of names, such as habits or stimulus-response bonds. Always, however, there is a concentration on the responses that occur, on the stimuli (and perhaps other conditions) that elicit them, and on the ways that these relationships between stimuli and responses change with experience.

Cognitive interpretations are concerned with the cognitions (perceptions or attitudes or beliefs, which are more complex intervening variables) that individuals have about their environment, and with the ways these cognitions determine behavior. In these interpretations, learning is the study of the ways in which cognitions are modified by experience.

Common sense makes use of both kinds of interpretations. When discussing simple reactions or more complex physical skills, we are likely to say, "I guess it's just a bad habit I've learned," or "With all that practice, her reactions have become very fast and smooth." These are connectionist interpretations. When discussing matters that involve words or deliberate decisions, we often say things like, "He has acquired a lot of knowledge on that subject," or "You'll have to learn that people don't like to be treated that way," or "Now I really understand geometry!" These interpretations are all cognitive.

Whether a given psychologist will prefer a connectionist or a cognitive theory of learning depends partly on the kind of learning in which that person is most interested. A specialist in the study of conditioning may find a connectionist interpretation better suited to his needs, while a specialist in problem solving may find a cognitive interpretation more useful. However, specialists tend to believe that the theory they prefer is best, not only for their own field of study, but for the whole psychology of learning. This tendency reflects a desire for unity and simplicity that is one of the reasons why theories are developed in the first place. As a result, some people adopt general cognitive theories of learning and others adopt general connectionist ones.

The distinction between connectionist and cognitive theories is not, of course, an all-or-nothing matter; there are numerous middle positions and combinations. Nevertheless, the distinction forms a convenient and useful basis for classifying the interpretations of learning that we will be investigating here. We will look first at a number of connectionist theories, since that is the kind of theory which has traditionally been most popular with psychologists of learning in the United States. Next we will consider some cognitive theories. After that we can look at various efforts to combine the best features of both kinds of theory and at some special topics and problems in learning theory. Finally we will speculate a bit on the possible future of learning theory. It is hoped that this survey will indicate what learning theories are, what they try to accomplish, how successful they are, and what they can contribute to our understanding of the learning process.

chapter 2

Connectionist Theories Emphasizing Contiguity

Human interest in psychology has a long history. At least since the time of the ancient Greeks, philosophers have been speculating about topics that are now considered part of psychology. How do we think and feel and learn and know and make decisions and act on them? Attempts to answer these questions make up a considerable part of the history of philosophy. It was not until the nineteenth century, however, that attempts were made to study these topics experimentally. The first psychological laboratory was founded by Wilhelm Wundt in Germany at a time traditionally given as 1879. Although research in psychology had been going on before then, this date marks the point at which modern scientific psychology was placed on a definite institutional footing.

Wundt and his colleagues in early scientific psychology, like the philosophers from whom they drew much of their inspiration, were largely interested in conscious experience. They wanted to understand human sensations and thoughts and feelings. They wanted to take the continuous flux of conscious awareness and analyze it into its basic components. Are memory images the same as sensations? Are feelings a special kind of sensation or are they something radically different? How is the intensity of a sensation related to the intensity of the physical stimulus that produces it? These were the sorts of questions that the early experimental psychologists studied.

This kind of psychology, developed in Germany, became to a great extent the standard for the rest of Europe and for America. The research in psychological laboratories and the discussion in textbooks of psychology were based principally on this approach. Its acceptance, however, was never complete. In both Russia and the United States there was always a considerable trend toward the study of objective behavior as well as of conscious experience and interest in what people did as well as in what they thought and felt. These trends gave rise to two major traditions of studying behavior, one Russian and one American, to which we now turn.

PAVLOVIAN CONDITIONING

In 1904, Ivan P. Pavlov (1849–1936) won the Nobel prize in physiology and medicine for his work on digestion. To do this research, he had to perform a difficult operation, opening a fistula in the wall of a dog's stomach. He noticed that the stomach secretions he was studying were first triggered not by food reaching the stomach but by the chewing or even just the sight of food, and he began to find this anticipatory secretion the most interesting aspect of the digestive process. To study it, he changed to a different part of digestion, the secretions of the salivary glands, which could be measured through a much simpler operation, placing a duct in a dog's salivary gland. When he presented food to a dog with such a duct in its cheek, drops of saliva fell into a beaker where they could easily be counted. Soon these drops of saliva began to appear in response not only to food but also to a variety of other stimuli in the lab. At the time the standard way of explaining this extra salivation would have been to say merely that these other stimuli had become associated with food. Pavlov decided that this was not an exact enough answer, and devoted the rest of his long life to studying this process in precise detail. Through this new line of research he became even more famous as the father of conditioning (Pavlov 1960).

We saw the basic elements of conditioning in Chapter 1. The experimenter starts with a stimulus (the unconditioned stimulus) that will reliably elicit a specific response (the unconditioned response). In Pavlov's research, the unconditioned stimulus was meat and the unconditioned response salivation. What was to become the conditioned stimulus could be any of a great variety of stimuli: a bell, a ticking metronome, a triangle drawn on a large card, etc. If this stimulus was presented repeatedly just before the meat, it too came to elicit salivation, the conditioned response, and it thus became a conditioned stimulus. Since the term "conditioning" came to be applied quite broadly, this particular kind of conditioning, being the first studied, came to be called classical conditioning (Hilgard & Marquis 1940). More recently, as it has become increasingly common to name everything from diseases to measuring units after people, classical conditioning has increasingly come to be called Pavlovian conditioning. Though there is some question as to how much of the credit Pavlov should share with such other Russian pioneer researchers as I. M. Sechenov and V. M. Bekhterev, his work was clearly of central importance and deserving of the tribute.

The terms "unconditioned stimulus" and "conditioned stimulus" may seem a bit odd, considering what they mean. It is now generally agreed that these terms are poor translations of the Russian words that Pavlov used. What is meant is that the meat is an unconditional stimulus (not conditional on any previous training), while the bell (or whatever stimulus precedes the meat) is a conditional stimulus for salivation—conditional on having been paired with the meat. By an error in translation, however, generations of English-speaking psychologists have been stuck with the strange terms "conditioned" and "unconditioned." Though occasionally someone tries to correct the error by using "conditional" and "unconditional," most writers stick with long-standing tradition and use the less appropriate but more familiar terms.

Excitation and Inhibition

Since Pavlov was a physiologist, it was natural that he should try to explain conditioning in physiological terms. He suggested that two processes go on in the cerebral cortex of the brain during the conditioning process. The more basic process, since it is always involved in conditioning, is *excitation*. Both the conditioned stimulus and the unconditioned stimulus produce excitation in the cortex. Since the unconditioned stimulus (food) is something important to the dog's survival, while the conditioned stimulus is typically much more neutral, even trivial, the excitation produced by the unconditioned stimulus is the stronger of the two. Excitation is drawn from the weaker toward the stronger, with the result that the excitations from the two stimuli make contact. However, the fact that the conditioned stimulus comes before the unconditioned is also part of the reason that excitation moves from the site of the conditioned to the site of the unconditioned stimulus rather than vice versa. The effect of repeated conditioning trials is that the excitation from the conditioned stimulus comes to travel to the place on the cortex where the excitation from the unconditioned stimulus normally occurs, even on trials when there is no unconditioned stimulus presented. This excitation then produces the same effect as if it had been produced by the unconditioned stimulus, namely, to elicit the same response that the unconditioned stimulus normally elicits. However, since the excitation at that point on the cortex is weaker than if it had been produced directly by the unconditioned stimulus, the response is also weaker than the unconditioned response would have been. This weaker version of the unconditioned response, produced by the conditioned stimulus rather than by the unconditioned, is of course the conditioned response.

Excitation tends to *irradiate,* that is, to spread out from its original focus in all directions over the surface of the cortex. The closer any spot on the cortex is to the center of excitation from the conditioned stimulus, the more quickly and strongly the excitation from the conditioned stimulus will irradiate to that point. When it does, that point also shares in the conditioning, forming a connection (though to a lesser degree) with the cortical site for the unconditioned stimulus. Because of the way the cortex is organized, points that are close together on the cortex are typically the sites for similar stimuli. Consequently, the derived conditioning resulting from irradiation has its principal effect on stimuli similar to the conditioned stimulus. This, of course, is the phenomenon known as *generalization.*

Although excitation is the more basic concept, it is scarcely more important than its opposite, *inhibition.* Inhibition is a cortical process that counteracts excitation, reducing the response of whatever cells are involved. Though inhibition is opposite in its effect to excitation, the two processes are otherwise much alike; for example, inhibition as well as excitation irradiates over the surface of the cortex. Inhibition serves to keep excitation from producing excessive effects, and according to Pavlov the interaction between these two processes explains most of what goes on in conditioning.

Inhibition appears for many reasons. *External inhibition* results from the presentation of an irrelevant stimulus during conditioning. Such a distracting stimulus momentarily reduces the tendency to give the conditioned response. The stimulus that produces external inhibition can be any stimulus that is reasonably strong and noticeable; it need not have any particular relationship to either the conditioned or the unconditioned stimulus. The inhibition thus comes from a source external to the whole conditioning process.

Another form of inhibition is *protecting inhibition*. This form of inhibition serves to protect the cells from damage by excessive excitation. In general, the stronger the conditioned stimulus and the stronger the unconditioned stimulus, the greater the response. However, once excitation reaches the *top capability* of the cells, protecting inhibition takes over to protect the cells. Various paradoxical effects can then occur, such as that only weak stimuli can produce a conditioned response, while stronger stimuli cannot, because of the extra effect of protecting inhibition on them.

There are several forms of *internal inhibition*, internal both in that its source is within the organism and that it is intrinsic to the conditioning process. One form of internal inhibition produces extinction: when the conditioned stimulus is no longer followed by the unconditioned stimulus, inhibition gradually builds up at the cortical site of the conditioned stimulus and weakens the conditioned response. A second form occurs in cases where there is a substantial delay between the beginning of the conditioned stimulus and the beginning of the unconditioned stimulus. At first the conditioned response tends to occur as soon as the conditioned stimulus begins, but after a good deal of training it does not come until shortly before the unconditioned stimulus is due to arrive. This delay in the conditioned response is attributed to inhibition. A third form is involved in discrimination training, where one conditioned stimulus is followed by the unconditioned stimulus and another, similar stimulus is not. Because of irradiation (generalization), excitation builds up to the stimulus that is not followed by the unconditioned stimulus as well as to the one that is. However, inhibition also builds up to the one that is not followed by the unconditioned stimulus, so that eventually a discrimination is formed.

A more extreme version of the inhibition formed in discrimination learning is seen in a special process called *conditioned inhibition*. This occurs when a conditioned stimulus is followed by the unconditioned stimulus when the conditioned stimulus appears by itself, but not when it is combined with another stimulus. For example, there might be two kinds of trials. In one kind, a bell (conditioned stimulus) is followed by meat (unconditioned stimulus); on the other, a bell and a light together are not followed by meat. At one level of analysis, this is simply an example of discrimination training. However, since the bell is both the stimulus that is followed by the unconditioned stimulus and also part of the stimulus that is not, it is a special kind of discrimination training in that the light becomes a conditioned inhibitor. It does not elicit the conditioned response, and can partially prevent other stimuli from eliciting it. If we now tried to condition salivation to still another stimulus, say a triangle drawn on a card, it would be harder to do so if the light were on than if it were off. We would thus have evidence that the light was indeed functioning as a conditioned inhibitor.

When excitation and inhibition are operating in the same place at the same time, they tend to counteract each other. Under other conditions, however, they can enhance each other. For example, if a conditioned stimulus is presented shortly after a conditioned inhibitor, there will be a larger conditioned response than at other times. The inhibitory stimulus has strengthened the excitation to the conditioned stimulus, a process called *positive induction*. Likewise, a conditioned inhibitor has a stronger inhibitory effect if it comes shortly after a positive conditioned stimulus has been presented, a process of *negative induction*.

Applications and Implications

Pavlov believed that the principles of conditioning could be used to explain a variety of phenomena. In particular, he related these principles to personality, considering that one of the most fundamental differences among dogs and among humans is the balance between excitation and inhibition. Excitatory personalities tend toward too much unrestrained activity ("when in doubt, do something, do anything!"), whereas inhibitory personalities tend toward unresponsiveness ("when in doubt, the safest thing to do is nothing"). Finally, he considered conflict between excitation and inhibition the basis of neurosis. He found that when a dog learned a discrimination between a circle and an ellipse and then the ellipse was gradually changed in shape to resemble more and more closely a circle, the dog would eventually reach a point where discrimination broke down completely. Excitatory dogs would respond to both stimuli, inhibitory dogs to neither. This failure to discriminate was not just a calm adoption of the same response to both stimuli. Rather, the dogs barked, tried to leave the experimental room, and generally appeared anxious, frustrated, and upset. These symptoms seemed so similar to those of humans in difficult conflict situations that Pavlov labeled the syndrome "experimental neurosis."

Pavlov's work earned him tremendous prestige in Russia. Remarkably, this prestige held during both the Czarist regime in which he began his work and the Communist regime that followed it, even though his own reaction to the new Soviet government was far from enthusiastic. Various aspects of Pavlov's system probably helped to make him popular with the Soviet government: his emphasis on reducing "higher mental processes" to conditioning appealed to Communist materialism, and his emphasis on learning was consistent with the Communist philosophy of environmental determinism. Pavlov's system became so much a "state system" that citation of Pavlov in an article became almost as much a symbol of loyalty as citation of Karl Marx. Though a good deal has been added to Pavlov's system by other eastern European psychologists and physiologists, as we will see in Chapter 7, the basic system has remained little changed.

In the Western world, also, Pavlov's work was received with a good deal of enthusiasm. Americans, in particular, were ready for the idea of conditioning. However, it was primarily the idea that Americans adopted, rather than the details of either research or theory. The empirical findings of Pavlov's research were widely quoted but little studied: some Americans studied the conditioning of the eye-blink reflex or the GSR, but not of salivation, and the majority of researchers on animal learning did not study classical conditioning at all. Moreover, a number of the phenomena that Pavlov described, such as conditioned inhibition or induction, were little studied. As for Pavlov's theory, even those Westerners who admired Pavlov's pioneering research tended to dismiss it. The irradiation of excitation and inhibition was almost entirely inferred from behavior, rather than from any direct study of the brain, and did not seem to most Westerners like very useful theory anyway. Thus, outside of eastern Europe, Pavlov was widely admired as a pioneer, widely cited, widely followed in general outline, but nonetheless largely neglected as regards many of the details of his system. Only fairly recently have psychologists in the West begun to look more carefully at the details of his system. They have since confirmed some of his findings, challenged others, and found still others hard to check because the research reports were so brief and so casually written. Though Pavlov's theories are still not much admired in the West, those of some of his followers have turned out to resemble those of some Westerners, developed independently. Pavlov has, however, survived the mixture of adulation, contradiction, and partial neglect that he has received, to remain one of the great pioneers in the psychology of learning.

WATSON'S BEHAVIORISM

About the same time that Pavlov was working in Russia, the trend toward the study of objective behavior in American psychology was bringing it more and more into conflict with the German tradition. Pressure increased to break the traditional mold and to develop a psychology that was frankly oriented toward objective behavior and practical usefulness. To varying degrees, psychologists were taking up the cry, "Enough of studying what people think and feel; let's begin studying what people do!" This movement found its most vocal spokesman in John B. Watson (1878–1958). It was through his vigorous attacks on traditional psychology and his attempts to build a radically different system that American theoretical psychology came into its own.

In 1903 Watson received the first Ph.D. in psychology granted by the University of Chicago. His dissertation was a study of maze learning by rats, and this concern with animal behavior was typical of his early interests. He was impressed by the fact that in studying animal behavior it is possible to dispense with consciousness and simply study what the animal does. Why, he asked, can't we do the same with humans? Behavior is real and objective and practical, while consciousness belongs to the realm of fantasy. Let us abolish consciousness from our discussions and study behavior! Watson's professors at Chicago agreed with many of his objections to traditional psychology, but considered his solution too radical. Perhaps they thought that, like so many young rebels, he would become more conservative with age and responsibility. In Watson's case, however, this change did not occur. After joining the faculty at the Johns Hopkins University in 1908, he became all the more convinced that his extreme position was the answer to psychology's problems. A few years later, Watson (1913) published the first formal statement of his position, an article entitled "Psychology as the Behaviorist Views It," and the psychological revolution known as behaviorism was under way.

The reason for the name "behaviorism" is clear enough. Watson was interested only in behavior, not in conscious experience. Human behavior was to be studied as objectively as was the behavior of machines. Consciousness was not objective; therefore it was not scientifically valid and could not be meaningfully studied. And by "behavior" Watson meant nothing more abstruse than the movements of muscles. What is speech? Movements of the muscles of the throat. What is thought? Subvocal speech, talking silently to oneself. What are feeling and emotion? Movements of the muscles of the gut. Thus did Watson dispose of mentalism in favor of a purely objective science of behavior.

It is easy to satirize such a position. (Estes, for example, has suggested that a behaviorist might change the familiar motto from "Think!" to "Behave!" and finally to "Twitch!") But we must not overlook the tremendous importance of this position for the development of modern psychological science. Though much objective study of behavior antedated Watson, he stands out as the great popularizer, the man who turned this sort of study into a national movement and philosophy.

Watson's opposition to admitting anything subjective into psychology led him to reject much more than the study of consciousness. Another of his targets was the analysis of motivation in terms of instincts. At the time Watson's career began, it was common to explain almost any form of behavior as due to a particular instinct. Sociability was attributed to an instinct of gregariousness, fighting to an instinct of pugnacity, and so forth. These were assumed to be innate and to determine in considerable measure what behavior people would show. These instincts were too mentalistic for Watson. He asserted that our behavior is, on the contrary, a matter of conditioned reflexes, that is, of responses learned by what is now called classical conditioning. We do not show sociability or aggression because we are born with an instinct to do so, but because we have learned to do so through conditioning.

Watson's demolition of theories extended not only to instincts but to other supposedly innate mental characteristics of humans. He denied that we are born with any particular mental abilities or traits or predispositions. All we inherit is our bodies and a few reflexes; differences in ability and in personality are simply differences in learned behavior. Thus Watson was in several respects a strong exponent of environment as against heredity in the familiar nature-nurture controversy. What we are (except for clearly anatomical differences) depends entirely on what we have learned. And since what has been learned can be unlearned, this contention meant that human nature, either in general or in a particular person, was greatly subject to change. There was practically no limit to what a person, properly conditioned, might become. As Watson expressed it in his most famous quote: "Give me a dozen healthy infants, well-formed, and my own specified world to bring them up in and I'll guarantee to take any one at random and train him to become any type of specialist I might select—doctor, lawyer, artist, merchant-chief and, yes, even beggar-man and thief, regardless of his talents, penchants, tendencies, abilities, vocations, and race of his ancestors." (Watson 1966, p. 104).

This combination of objectivity with faith in the power of learning swept American psychology and captured the popular imagination. Combined with some more specific ideas about learning, it had great implications for child rearing, education, advertising, and social organization. When we consider how well Watson's ideas fitted in with the American belief in equality of opportunity, emphasis on unemotional practicality, and faith in progress, it is no surprise that behaviorism came to occupy the center of the American psychological stage.

We cannot, of course, picture Watson as suddenly presenting behaviorism and having it promptly and universally adopted. When Watson published "Psychology as the Behaviorist Views It," the trends to objectivity and to environmentalism were already under way. The demolition of instinct doctrine was more the work of L. L. Bernard and of Z. Y. Kuo than of Watson. Moreover, Watson owed many of his ideas to sources as diverse as the philosophy of John Locke in England and the physiological psychology of Ivan Pavlov in Russia. Finally, alternative points of view continued to be defended, and Watson faced much opposition. Nevertheless, there was a marked change in American psychology during this period, and Watson was the keynote speaker around whom any discussion of the change is likely to center. He gave behaviorism its name, its loudest voice, and its sense of mission.

Watson's Interpretation of Learning

What, then, was Watson's interpretation of learning? We have already seen that he regarded all learning as classical conditioning. We are born with certain stimulus-response connections called reflexes. Examples are sneezing in response to an irritation of the nose and the knee-jerk response to a sharp tap on the knee. These reflexes, according to Watson, are the entire behavioral repertoire that we inherit. However, we can build a multiplicity of new stimulus-response connections by the process of conditioning. If a new stimulus occurs along with the stimulus for the reflex response, after several such pairings the new stimulus alone will produce the response. This conditioning process, first described by Pavlov, makes it possible for each response in the original repertoire of reflexes to be elicited by a great variety of new stimuli in addition to the ones that originally elicited it. This, according to Watson, is how we learn to respond to new situations.

Such conditioning, however, is only part of the learning process. We must not only learn to respond to new situations; we must also learn new responses. Sneezes, knee jerks, and the like would not carry us very far in dealing with complex situations. How can complex new habits be learned? The answer, according to Watson, is by building up a series of reflexes. Walking, for example, is a sequence of many responses, such as putting the weight on one foot, swinging the other foot forward, bringing it down, thrusting the weight forward from one foot to the other, and so forth. All these responses occurring in proper order constitute the skilled performance of walking. The building up of such a sequence is possible because each response produces muscular sensations that become stimuli for the next response. Thus new and complex behavior is acquired through the serial combination of simple reflexes.

Let us look at this kind of learning in more detail. Consider one response in the sequence, such as swinging the leg forward. Originally the stimulus for this response is, perhaps, the sight of the place toward which one is walking. However, the person can swing his leg forward only if his weight is on the other foot. Hence, whenever he swings his leg forward, he does so in the presence of those sensations from his own body that result from having his weight on the other foot. Those sensations thus are paired with the response of swinging the leg, and through repeated pairings they come to elicit leg swinging. Hence, in the well-learned habit of walking, the sensation of having weight on one foot automatically elicits the conditioned response of swinging the other leg forward. This response merges with the others in the sequence, each providing the stimulus for the next response. The sequence eventually becomes so well integrated that for practical purposes we can speak of the whole process of walking from one place to another as a single response, even though it is actually a complex sequence of stimulus-response connections.

A reader of the above discussion is very likely dissatisfied with Watson's explanation of complex learning. What, one may fairly ask, determines that this particular sequence of stimulus-response connections will be formed? Why does the sensation of weight on one foot elicit the response of swinging the other leg forward? Reading between the lines in Watson's last book (*Behaviorism,* first published in 1924), one gets the feeling that he was still seeking the answer to this problem (1930). He had two different answers, neither completely adequate, and the relation between the two was still unclear. One answer was to say that the stimulus-response connections that make up the skilled act are conditioned reflexes. Each response produces sensations that become conditioned stimuli for the next response, and thus the whole sequence of conditioned stimulus-response connections is formed. This formulation gave Watson the satisfaction of having reduced complex habits to their simple building blocks—conditioned reflexes. Now, he said, we can turn to the physiologists to explain why conditioning occurs; we as behaviorists have done our job. However, Watson never really carried the analysis through in detail. If feeling one's weight on the left foot is the conditioned stimulus and swinging the right leg forward is the response, what is the unconditioned stimulus which always guarantees that the response will occur so that conditioning can take place? To this crucial question, Watson had no answer. As a result, his reduction of complex behavior patterns to sequences of conditioned reflexes is more apparent than real.

Watson's other explanation of this form of learning is in terms of two principles: *frequency* and *recency.* The principle of frequency states that the more frequently we have made a given response to a given stimulus, the more likely we are to make that response to that stimulus again. Similarly, the principle of recency states that the more recently we have made a given response to a given stimulus, the more likely we are to make it again.

Watson illustrates these principles with the example of a 3-year-old child learning to open a puzzle box with candy inside. The child turns the box around, pounds it on the floor, and makes a variety of other useless responses. Finally, by chance, he presses a button on the box, which is the one response that will release the lid so he can open the box and obtain the candy. Since the box is now open and the candy obtained, the child is no longer in the presence of the stimuli that kept him working at the box. The last response he made in the presence of those stimuli was the response of pressing the button. The next time his father puts candy in the box and closes the lid, the child will go through much the same sequence of trial and error as before. However, by chance, he will try some new responses and leave out some of those from last time. Again, however, the last response he makes will be that of pressing the button, since that is the one which changes the stimulus situation. Every time he works with the box, pressing the button occurs, whereas other responses may or may not. Thus in the long run button pushing gains a lead in frequency. Since it is always the last response, it always has a lead in recency. As a result, button pushing occurs sooner and sooner on successive experiences with the box. Since button pushing solves the problem, other responses have less and less chance to occur on successive experiences with the box. Button pushing as a response to the stimulus of the closed box has been learned.

This illustration shows only how a single response, pressing a button, is learned. The problem might, however, have required the child to make a series of several successive responses to open the box, with each response changing the situation so that the next response could be made. Pressing the button, for example, might have opened an outer lid and revealed a lever that had to be moved sideways in order to open the inner lid. In this case both button pushing and lever moving would be learned in the same way, since each would change the stimulus and thus become the last response to the old stimulus. Such a series of responses could be extended indefinitely.

Why, then, does one particular response rather than others occur to the stimulus at a given place in a complex sequence? Watson's answer is that during learning many different responses occur to the stimulus, but that through the process described above, most of them drop out. The response that changes the situation gains in frequency and recency until it comes to occur as soon as the stimulus is presented. That particular stimulus-response unit in the sequence is then complete.

All of these statements about the learning of new responses are left rather undeveloped in Watson's treatment. How are conditioning, the principle of frequency, and the principle of recency related? How does the fact that the learner may at first make some wrong response much more often than the right one, yet still eventually learn the right one, fit in with the principle of frequency? Watson does not tell us. He was confident that complex learning could be explained by simple principles, but his attempted explanations were tentative and were never organized into a clear and consistent theory.

Special Kinds of Learning

What about the learning of emotional reactions? Here Watson makes a concession to heredity, beyond what he has already made by recognizing the existence of innate reflexes, since he recognizes three innate patterns of emotional reaction. In principle these reaction patterns are the same as reflexes, for we can state what movements (including those of the internal organs) they involve and what stimuli will produce them. However, they are more complicated than what is usually meant by a reflex. The three emotional reaction patterns may for convenience be labeled as fear, rage, and love. We must note, however, says Watson, that these labels refer to patterns of movement, not to conscious feelings. If we bang a gong close to a child, and he starts to cry, we may describe this event by saying that the stimulus of a loud noise has produced the emotion of fear. However, we are simply giving a name to the behavior we see, not commenting on the child's feelings.

Emotional learning involves the conditioning of these three patterns of emotional response to new stimuli. The above example of innate fear was taken from a famous experiment of Watson's, which can also be used to illustrate conditioned fear. Little Albert, aged 11 months, was permitted to play with a white rat, which he did happily and with no sign of fear. A metal bar was then hit with a hammer close behind him. He started and fell sideways. This sudden loud noise was repeated a number of times just as the rat was presented to him, and each time he reacted in the same way, sometimes also whimpering. These responses indicate that the noise was an unconditioned stimulus for fear. After this training, the rat was presented without the noise. Albert fell over, cried, and crawled away from the rat as fast as he could. This change indicates that through the training procedure the rat had become a conditioned stimulus for fear. According to Watson, such conditioned and unconditioned responses account for all of our emotions.

What about the acquisition of knowledge? Can conditioning be used to explain how one learns, for example, the facts of history? Certainly, says Watson, for this knowledge consists simply of saying certain words, aloud or to oneself. The response sequence involved in saying "William the Conqueror defeated Harold the Saxon at Hastings in 1066" is in principle no different from that involved in walking across a room. A question, such as "How did the Norman conquest occur?" elicits the statement, which is itself a sequence of words with each word a conditioned stimulus for the next one. Acquiring knowledge is a process of learning to give the proper sequence of words in response to a question or other conditioned stimulus.

All of our behavior, says Watson, tends to involve the whole body. When we think, we may pace the floor or furrow our brows. We announce our opinions with smiles or waves of the arm as well as with words. We cannot therefore really say that emotions are responses of the gut or that thinking is made up of vocal responses. These are the dominant but by no means the only responses involved. Everything we think, feel, say, or do involves activity of, to varying degrees, the entire body. This is probably the most fundamental credo of behaviorism.

Evaluation of Watson

Watson's great contribution to the development of psychology was his rejection of the distinction between body and mind and his emphasis on the study of objective behavior. This battle was so effectively won that most of the learning theory in America, at least through the 1950s, was behavioristic in the broad sense of the term. Since then more of the field has gone in directions that are no longer commonly called behavioristic, but that still reflect the legacy of behaviorism.

In this book we will see a number of theoretical systems that represent different variations on the behaviorist theme. All of them have in common a concern with objective behavior, a strong interest in animal studies, a preference for stimulus-response analysis, and a concentration on learning as the central topic in psychology. This fact makes Watson in some ways the intellectual father or grandfather of a large portion of the systems we will be considering here.

Watson, however, was much less thorough than he might have been in dealing with the detailed problems of learning. We have already seen the incompleteness and inconsistency in his treatment of complex learning. In his eagerness to build an objective psychology, he was somewhat cavalier with the matter of logical thoroughness. Perhaps if he had worked on his theory longer he would have extended his system to deal with some of these problems. More likely, however, his zeal for freeing psychology from subjectivism and nativism was incompatible with laborious theoretical completeness. In any case, he left the academic world in 1920 as a result of a sensational (for its day) divorce scandal and, though continuing to write about behaviorism for a short time afterward, devoted most of the rest of his life to the applied psychology of advertising. Watson is now admired mainly for his philosophical trail blazing rather than for his detailed system building. It has remained for others to try to build, within the behavioristic framework, a more complete theory of learning.

GUTHRIE'S INTERPRETATION OF LEARNING

Of those who have continued in the behaviorist tradition in recent years, the one who has remained closest to Watson's original position is Edwin R. Guthrie (1886–1959). From 1914 until his retirement in 1956, Guthrie was a professor at the University of Washington. His university teaching career thus began only 10 years later than Watson's, and he himself never studied with Watson. His graduate education was more in philosophy than in psychology. Nevertheless, his interpretation of learning sounds much like what Watson's might have been if he had had another decade to work on the topic. His definitive work, *The Psychology of Learning,* was published in 1935, revised in 1952, and reprinted in 1960, and his final theoretical statement was published in 1959. Thus Guthrie, though scarcely recent, can still be regarded as more nearly a contemporary theorist than Watson.

Among theories of learning, Guthrie's is one of the easiest to read in his own words, but nonetheless hard for someone else to discuss. It is easy to read because he wrote in an informal style, making his points with homely anecdotes rather than with technical terms and mathematical equations. It is hard to write about because his casual presentation contains the germ of a highly technical, deductive theory of learning. Reading Guthrie is like reading an exciting novel that contains a difficult allegory, so that he can be read on an easy or a hard level. At the heart of his system, is one basic principle of learning. Interpreted loosely, this principle is a source both of entertaining interpretations of learning and of valuable advice about the management of learning situations. Interpreted rigorously, it becomes the chief postulate of a deductive theory. This theory, so deceptively simple at first glance but so maddeningly complex on closer investigation, stands as a challenge to students of learning. Has Guthrie actually succeeded in summing up the whole field of learning in one key postulate?

The Basic Principle of Learning

Guthrie's basic principle of learning is similar to the conditioning principle that was basic for Watson, but it is stated in a still more general form. Guthrie says, "A combination of stimuli which has accompanied a movement will on its recurrence tend to be followed by that movement" (1960, p. 23). The principle may be paraphrased as, "If you do something in a given situation, the next time you are in that situation you will tend to do the same thing again." This principle is more general than the principle of classical conditioning, in that it says nothing about an unconditioned stimulus. It says only that if a response accompanies a given stimulus once, it is likely to follow that stimulus again. In classical conditioning, the response occurs with the (conditioned) stimulus during training because the unconditioned stimulus elicits it. This sequence of course fulfills Guthrie's conditions for learning. However, it does not matter to Guthrie whether the response is elicited during training by an unconditioned stimulus or in some other way. As long as the (conditioned) stimulus and the response occur together, learning will occur.

In claiming to sum up the whole field of learning in that one statement, Guthrie was inevitably challenging others to find inadequacies in the summary, and psychologists were quick to answer the challenge. The first difficulty with this principle is that one often does many different things in the same situation. Which one will occur next time? This challenge is no problem for Guthrie; he simply replies, "The last one." A person struggling with a mechanical puzzle tries many responses. If he finally makes the correct response, he will tend to make this same response when next confronted with the puzzle. We say, then, that he has learned how to do the puzzle. Suppose, however, that he finally gives up and puts the puzzle aside unsolved. The next time he sees the puzzle he will tend to do what he did last, namely put it aside. In that case we do not say that he has learned how to do the puzzle, but he has still learned something. In both cases he was presented with a combination of stimuli from the puzzle. In each case there was a movement that removed the stimuli. To the observer, one of these movements represented success and the other failure, but to Guthrie they both represented responses that removed the stimuli of the unsolved puzzle and that therefore became more likely to occur again. In both cases a response was learned, and in both cases the last response that the learner made to the stimuli was the one that he learned.

This aspect of Guthrie's system sounds much like Watson's principle of recency, since the last thing that occurred in a situation is the one that will occur again. However, Guthrie does not use Watson's other principle, frequency. Whereas for Watson a stimulus-response connection is something that varies in strength and grows stronger with practice, for Guthrie it is an all-or-nothing bond. The connection is either present or absent, with no intermediate variation in strength. Hence the conditioning of a movement to a combination of stimuli takes place completely in one experience, and further practice adds nothing to the strength of the connection.

At first glance this assumption seems contrary to well-known laws of learning. While practice may not make perfect, it usually does produce gradual improvement. How can Guthrie say that all the improvement takes place in a single experience? We must beware, replies Guthrie, of treating a "movement" as the same thing as an act or an accomplishment. Guthrie is referring in his principle of learning to specific small movements of particular muscles. It takes many such movements working together to make up a skilled act. Moreover, competent performance involves not just one but many skilled acts, each in response to a particular combination of stimuli. Hence learning how to do something involves learning an enormous number of specific stimulus-movement connections. Improvement in the skill is gradual even though the learning of each minute part occurs suddenly.

Consider a particular skill, such as riding a bicycle. For each possible position of the bicycle, a different motion is required in order to keep it upright. Each of these motions, in turn, is made up of movements of the arms, torso, and legs. A particular movement of the left arm to help correct a particular kind and degree of tilt may be learned in one experience, but it certainly does not follow that the whole skill of balancing the bicycle will be learned so quickly. If we also consider all the other aspects of bicycle riding, the distinction between learning a movement and gradually mastering a skill becomes evident. This illustration does not show that Guthrie is necessarily correct when he says that a movement is learned in one trial, but it does make this interpretation more plausible.

This explanation, however, introduces some ambiguity into Guthrie's theory. In many cases "the last thing one did in a situation" refers to an act, such as lighting a cigarette or making a remark. These, however, are skilled performances made up of many specific movements. Why does Guthrie treat them as if they were single movements that could be conditioned in one trial? Presumably what is needed here is an analysis in terms of hierarchies of complexity. Lighting a cigarette is a skill made up of many stimulus-movement connections that must be conditioned. However, once learned, this whole act behaves like a single movement and can be conditioned as such to combinations of stimuli. Guthrie does not concern himself with this relationship, but applies his principle of learning sometimes to movements and sometimes to acts, depending on the point he wants to make. Fortunately, this ambiguity is unimportant in most situations.

Guthrie's Substitute for Reinforcement

The aspect of Guthrie's theory that has been most attacked is his lack of concern with success and failure, with learning to do the "right" thing. Whatever one did last in the situation, right or wrong, is what one will do again. Guthrie makes no use of the concept of reinforcement. He does not say that we learn to make those responses that work, or that obtain reward. Whether or not something we do becomes learned as a response to the situation depends only on whether it changes the situation into a different situation, so that it becomes the last thing done in the old situation. Success has this result, since a solution changes a problem situation into a situation without a problem. Thus the successful act is the last one that occurs in the problem situation, and it will tend to occur if the problem is presented again. However, if the individual can somehow escape from the situation without solving the problem, the escape response will be learned. Inefficient methods may be learned and retained as well as efficient ones, since both get the person out of the situation. Mistakes may be repeated over and over again. We learn, not by success or by reinforcement, but simply by doing.

A number of testable predictions follow from this position. As an example, consider a hungry rat that can obtain food by pressing a lever. The rat learns to press the lever more and more rapidly. According to Guthrie, the rat learns because the food changes the situation through its effect on hunger and on the sensations in the mouth. Thus pressing the lever becomes the last thing the animal did in the old situation, and it becomes increasingly likely to occur. Suppose instead of getting food after each pressing of the lever the rat was simply taken out of the box as soon as it pressed the lever. This would change the situation even more than food did, so the rat should be even more likely to press the lever at the next opportunity than if it had been fed. This experiment has been done, and the results did not confirm the prediction (Seward 1942). The rats receiving food showed far more lever pressing than those removed from the box, contrary to what would be expected from Guthrie's theory. This experiment and others like it cast doubt on Guthrie's view that reward has nothing to do with learning.

It may be, however, that our interpretation of this experiment is not altogether fair to Guthrie. Although the food produced less change in the total stimulus combination than did removal from the box, the food did produce a marked change in certain particularly important stimuli. These were the *maintaining stimuli*—those stimuli that kept the rat active in the situation. In this particular case the maintaining stimuli were those resulting from food deprivation —in other words, the stimuli of hunger. In other situations they might be the stimuli of thirst or pain or sexual arousal or anger or fear. At some places in his writings Guthrie suggests that it is changes in the maintaining stimuli that are crucial for learning. If a response removes the maintaining stimuli, by definition it solves the problem and thus becomes the last response in the problem situation. If it fails to remove the maintaining stimuli, then no matter what other changes it may produce it cannot be the last response in the problem situation. By this interpretation, we can see why food might be expected in Guthrie's theory to produce more learning than removal from the box.

However, this interpretation also raises other problems. In some cases responses are learned that do not remove the maintaining stimuli. A softball player learns those responses that produce successful batting and fielding, even though a base hit or a good catch does not reduce the competitive excitement that provides the maintaining stimuli for playing. A rat in a maze learns the correct turn at each choice point, even though only the last turn is followed by any change in the maintaining stimuli. In both cases, however, the response does change the overall stimulus combination, so that it is in one sense the last response in the situation. Thus we are faced with the problem that sometimes only changes in the maintaining stimuli are crucial, while at other times changes in other stimuli are important. How do we know which times are which? Guthrie does not tell us. By sometimes considering all stimuli and sometimes considering only maintaining stimuli, Guthrie can explain any case of learning after it has occurred, but he cannot do so well at predicting what learning will take place.

By now the reader can see more clearly why Guthrie's system is difficult to treat as a formal logical theory. When are we talking about movements and when about acts? When should we look at all stimulus changes and when only at changes in the maintaining stimuli? Because he concentrates on presenting simple, entertaining interpretations of learning, Guthrie never gives clear answers to these awkward questions. As a result, his theory, which at first glance seemed so direct and precise, turns out to be discouragingly vague. His attempt to reduce all learning to one basic principle is, in any precise sense, inadequate.

His loose, anecdotal approach reflects the fact that Guthrie was more interested in the undergraduate teaching of psychology than in detailed research. He himself produced only one major experiment bearing on his theory, a demonstration of the stereotyped behavior of cats in escaping from a cage (Guthrie & Horton 1946), which we will encounter again in Chapter 11. Perhaps because of this lack of emphasis on research he has had many sympathizers but few active followers. There has never been a long and active tradition of research within the framework of Guthrie's theory (though Fred Sheffield and Virginia Voeks, at Yale, and Arthur Lumsdaine, currently at the University of Washington, did make some starts toward one and we will see his influence on Estes in Chapter 8). However, many psychologists have found that, once they stop treating Guthrie's system as a formal deductive theory and concentrate on its informal implications, its basic principle of learning turns out to be quite useful. In any situation, says Guthrie, if you want to know what an individual will learn, look at what he does. What he does, right or wrong, is what he will learn. As a formal postulate, this statement is inadequate, but as an informal source of advice, it turns our attention to aspects of learning that we would otherwise be very likely to neglect. We can best appreciate Guthrie's contribution by looking at his discussions of some practical learning situations.

The Breaking of Habits

Perhaps the best known of these applications is in Guthrie's three methods for changing a bad habit. All three methods depend on finding out what stimuli evoke the undesirable response and then finding a way of making some other response occur in the presence of those stimuli. This other response should then occur again the next time the stimuli are presented. The emphasis is on the exact stimulus and the exact response that are connected. Guthrie gives the example of a 10-year-old girl who, whenever she came in the door of her house, threw her hat and coat on the floor. Time and again her mother scolded her and made her go back and hang them up, but to no avail. Finally the mother realized that the stimulus for the girl to hang up her wraps was the mother's nagging. The next time the girl threw down her wraps, her mother insisted that she put them on again, go outside, come in the door again, and hang up her coat and hat at once. After a few trials of this procedure the girl learned to hang up her wraps. The desired response had been attached to the stimuli of coming in the door, and the habit of throwing down the wraps had thus been replaced by the habit of hanging them up. This procedure worked where the previous nagging had failed because this time the mother saw to it that the girl hung up her wraps in the presence of the particular stimuli (those resulting from having just come through the door) that had previously led to the response of throwing the wraps down.

The first method, which may be called the *threshold* method, involves presenting the stimuli so faintly or weakly that the undesirable response does not occur. (The stimuli are then said to be below the threshold intensity for the response, hence the name.) The stimuli are then increased in strength so gradually on successive occasions that the response never occurs. These repeated experiences with the weak stimuli raise the threshold so that stronger stimuli will also be below threshold. Eventually the stimuli can be presented at full strength without eliciting the undesired response, since the individual has been making some other response repeatedly in the presence of the stimuli. This method is useful mainly for emotional responses, involving anger, fear, or the like. Guthrie gives the example of the old cavalry method of training saddle horses. If an untrained horse is saddled and ridden, it will buck wildly. This reaction can be avoided by employing the method of thresholds to replace the bucking response with a response of standing quietly. First a blanket is put on the horse's back. This pressure on its back is the sort of stimulus that induces bucking, but the blanket alone is too weak a stimulus to have this effect. After some experience with the blanket the horse is saddled. Prior to experience with the blanket, the saddle might have produced bucking, but now it does not. Eventually, after the horse's experience with the saddle, a rider can mount without producing bucking, though the horse would certainly have bucked if mounted before the training with blanket and saddle. The experience of not bucking while successively heavier weights were placed on its back has eventually resulted in the horse's standing still even for the weight of a rider.

The second method may be called the method of *fatigue*. The response to be eliminated is elicited again and again, until the individual is so tired that he stops making the response and does something else (if only resting) instead. This other response is then the one likely to occur when the stimuli are presented again. Again Guthrie has an example of a disobedient small girl, though we are not told whether it is the same one who would not hang up her clothes. This girl had a habit of lighting matches. After scolding and punishment failed, her worried mother finally eliminated the habit by making the girl light a whole box of matches in quick succession. Long after the girl was thoroughly tired of lighting matches, her mother insisted that she continue. Eventually she began actively resisting, throwing the box of matches down and pushing it away. At this point new responses, incompatible with match lighting, had been attached to the stimuli from the match box. The next time she had a chance to light matches, the girl showed no inclination to do so. This method illustrates in extreme degree Guthrie's reliance on his version of the law of recency (doing again what one did last in a given situation) and his rejection of the law of frequency. The girl had lighted matches more frequently at the end of this experience than at the beginning, but the last thing she did was to push the match box away. Pushing it away was therefore what she tended to do when she next encountered a match box.

In the third method, which we may call the method of *incompatible stimuli,* the stimuli for the undesired response are presented along with other stimuli that can be counted on to produce a different, incompatible response. The original stimuli then become attached to the new response. Guthrie illustrates this method with the case of a woman college student who could not study because of the distracting noise. She solved this problem by spending a period of time reading absorbing mystery novels instead of studying. These stories held her attention so well that she ignored the distracting noises. The stimuli of noise thus occurred along with the responses of reading and became attached to these responses. When she then changed back (however reluctantly) from reading mysteries to reading textbooks, she found that the noises no longer distracted her, for they were now attached to reading responses instead of listening responses.

It is noteworthy that there is no reference to punishment in any of these methods. Someone might suggest that it was punishing for the one little girl to go out of the house, come in again, and hang up her clothes, and also punishing for the other girl to light so many matches at once. True, says Guthrie, but remember that other forms of punishment had previously failed. The important question is not whether these experiences were punishing but what they led the individuals to do. Inflicting pain on someone, says Guthrie, cannot be expected to change his habits if the pain does not occur in the presence of the stimuli that produce the behavior. Scolding the one girl after her clothes were already on the floor, or slapping the other girl after she had finished with the matches, would be irrelevant to the habits in question. Only when the punishment resulted in a new response to the same stimuli, incompatible with the old response, was it effective. Moreover, as the threshold method indicates, absence of punishment may be just as good a way of producing new responses as is punishment.

This attitude is characteristic of Guthrie's interpretation of punishment. Always look at what punishment makes the individual do. If punishment succeeds in changing the punished habit, it is because it elicits behavior incompatible with it. If punishment fails, it is because the behavior elicited by the punishment is not incompatible with the punished behavior. Thus, if you want to stop a dog from chasing cars, slapping his nose as he runs is likely to work, whereas slapping his rear is not. The two blows may be equally painful, but the one on the nose tends to make him stop and jump backward, whereas the one on the rear tends to make him continue forward all the more vigorously. Hence the blow on the nose, by eliciting behavior incompatible with running after the car, makes this nonrunning more likely to occur next time. The blow on the rear, however, has no such effect; it may even strengthen the chasing. Punishment works, when it does work, not because it hurts the individual but because it changes the way he responds to certain stimuli.

If one wants to use these methods of Guthrie's as cure-alls for bad habits, a problem at once arises. In order to obtain different behavior from the individual, one has to change the stimuli in some way. For the little girl, coming in the door and taking off her wraps was not the same when she had just been sent out the door by her mother as when she had just come in after a long time outside. For the army horse, not bucking to a blanket was different from not bucking to a rider. There was a considerable difference between the stimulus situation when lighting a fiftieth match under a mother's prodding and when lighting a first match for fun. Now, when the original stimulus situation is restored, how do we know whether the two situations are enough alike so that the last response in one will occur in the other? For example, will the dog that jumped back when presented with the stimulus of moving-car-plus-blow-on-the-nose also jump back when presented with moving-car-alone? The answer in all of these cases seems to be: try it and see. This difficulty weakens the general usefulness of Guthrie's advice, not to mention the problem of relating the advice clearly to the theory. However, we can scarcely expect to get advice that will work infallibly in every situation without any ingenuity on the part of the person taking it. Guthrie's interpretation of punishment and his methods for changing habits are valuable tools for interpreting situations as well as useful suggestions for dealing with them. A theorist who can give us this much need not be ashamed of his practical contributions.

Some Special Topics

Guthrie's emphasis on responses to stimuli and the ways of changing them shows up in other contexts, too. What of extinction? Since Guthrie does not talk about reinforcement, he cannot talk about extinction as resulting from the removal of reinforcement. Instead, he says that extinction is simply learning to do something else. The response was learned because it changed the stimulus situation into a different one, thus becoming the last thing that was done in the original situation. If, now, the learned response no longer produces this change, the individual will go on doing various things in the situation until some other response does change the situation. That new response will then be the one that tends to occur next time. If this new response consistently terminates the situation, it will replace the old response. If, however, there is no longer any consistency in what response will terminate the situation, behavior will be variable from time to time. No particular new response will be learned, but the old response will still be replaced by new responses, in this case, many new ones. If a dog has learned to get out of his yard by crawling through a hole in the fence, and if this hole is now mended, he may or may not discover some other mode of escape. In any case, however, the response of going to the place where the hole was will be replaced by some other response.

Guthrie's interpretation of forgetting is similar. Habits do not weaken with disuse; they are replaced by other habits. If we forget the German vocabulary we have learned, it is because the English words as stimuli have become attached to other responses than the German words. If we lose our skill at horseback riding, it is because we have practiced other, competing responses in situations that were somewhat similar to being on horseback (such as being on a bicycle). In most cases the details of the relearning process are obscure, and it would be difficult to predict with accuracy how much of some knowledge or skill one would forget under a given set of circumstances. However, this interpretation of forgetting does provide a good starting point for studying the factors that influence forgetting. Even this start is more than many theorists have provided for this topic.

Forgetting, like acquisition, is usually gradual because of the many specific stimulus-response connections that make up a complex habit. If the correct responses have been attached to many different stimuli, it will take longer for new responses to get attached to all of these stimuli. Hence it is possible to make one definite prediction from Guthrie's interpretation of forgetting. We can predict that a habit will be better retained if it has been practiced in a number of different situations (i.e., in the presence of a number of different stimulus combinations). In the course of forgetting, new responses may replace the old, correct ones quickly in any one of these situations, but the old response will still be conditioned to many other stimulus combinations. On another occasion when the stimulus combination is different, the old response is likely to reappear. Forgetting, like learning, is specific to the situation, and what is forgotten in one situation may well be remembered in another. The "forgotten" response to the changed stimulus will occur only, however, if the response in question was originally learned to a variety of different stimulus combinations. Hence we can increase the resistance of a habit to forgetting (including those verbal habits that we call knowledge) not only by practicing it more but by practicing it in a variety of situations.

The impression one gets from most of Guthrie's writing is that human behavior is a very mechanistic matter. Behavior is rigidly controlled by stimuli, and changes in the stimulus-response connections follow simple mechanical laws. However, Guthrie has been more receptive than Watson to such concepts as desire and purpose. He recognizes that much behavior has a goal-directed character. Rather than ignoring this, as Watson was inclined to do, he attempts to interpret it in rigorously physical terms.

What does it mean to say that someone has a desire, a purpose, or an intention to do something? Guthrie recognizes four components: (1) a complex of maintaining stimuli that keeps the organism active; (2) something that blocks any simple, direct action that would remove the maintaining stimuli at once; (3) muscular readiness to make certain responses; and (4) muscular readiness for the consequences of this action. Consider a person in a burning building who has the intention of jumping to safety. In this case the four components are as follows: (1) heat from the fire, choking sensations from the smoke, and fear; (2) the fire and the height that block him from simply running away; (3) the tensing of his muscles for the jump; and (4) the preparation of his body for the shock of the fall. These four components, says Guthrie, are all that we need to describe an intention.

If someone suggested to Guthrie that the intention is something mental, over and above these four physical components, he might have replied with his story about a strange murder case. A man resolved to shoot his neighbor, and he hid outside the neighbor's house with a rifle pointed at the door and his finger on the trigger. While sitting there, he began to think better of his plan. He was about to get up and go away when the neighbor came out the door. He pulled the trigger and the neighbor fell. At his trial, the question arose as to whether or not he fired intentionally. According to Guthrie, this is a meaningless question. That part of his intention which took the form of words to himself had changed, but the part that involved a ready trigger finger had not changed. There was no one intention, only a variety of bodily adjustments which did or did not prepare him to shoot.

What is attention? A variety of responses that orient the sense receptors toward certain stimuli, as in looking or listening. There may even be scanning, involving searching movements that end when a certain stimulus is perceived. This formulation of attention makes it possible for Guthrie to reword his basic principle of learning in the form: "What is being noticed becomes a signal for what is being done" (1959, p. 186).

In all of these interpretations, Guthrie is insisting that the processes involved, though they may be called by subjective terms, refer to objective physical movements. They may be hard to observe, but they are there just as surely as any other movements. Guthrie particularly emphasizes the role of *movement-produced stimuli,* the sensations produced by our own movements. These play an important part in thought, purpose, the coordination of sequences of behavior, and responses to stimuli that are no longer present. Though they often function like intervening variables in his system (since they are often impractical to observe directly), he hesitates to call them intervening variables since for him they are just as objectively present as the independent and the dependent variables.

Guthrie's final theoretical statement (1959), written shortly before his death, is both more technical and more tentative than most of his earlier work. He seems to be trying to clarify both his own ideas and his relationships to other theorists. In this statement he is concerned both with the concept of attention and with the formal structure of his theory. However, it is likely that Guthrie will be remembered not so much for his attempts, successful or not, at formal theory building as for his informal contributions to our thinking about the learning process.

In trying to understand or to control any learning situation, Guthrie reminds us to look at the particular response that is being made and the particular stimuli that are eliciting it. He warns us not to rely on vague exhortations, not to look for magic in the administration of rewards and punishments, but to concentrate on eliciting particular patterns of behavior in particular situations. Though he tends to draw his examples largely from child rearing and animal training, Guthrie has much that is useful to offer adult human learners as well.

College students often complain that they know the material they have studied but that they somehow cannot present it on examinations. A familiarity with Guthrie's thinking would lead one to say, "If the behavior you want to produce is the behavior of writing essays about certain topics, practice writing essays, and practice in a situation as close as possible to that of an exam." A similar example is seen in military training, where studies of combat effectiveness have resulted in training situations being made more and more like combat. As a result, infantrymen in training spend less time practicing exact marksmanship with bull's-eye targets on the known-distance range and more time practicing rough and ready marksmanship with silhouette targets that pop up to confront the trainee as he advances. Though we cannot say that these examples represent Guthrie's direct influence on the applied psychology of learning, we can say that Guthrie more than any other major theorist has emphasized the importance of such precise analysis of stimuli and responses. Guthrie's approach can stand one in good stead in many learning situations.

A FINAL WORD ON CONTIGUITY THEORY

Watson and Guthrie of course have in common all the characteristics of behaviorism in the general sense of that term. In addition, there is one respect in which the two of them differ from the other behavioristic theorists we will be discussing, namely, in that they do not regard learning as depending on reinforcement. Watson ridiculed the idea that reward could determine what was learned, regarding it as a magical notion unfit for a scientific explanation. (Pavlov spoke of the unconditioned stimulus as a reinforcer for the conditioned response, but Watson ignored this aspect of conditioning.) Guthrie similarly avoided making any reference to the reinforcing effects of rewards. In their systems, learning is assumed to depend only on the contiguity of stimulus and response, in other words, on the fact that they occur together. Hence Watson and Guthrie are called *contiguity theorists*.

In taking this position, Watson and Guthrie stand in contrast to another group of behavioristic theorists, known as *reinforcement theorists*. This latter group is just as dedicated to objectivity and just as much attached to the stimulus-response language in describing learning. They do not, however, see any objection to recognizing the reinforcing effect of reward in their theories; in fact, they consider this effect essential to the analysis of learning. It is to this group of connectionist theorists that we turn in the next chapter.

chapter 3

Connectionist Theories Emphasizing Reinforcement

The idea that pleasure and pain as consequences of our acts are important determiners of behavior has a distinguished history in psychology. It forms the basis of the theory of psychological hedonism that was developed by Jeremy Bentham and adopted by a number of other British philosophers. According to this view, we all do those things that give us pleasure and avoid those that give us pain. However, it remained for Edward L. Thorndike (1874–1949) to make a similar view central to the psychology of learning.

THORNDIKE'S EARLY CONNECTIONISM

Thorndike was a pioneer in experimental animal psychology. Instead of relying on stories about the intelligent feats of this or that animal, he took animals into the laboratory, presented them with standardized problems, and made careful observations of how they solved the problems. His monograph, "Animal Intelligence" (1898), is one of the classics in the field. His most widely quoted study was with cats in a problem box. A hungry cat was confined in a cage with a tempting morsel of fish outside. The cat could open the door by pulling a loop of string hanging inside the cage. Usually a cat went through a long process of walking around, clawing the sides of the cage, and other responses before it pulled the loop of string and was able to leave the cage. On successive tests in the cage, animals took shorter and shorter times to pull the string. However, this improvement was very gradual. Even after several experiences of opening the door by pulling the string, animals on a given trial would still spend considerable time in other behavior before pulling the string. This led Thorndike to conclude that the cat's learning to pull the string involved not an "intelligent" understanding of a relation between string pulling and door opening but a gradual "stamping in" of the stimulus-response connection between seeing the string and pulling it.

At the time Thorndike published these studies, they were radical in two respects: their careful observation of animal behavior under controlled conditions and their concern with the gradual strengthening of stimulus-response bonds. They were Thorndike's answer to the argument about whether animals solve problems by reasoning or by instinct. By neither, said Thorndike, but rather by the gradual learning of the correct response.

In relation to Watson and Guthrie, however, another point is noteworthy. Whereas both Watson and Guthrie were contiguity theorists, Thorndike was a reinforcement theorist. Watson's laws of frequency and recency and Guthrie's basic law of learning both state that stimulus-response bonds are strengthened simply by the response occurring in the presence of the stimuli. Thorndike did not completely reject this view, which he summarized as the *law of exercise*. His primary law of learning, however, was the *law of effect*. This stated that the stamping in of stimulus-response connections depended not simply on the fact that the stimulus and response occurred together but on the effects that followed the response. If a stimulus was followed by a response and then by a *satisfier*, the stimulus-response connection was strengthened. If, however, a stimulus was followed by a response and then by an *annoyer*, the stimulus-response connection was weakened. Thus satisfying and annoying effects of responses determined whether the stimulus-response connections would be stamped in or stamped out.

The terms "satisfier" and "annoyer" sound startlingly subjective for a theory concerned with the mechanical stamping in and stamping out of stimulus-response bonds. This language is much more like that of the hedonistic philosophers than like that of the behaviorist psychologists. Thorndike was indeed criticized by behaviorists for this way of talking about learning. Actually, however, he defined these terms in a quite objective way.

> By a satisfying state of affairs is meant one which the animal does nothing to avoid, often doing things which maintain or renew it. By an annoying state of affairs is meant one which the animal does nothing to preserve, often doing things which put an end to it [Thorndike 1913, p. 2].

Thorndike says nothing here about the animal's feelings, only about what the animal does. Thus he adheres to the concern of behaviorism with what individuals do. His language may sound subjective, but his meaning is as objective as Watson's. Working at the height of the behaviorist movement, Thorndike had his disagreements with its extreme supporters, but actually he and they were close together in interests and objectives. In the broader sense of the term, Thorndike was certainly himself a behaviorist.

Later in his career, Thorndike modified the law of effect to make satisfiers much more important than annoyers. Reward, he decided, strengthens connections, but punishment does not directly weaken them. If punishment is effective in weakening the tendency to do something, it is because it produces variable behavior and thus gives some new response a chance to be rewarded. This position, except for the emphasis on reward, sounds much like Guthrie's. With this modification, the law of effect became the now familiar statement (but not at all familiar when Thorndike presented it) that satisfying consequences serve to reinforce stimulus-response bonds.

Thorndike was a man of practical interests, and he took a special interest in the psychology of education. For many years he served on the faculty of Teachers College, Columbia University. Throughout his professional life, his studies on the "pure" psychology of learning with both human and animal subjects were interspersed with studies on the applied psychology of education. His emphasis on specificity in learning and on the mechanical stamping in of stimulus-response connections has been both praised and condemned by educators over the years. (It is to him, indeed, that we owe the term "connectionism.") For our purposes, however, these aspects of Thorndike's work are too similar to Watson's and Guthrie's to require further comment here. Thorndike was no less a pioneer of objective psychology than Watson; indeed, his original contributions were quite likely more important than Watson's. However, our concern here is that he incorporated within his objective psychology of learning the law of effect, and thus became the first real reinforcement theorist.

Thorndike's view of learning—that it involves the formation of stimulus-response bonds through the operation of reinforcement—became the dominant view in American learning theory. Not only was some version of this view held by the majority of learning theorists until well beyond the middle of the twentieth century, but even those who held other views found that much of their energy went into disagreeing with Thorndike's approach. As Tolman later wrote (1938), one might agree with Thorndike or disagree with him or try to improve on him in various ways, but he remained the starting point for any discussion of learning. However, these attempts to improve on him achieved increasing prominence, and constitute most of this chapter.

MILLER'S INTERPRETATION OF LEARNING

We turn now to another connectionist reinforcement position, that of Neal Miller (b. 1909), who was a professor of psychology at Yale through much of his career, but who moved to Rockefeller University in 1966. Miller's system represents to a great extent a simplification of the theory of Clark Hull, which will be considered in detail later. Treating Miller before Hull, though it reverses the natural chronological sequence, may serve as an introduction to the more technical study of Hull's system.

Much of Miller's importance as a theorist comes from the applications of his theory to topics in personality, social, and abnormal psychology. These applications were worked out jointly by Miller and John Dollard (1900–1980). Miller's background in experimental psychology and Dollard's in clinical psychology and the social sciences made possible a very fruitful collaboration on these topics. The theoretical analysis of learning is primarily Miller's, with a heavy debt to Hull, but the applications are largely Dollard's.

The Four Elements of Learning

Central to Miller's interpretation of learning and motivation is the concept of *drive.* A drive is an aroused state of the organism, one that goads the individual into action. For Miller, a drive always involves a strong stimulus; moreover, any stimulus, if strong enough, acts as a drive. The drive stimulus may be either external or internal. Pain is an example of a drive produced by an external stimulus, while hunger and thirst are drives produced by internal stimuli. Some drives are produced by stimuli from an individual's own emotional responses. When we are angry or afraid, physiological changes take place in our bodies. Some of these produce strong internal stimuli, which are responsible for the drives of anger and fear. Whatever its source, a drive arouses the individual and keeps him active. Drive is thus the basis of motivation.

In an infant, or in an older individual in a highly unfamiliar situation, the activity produced by the drive has little direction. All sorts of different responses are made. It may happen that one of these responses serves to reduce the strength of the drive. If the drive is hunger, eating food will reduce it. If the drive is pain from electric shock, moving away from the electrically charged conductor will reduce it. When the drive is reduced (which often, but not always, means that it is completely removed), the individual becomes less active. Thus one thing we say about drive is that a strong stimulus increases activity and the removal of the strong stimulus decreases activity.

So far this is only a statement about motivation, not about learning. However, a reduction in the strength of a drive has a very important property: it reinforces whatever response came just before. Thus whatever response serves to reduce the drive is reinforced and therefore tends to be learned. As a result, the behavior produced by drive in a familiar situation is quite different from the "trial and error" in an unfamiliar situation. The individual now quickly makes the learned response that has reduced the drive in the past and thus immediately reduces it again. Drive reduction is thus the basic operation in learning.

So far we have a drive, a response, and a resultant reduction in drive. One more element needs to be added: the collection of stimuli that guides the response. One does not simply learn a response to reduce a given drive whenever or wherever the drive occurs; the response depends on conditions. Under some conditions one reduces hunger by going to a restaurant, under others by cooking a meal. The stimuli that guide the response and that determine which response will occur are known as *cues.* Finally, the drive reduction that ends the learning sequence may of course be called a *reward.* This is the fourth of the elements in learning that became Miller and Dollard's trademark: *drive, cue, response,* and *reward.* In Thorndike's puzzle box, for example, the drive was hunger (plus, very likely, exploration), the most important cue was the loop of string, the response was pulling the string, and the reward was escape and food.

This position, though more similar to Thorndike's, also bears some resemblance to Guthrie's. A strong (drive) stimulus acts as a maintaining stimulus, in Guthrie's terms. Its removal, however, acts as what Thorndike called a satisfier and Miller calls a reward. This reward functions as a reinforcer, increasing the tendency for the rewarded response to occur again. This emphasis on reinforcement distinguishes both Miller and Thorndike from Watson and Guthrie, and makes them representatives of a different tradition in learning theory.

Imitation

In their first book, *Social Learning and Imitation,* Miller and Dollard (1941) state their basic interpretation and then proceed to apply it to a variety of complex situations. They note that much human learning behavior involves imitation. In a great many situations people solve problems, not by trying one response after another until one is rewarded, but by doing what they see someone else doing. How does this behavior fit into the simple Miller-Dollard model of learning? The answer is that the tendency to imitate is itself learned. When an individual makes a response, it is often done in the presence of cues produced by the behavior of others. His own response may be either like or unlike that of another individual. If the response is like that of someone else, and if the response is followed by drive reduction, the individual has been rewarded for using the cues from another individual to model his response after the other's. If the response is different and is not followed by drive reduction, the tendency to behave differently from the other is not rewarded and starts to extinguish. Thus imitative behavior is rewarded and other behavior not, so that the individual learns to do what he sees the other do.

Miller and Dollard give an example of two little boys, aged 6 and 3, playing a game with their father. The father hid a piece of candy for each and then the two boys looked for them. Wherever the older boy looked, his younger brother tagged along and looked also. When the older boy found his candy and stopped looking, the little one had no idea where to look next. The only strategy he knew in this game was to imitate his brother exactly.

How had this pattern of imitation, so self-defeating in this case, been built up? Miller and Dollard refer to an earlier incident in the life of these brothers. On one occasion, the older boy heard his father's step and ran to greet the father as he came home from work. The younger boy happened to be running in the same direction at the same time. The father met both boys with presents of candy. Since the young boy had not learned to distinguish his father's step, he was not running to greet his father; the fact that he was running was purely coincidental. Nevertheless, he was rewarded for the running. Naturally, there had been many times in the past when he had run and not been rewarded for it. The cue that made this time distinctive was the sight of his brother running. Thus there was a learning situation for the younger boy, with hunger as the drive, the sight of his brother running as the cue, running as the response, and candy as the reward. It was through this incident and many others like it, Miller and Dollard decided, that the little boy eventually learned to imitate his brother. Having often been rewarded for imitating his brother, he did so even in situations such as the hiding game where it was useless.

It is easy to think of such situations in which people are rewarded for imitating others. Miller and Dollard were not satisfied, however, merely to cite such examples. They went on to do experiments in which both humans and animals were taught to imitate. In one such experiment, the subject (a first-grade child) could get candy from a machine sometimes by turning the handle and sometimes by pressing it down. If the child made the wrong motion, he got no candy on that trial. Paired with each child was another person, who took a turn at the machine just before the subject did. Sometimes this other person was another child and sometimes an adult. If the adult turned the handle, turning the handle would also be correct for the child. If the other child turned the handle, however, only pressing the handle would work for the subject. In other words, in this situation the children were rewarded for imitating adults but not for imitating other children. The children not only learned to imitate the adult and not the other child, they also generalized this behavior to other adults and other children. Some other children were rewarded for imitating children but not adults, and they too learned. This one experiment illustrates not only the learning of imitation, but also generalization of imitation from one person to another and discrimination between people to be imitated and people not to be imitated.

Miller and Dollard go on to apply these principles to a variety of social situations. They point out, for example, that we learn to imitate high-prestige people more than those of low prestige. A child is likely to be rewarded for imitating "those nice (middle-class) children" and not rewarded for acting like "those nasty (lower-class) children from across the tracks." The results of such learning to imitate high-prestige people may be seen in adolescent girls who try to dress and act like movie stars and in adult men who buy cars beyond their means in order to keep up with the Joneses. Miller and Dollard also apply the principles of imitation to the behavior of crowds. Mobs, they suggest, consist of people imitating one another and thus stimulating one another to deeds that few of the people would ever commit as isolated individuals. This argument is illustrated with a gruesome description of a lynch mob.

Fear and Neurosis

In their second book, *Personality and Psychotherapy,* Dollard and Miller (1950) consider the learning of personality characteristics and particularly the learning and unlearning of neuroses. They begin by pointing out three characteristics of the neurotic person: that he is miserable because of his conflicts, that he is stupid about certain aspects of his life, and that he has symptoms. They then proceed to explain these three characteristics according to the neurotic's previous learning. The crucial element in this learning is the learned drive of fear. This drive is the basis of the conflict, the source of the misery, and the cause of the stupidity.

What is a learned drive? Dollard and Miller begin their discussion of the topic with an experimental demonstration involving rats. A rat is placed in a box with two compartments, one of which has white walls and a grid floor, the other black walls and a wooden floor. The rat explores both parts and shows little preference between them. Then it is placed in the white compartment and given strong electric shock through the grid floor. Most rats soon escape the shock by running into the black compartment. This sequence of shock in white and escape to black is repeated several times. Then the rat is placed in the white compartment without shock. It runs rapidly to the black compartment. Since there is no longer a pain drive to motivate this escape behavior, Dollard and Miller explain it on the ground that a learned drive of fear has been conditioned to the cues of the white compartment.

What is the nature of this learned drive? Like all drives, say Dollard and Miller, it involves strong stimulation. These strong stimuli are produced by the rat's own responses. When the rat was first shocked in the white compartment, it made a variety of responses to the shock, such as tensing the muscles, increasing the heart rate, and other such involuntary indicators of emotion. These in turn produced strong stimulation which was added to the drive produced by the pain of the shock. These strong stimuli produced by the emotional responses make up the drive of fear. These emotional responses became conditioned to the cues of the white compartment, owing to the fact that they occurred in the presence of those cues and were followed by drive reduction when the rat escaped the shock. Now when the cues of the white compartment are presented without shock, they produce the emotional responses which in turn produce stimuli of the fear drive.

The fact that fear is a drive can be demonstrated by using it as the basis of new learning. This demonstration was done by closing the door from the white to the black section and making it possible for the rat to open the door only by turning a wheel on the wall near the door. The animals learned to turn the wheel and then run into the black compartment, even though there was no shock in the white compartment. In this case fear was the drive, sight of the wheel the cue, turning the wheel the response, and escape from fear (by escaping from the white compartment) the reward. Then the situation was changed so that turning the wheel would not open the door but pressing a lever would. As a result, the wheel-turning response was extinguished and the lever-pressing response was acquired. Thus the learned drive of fear operated like a primary drive to motivate learning.

How does this kind of learning occur when we go from experimental rats to neurotic humans? Let us consider a child who is severely punished for any kind of self-assertive behavior. Whenever she tries to get her own way, she is subjected to pain, which produces emotional responses, which produce the learned drive of fear. These fear-producing responses become conditioned to the stimuli which are present at the time, including the cues that come from her own self-assertion. As a result, any self-assertive behavior comes to produce fear, while submissiveness reduces the fear. Moreover, the fear is not merely of overt self-assertive behavior, but even of those self-assertive thoughts and feelings that go with it. The child is then afraid of self-assertion in the same way that the rat is afraid of the white compartment, and the child's submissiveness (in thoughts as well as deeds) is an escape from fear-provoking cues just as the rat's running to the black compartment is an escape from the fear-provoking white compartment.

However, the child's problem is worse than the rat's. As long as the rat is able to run to the black compartment its fear is brief and does not disrupt its life. The child, however, is often placed in positions where self-assertive behavior might get her things that she wants. These positions occur even more often after she becomes an adult. The fact that she is afraid to be self-assertive is a great handicap in such situations. She is placed in a conflict between her desire for something and her fear of the self-assertive behavior that would get it for her. This conflict, in which she loses no matter what she does, is a source of misery. If she recognized the great difference between her present situation and that in which she was punished for self-assertion, she might be able to relieve the fear and resolve the conflict. However, this course requires that she recognize her problem and think about it. But she cannot do either since she has become afraid not only of behaving self-assertively but even of saying (to others or to herself) that she would like to be self-assertive. It is this fear of saying or even thinking that she would like to be self-assertive that makes her behavior stupid. She cannot make the thinking responses that would help her to understand and to solve her problems. She can, however, obtain some relief in a variety of ways. She may, for example, become so dependent, perhaps through symptoms of apparent physical illness, that others will feel obliged to take care of her and provide her with some of the things she wants. This would not be a deliberately adopted policy but a response learned through its drive-reducing effects. The "illness" would be called a symptom. It is, however, only a partial solution to the problem posed by fear and conflict, and it interferes with finding a more effective solution. This individual has all the characteristics of the neurotic; she is miserable, in conflict, stupid about her troubles, and has symptoms.

How can the neurosis be eliminated through psychotherapy? Since fear is the crucial cause, extinguishing fear is the crucial element of the cure. If the rat is given enough experience in the white compartment without shock, its tendency to make the fear-producing responses will eventually extinguish. Similarly, if the neurotic can be persuaded to make self-assertive responses (or do whatever else it is that she is afraid of) under conditions where she will not be punished, her fear will extinguish. Since the cues for fear come from the individual's own responses, she must gradually be induced to make these responses, first in very weak and indirect form, later more directly and strongly. Thus in the early stages of therapy the neurotic may timidly say that she sometimes thinks that if she were permitted to she could make helpful suggestions to her boss, while in the later stages she may express a violent desire to tell the boss off with assorted insults. As the patient extinguishes her fear of making self-assertive statements, she becomes more able to think sensibly about her conflict. Since talking about an act and doing it are somewhat similar, she also becomes by stimulus generalization less afraid of overt self-assertive behavior. Thus Dollard and Miller, through a considerably different theoretical system, come to a practical conclusion very much like Guthrie's threshold method for the elimination of undesirable emotional habits.

In the years since his collaboration with Dollard, Miller has gone on to make many additional contributions, particularly dealing with biofeedback, which is considered in Chapter 11. He has also explored the possibility that reinforcement may not be simply a matter of drive reduction (Miller 1963). In 1975 this lifetime of diverse contributions to psychology led to his receiving the annual Gold Medal from the American Psychological Foundation. In some ways it is unfair to Miller to describe his earlier rather than his later ideas, but they are the theory (as distinguished from experimental findings) for which he is most remembered, and they have played a major role in the history of learning theory.

HULL'S DEDUCTIVE THEORY

The most ambitious of the connectionist learning theories is that of Clark L. Hull (1884–1952). Long a professor at Yale, Hull was the most influential learning theorist of his time. He was a behaviorist, but far more sophisticated than Watson in the philosophy of science. His early training, before he became a psychologist, was in engineering, and something of the engineer's outlook is evident in his desire to construct an elaborate, formal, precise structure of psychological theory. In him we see the full logical flowering of the connectionist reinforcement tradition.

The Postulational Method of Theory Construction

Hull's concept of the ideal theory was a logical structure of postulates and theorems, similar to Euclid's geometry. The postulates would be statements about various aspects of behavior. They would not be laws taken directly from experiments, but more general statements about the basic processes involved. Like the postulates of geometry, they would not themselves be proved but would be taken as the starting points for proofs. From these postulates, a great variety of other statements, called theorems, could be logically derived. Each theorem could be proved by arguing logically from some combination of postulates. These theorems would be in the form of laws of behavior.

So far, such a theory is simply a logical creation. We have said nothing about whether its statements are true or false, only about how they hang together logically. When a theorem is proved, all this means is that if the postulates are true, the theorem must also be true. In order for the theory to have any value as a description of the real world, it is necessary to compare the theorems with actual laws of behavior as determined by experiments. In other words, after the theorist has determined by logic that the theorems follow from the postulates, he must then determine by experiment whether they are true. If they are, the whole theory is supported; if not, the theory is weakened and requires revision.

To anyone not acquainted with the philosophy of science, this approach may seem backward. The theorists start with postulates that may or may not be true. They then prove logically that if the postulates are true, certain theorems must also be true. Next they determine by experiments whether each theorem is in fact true. Finally, they use the truth or falsity of the theorems to argue indirectly about the truth or falsity of the postulates. If a theorem turns out to be false, they know that at least one of the postulates from which the theorem was proved must also be false, since it led logically to a false conclusion. In consequence, some postulate (the theorists may not yet know which one) must be changed so that the theorems which follow from it will be true. If, instead, all the theorems turn out to be true, this verification increases their confidence that all the postulates are true. However, they can never be absolutely sure that the postulates are true, since false postulates can sometimes lead to true theorems. As more and more theorems turn out to be true, they become more confident that the postulates are true, but there is always the possibility that eventually a theorem derived from the postulates will turn out to be false.

Although this theoretical approach may sound both complicated and strange, it is actually rather similar to what we do in many familiar situations. Consider a teacher who is concerned about the poor performance of a certain student, one who has a high IQ. She suspects that his difficulty may reflect two factors: (1) a fear of competition, and (2) a tendency to react to fear by "freezing up" and being unable to act effectively. These guesses are the equivalent of postulates. Either or both of them may be either true or false. They cannot be tested directly, since fear is not directly observable. They can, however, be tested indirectly. To test them, the teacher must first figure out how a student who had this fear and this reaction to fear would behave in certain situations. This is the process of deducing theorems from postulates. Thus, if the teacher's "postulates" about the student are true, it should also be true that: (1) the student will do better on test items if they are presented to him casually in conversation rather than as part of a test; (2) if given an opportunity to compete for a prize, he will refuse; and (3) if offered a chance to give a talk to the class on some topic that interests him, he will accept. The teacher may try each of these approaches and see what happens. These, then, are three experiments, each designed to test one of the teacher's "theorems." (We assume the design is sound.) If in each case the student does what the teacher predicted, her confidence in her interpretation (i.e., in her "postulates") will increase. She cannot, however, rule out the possibility that all of his behavior is really due to some other combination of factors, and that eventually he will do something that does not fit at all with her interpretation. She can become more and more confident that her interpretation is correct, but she can never be absolutely sure of it.

If it turned out that her first two predictions were confirmed, but the third was not, she would know that her "postulates" were not entirely correct. She might decide, since he refused to address the class even when no competition was involved, that his fear was not merely of competition but of any situation in which he was threatened with failure or disapproval. She could then look for new situations in which to test this revised "postulate." In this way her interpretation of his behavior would be a self-correcting process of making and testing assumptions.

The teacher's thinking in this example and Hull's thinking in constructing a scientific theory are, of course, markedly different in scope and in logical formality. These are differences of degree, however, rather than of kind. The teacher was concerned with very narrow interpretations, involving the behavior of a single student, while Hull was concerned with very broad ones, involving the whole range of human and animal behavior. In addition, Hull wrote down his postulates in detailed form and tested the theorems in controlled experiments, whereas the teacher merely developed hunches and tested them in a rough-and-ready fashion. Nevertheless, the two cases are basically similar enough to show the kind of reasoning that Hull followed in building his theory.

It should be clear from the above that Hull did not regard his theory as a final statement about the nature of learning. Rather, it was intended as a tentative formulation, always subject to revision to bring it in line with new data or new ideas. This tentativeness was a necessary characteristic of the kind of system he wanted to build. A set of postulates from which many laws of behavior are supposed to follow by strictly logical deduction has more chances of being wrong than does an informal system that makes fewer or less exact predictions. Watson's and Guthrie's theories, for example, are informal enough to leave considerable doubt as to just what they would predict in a particular situation. Hull, in contrast, intended to create a theory specific enough so that it would be easy to see when it was contrary to the evidence. A theory of this sort is practically certain to be wrong in some respects when it is first formulated, hence it must be open to change as errors are discovered.

It was Hull's plan to write three books expounding his theory. The first was to present and explain the postulate system. This appeared in 1943 as *Principles of Behavior.* Though various revisions of the postulate system were subsequently published, this book remains the cornerstone of Hull's theoretical writing. The second book was to contain detailed derivations of individual behavior in a variety of situations. This was published in 1952 as *A Behavior System.* It contains 133 theorems with their derivations from the postulates and the evidence bearing on their correctness as laws of behavior. The topics with which these theorems deal are as diverse as discrimination learning, locomotion in space, and the acquisition of values. As might be expected, this system of postulates and theorems is much more complicated and technical than any of the other systems we have discussed so far.

An invalid during the last few years of his life, Hull was barely able to finish this second major book. In the preface, he expressed his regret that the third book in the series, which was to present derivations of behavior in social interactions, would never be written. Four months later he died. Although his trilogy thus remains incomplete, it gives us a good picture both of the grandness of Hull's conception and of the many respects in which the actual system fell short of his aspirations. It is possible that if Hull had lived longer and had been in better health during his last years, many of the shortcomings of his theory would have been corrected. As it is, we must judge both his successes and his failures by his works as they stand.

The Four-Stage Analysis

Like most theorists, Hull wanted to develop a system for predicting the dependent variables of behavior from various independent variables. Recognizing the variety of independent and dependent variables with which he had to deal, he tried to simplify the task of prediction by introducing intervening variables. We saw in Chapter 1 how the use of such intervening variables makes it possible to summarize a great many details with a small number of concepts. Hull organized his intervening variables into a four-stage predictive scheme. The first stage consisted of the independent variables from which he was predicting, the fourth stage of the dependent variables to which he was predicting, and the second and third stages of intervening variables connecting them. Knowing the values (amounts or degrees) of the independent variables, he could compute the values of the intervening variables at stage 2. From these he could in turn compute the value of the intervening variable at stage 3, and from that finally predict the values of the dependent variables. The general outline of this elaborate scheme is given in Figure 3.1, which may serve as a guide to the explanation below.

The independent variables include all those that can be directly manipulated by an experimenter. These may be summarized briefly, since they are discussed in more detail in connection with the intervening variables. Some of the independent variables refer to the stimulation the learner is receiving at the moment, such as the brightness of a signal light or the intensity of electric shock. Others refer to immediately preceding events, such as the number of hours since the learner's last meal or the amount of muscular effort recently put forth. Still others refer to previous experience in the same learning situation, such as the number of times the subject has previously made the response to be learned or the magnitude of the reward received the last time the response was made. The

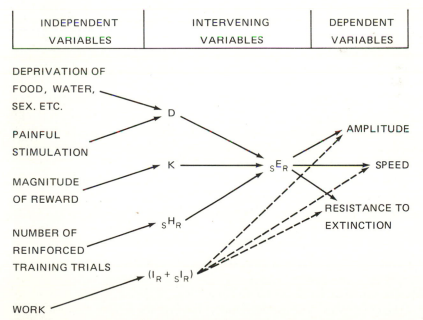

Figure 3. *A schematic representation of Hull's system.* The independent variables influence the intervening variables, which in turn influence the dependent variables. Solid arrows indicate that increases in the first variable tend to produce increases in the second; broken arrows indicate that increases in the first tend to produce decreases in the second. Note that $_sE_R$ is not an exact quantity but rather the mean of a range of oscillation.

number of such independent variables that could be mentioned is endless; the important thing for our understanding of Hull is the way that he has organized them in his system.

The second stage of the analysis introduces intervening variables. These are hypothetical states of the organism that cannot be observed but that are assumed to be directly controlled by the independent variables. The two most prominent ones, *habit strength* and *drive,* differ only in detail from the corresponding items in Miller's system of drive, cue, response, and reward. Habit strength refers to the strength of the learned connection between a cue or cues and a response, a connection built up through reinforced practice. Drive, for Hull as for Miller, is an activating state of the organism, and a reduction in drive serves as a reward.

Since Hull is a connectionist theorist, habit strength is a key concept in his system. It is the strength of the bond connecting a stimulus with a response. To indicate the nature of this connection, habit strength is abbreviated $_sH_R$ (pronounced S H R), with the H standing for habit and the S and R subscripts standing for the stimulus and the response that the habit connects. This habit is a permanent connection, which can increase but cannot decrease in strength. All long-term learning involves the formation and strengthening of habits. Each time a response occurs in the presence of a stimulus and this event is quickly followed by reinforcement, the habit strength of this stimulus-response connection increases. In this assumption (Postulate 3 in the final version of his system), Hull resembles all other reinforcement theorists. Like Miller, he goes on to say that all reinforcement involves a reduction in the strength of a drive stimulus. The rate at which habit strength builds up with successive reinforced responses (given by an equation in Postulate 4) follows the well-known "law of diminishing returns," so that each successive reinforced response contributes less to $_sH_R$ than the previous one. Eventually a point is reached at which additional reinforced responses contribute very little more to habit strength.

Drive is a temporary state of the organism, produced by deprivation of something the body needs or by painful stimulation. There are many different specific drive conditions, of which hunger, thirst, and pain are typical examples. Drives have two different functions. For one thing, each drive condition, such as hunger or thirst, produces a characteristic drive stimulus. This stimulus indicates the particular need from which the body is suffering. A rapid reduction in this drive stimulus is reinforcing. As a result, any response that occurs just before a reduction in a drive stimulus tends to be learned as a response to whatever stimuli are present. (We have already seen this relationship in connection with the postulate about the building up of habit strength.) The other function of drives is an activating or energizing one. All drive conditions combine to make up the total drive level of the organism. This total drive (abbreviated D) serves to raise the individual's activity level. This activating effect of D can be seen both in an increased level of general body activity and in the increased vigor with which all learned habits are performed. This analysis is essentially the same as Miller's (not surprisingly, since Miller based his on Hull's), but somewhat more detailed as well as more precisely stated.

Hull was also concerned with the size of the reward used as a reinforcer.

We are all familiar with the law that people tend to work harder for a larger reward than for a smaller one. In other words, the level of performance is commonly higher when a larger reward is given after the response occurs. How should this law be handled by the theory? In his earlier book, Hull (1943) treated the magnitude of the reward as one aspect of reinforcement. The larger the reward, the greater the reduction in drive, and hence the greater the increase in habit strength. However, this treatment proved not to be satisfactory. Experiments showed that changes in the magnitude of the reward produced very rapid changes in the level of performance, much faster than the slow growth of habit strength could explain. This difference was particularly difficult for Hull to explain when the change was from a larger to a smaller reward. If the reward was made smaller and performance became poorer, this result seemed to mean that the habit strength had become less. Yet habit strength involved a permanent bond, one that became stronger with reinforced practice but never became weaker. Here was a striking example of a discrepancy between theory and experiment. How would Hull deal with it?

Hull's answer, in the later versions of his theory, was to introduce a third intervening variable at the second stage of the analysis. Along with habit strength and drive he added *incentive motivation* (abbreviated K). The magnitude of the reward, in the new version, affects only K, not habit strength. The level of K depends on the size of the reward in the few immediately preceding trials. When the size of the reward is increased, at whatever stage of practice, K increases, and when the reward is decreased, K decreases. Incentive motivation thus refers, as the name implies, to the motivating effect of the incentive that is provided for making the response. The distinction between incentive motivation and reinforcement is subtle, since both depend on the reward, but the difference is nonetheless important. In order for a habit to increase in strength, the response must be followed by a reward that reduces a drive stimulus. The size of the reward makes no difference to the rate at which habit strength is built up; any reinforcement is as good as any other. The size of the reward does, however, affect the level of incentive motivation. Large rewards make for higher values of K, smaller rewards for lower values. When a rat learns to run down an alley for food, we see a gradual increase in its speed, an increase resulting from reinforced practice. However, over and above this slow increase in speed, we can increase or decrease the speed rapidly by changing the size of the food pellet we give at the end of each run. In the same way, it may be possible to increase a worker's output immediately by offering more pay for each item produced (thus increasing K), whereas it would take much longer to increase output by training the person in better work methods (increasing habit strength).

These three intervening variables, $_sH_R$, D, and K, work together to produce another intervening variable, which constitutes the third stage of the analysis. This is called *excitatory potential* and refers to the total tendency to make a given response to a given stimulus. It is abbreviated $_sE_R$, according to the same principle as $_sH_R$. It is equal to the product of the three other intervening variables; in other words, $_sE_R = {}_sH_R \times D \times K$. This equation means that the tendency to make a given response to a given stimulus depends on a habit built up through reinforced practice ($_SH_R$) and on two motivational factors, one depending on an internal state (D) and the other on an external incentive (K). For everyday purposes, one might refer to the $_SH_R$ for a given response as "knowing how to do it," to the K as "knowing what is to be gained by doing it," and to D as "wanting the thing that is to be gained." Hull, however, would not use this terminology, as he would consider it too vague for the precise and objective science of behavior that he wanted to promote. For Hull, $_SH_R$, D, and K are defined by the operations that produce them (reinforced practice for $_SH_R$, deprivation or painful stimulation for D, nutritive substance for K), not by any vague, everyday names that we might choose to give them.

The fourth and final stage of Hull's analysis is made up of the dependent variables, the aspects of behavior that can actually be observed and measured. Hull relates three of these to excitatory potential ($_SE_R$): (1) the amplitude or size of the response, (2) the speed of the response, and (3) the total number of responses that will occur, after reinforcement is removed, before extinction is complete. As $_SE_R$ increases, amplitude, speed, and number of responses to complete extinction all increase.

What Figure 3.1 shows, and what we have discussed, is only the barest outline of Hull's system (1952). The final version of his theory had 17 postulates and 15 corollaries (theorems that follow immediately from a single postulate), which he hoped would cover the whole range of known behavioral phenomena. For example, he postulated the existence of unlearned stimulus-response connections, but did not elaborate the topic and rarely referred to such innate connections in his theorems. He discussed the effect of a delay between the response and the reinforcement in weakening the response tendency. He went into considerable detail about generalization and about the way generalized habit strengths combine (i.e., what happens when the same response is learned to two different but related stimuli). These details are beyond the scope of this book.

Elaborations of the Theory

Other postulates and corollaries, however, are necessary in order to understand his derivations. One of these is *oscillation*. This refers to the assumption Hull makes that any given amount of excitatory potential is not an exact value but the average of a random distribution of values. When $_SH_R$ and D and K have been multiplied together to give the value of $_SE_R$, we still cannot predict with certainty what the amplitude or speed of the response will be. The reason is that the oscillation of $_SE_R$ may have carried the excitatory potential momentarily above or below the value computed. The oscillation in the value of $_SE_R$ is rapid and random (following approximately a normal distribution). The fact that Hull found it necessary to introduce this concept shows that his system, for all its complexity, could not hope to achieve perfect prediction of behavior. An element of random, unpredictable variation had to be introduced to make the system at all realistic.

When two incompatible responses have been learned to the same stimulus, so that two $_SE_R$'s are competing for expression, the principle of oscillation may be used to predict which will occur on any given trial. The oscillations of the two $_SE_R$'s are not synchronized, so that when one $_SE_R$ is momentarily high the other may be high, medium, or low. If the ranges of oscillation of the two $_SE_R$'s overlap, each response will occur on some trials. If the $_SE_R$ for one response is considerably stronger than that for the other, so that their ranges of oscillation overlap only slightly, the stronger will occur most of the time and the weaker only rarely. If the two are equally strong, so that their ranges of oscillation coincide, each will occur half of the time. All such situations involve the conflict between two response tendencies, and the degree of overlap of the two ranges of oscillation makes it possible to predict how often each of the two competing responses will occur.

Second, there is the concept of *reactive inhibition*. This is a tendency not to repeat a response that has just been made. The amount of reactive inhibition resulting from a response depends on the amount of effort required to make the response, so that reactive inhibition is roughly analogous to fatigue. Since this tendency not to respond works against and tends to cancel the effects of excitatory potential ($_SE_R$), it is subtracted from $_SE_R$ to give the net excitatory potential used in predicting the amplitude and latency of responses. The abbreviation for reactive inhibition is I_R. The fact that there is no subscript S indicates that the inhibition is against any making of that response, regardless of the stimulus that produces it. The total amount of I_R against a given response increases each time the response occurs but decreases with the passage of time. It is for this reason that subjects usually perform better on a learning task involving a lot of effort if their practice is *distributed,* with short periods of practice separated by short periods of rest. These rest periods provide an opportunity for I_R to dissipate. Hull also uses reactive inhibition to explain why extinction occurs. Once reinforcement is removed, successive responses no longer build up $_SH_R$ but continue to build up I_R. As a result, inhibition gradually overcomes $_SE_R$ until no further responding occurs. However, after a period of time the I_R dissipates and the response again occurs, giving spontaneous recovery.

There is a derivative of reactive inhibition called *conditioned inhibition,* which is somewhat different from Pavlov's intervening variable by the same name. This is abbreviated $_SI_R$ to indicate that it is a kind of habit connecting stimulus and response. Conditioned inhibition may be thought of as a habit of nonresponding produced by reactive inhibition. We can think of I_R as a negative drive that can be reduced by not making the response. Whenever the individual who has been responding ceases to respond, this "response of stopping responding" is reinforced by the fact that I_R starts to dissipate. The habit of stopping responding that is learned in this way is $_SI_R$. This $_SI_R$ explains, among other things, why spontaneous recovery is not complete. The I_R built up during extinction dissipates with time, but the $_SI_R$ learned in the process remains. It is noteworthy that Hull does not treat I_R and $_SI_R$ consistently as a drive and a habit, respectively. In his equation he simply subtracts both I_R and $_SI_R$ from $_SE_R$, so that net $_SE_R = {_SH_R} \times D \times K - I_R - {_SI_R}$.

We have said that Hull's goal was to derive the laws of behavior logically from a simple system of postulates. After considering the number of concepts and assumptions that Hull packed into his 17 postulates, the reader may not think that there is anything simple about the system. However, its relative simplicity is more evident if we note that *A Behavior System* contains 133 theorems, some with several parts, all following from the 17 postulates. Moreover, these 133 represent the limitations of Hull's time and energy rather than the limitations of the theory—there could have been many more. There is no question that the system represents an accomplishment of major proportions.

Strengths and Weaknesses of the System

Hull saw the value of his theory not so much in the particular intervening variables it included as in its rigorous quantification. The postulates do not merely state that certain variables are related; they give equations by which one can be computed precisely from the other. For example, the postulate regarding habit formation contains the equation $_sH_R = 1 - 10^{-.0305N}$, where N is the total number of reinforcements. Using this equation, one can state the exact level of habit strength for any given number of reinforcements. Similar equations are presented connecting the other second-stage intervening variables to the independent variables and also connecting excitatory potential to the dependent variables. The equation connecting the second-stage intervening variables to $_sE_R$, which involves simple multiplication, has already been given.

Hull dedicated much of his effort in the last years of his life to the problems of quantification. He wanted to develop a scale of measurement for excitatory potential that would be applicable to any response. How can $_sE_R$ for pressing a lever be made comparable to $_sE_R$ for running down an alley? Hull's answer (which will be meaningful only to those readers who have studied statistics) was to use the standard deviation of the oscillations of $_sE_R$ as an absolute measuring unit. This use of the standard deviation as a scaling unit is an idea Hull took over from the specialists in mental testing. He could then say that $_sE_R$ for a given response was two standard deviation units above zero, and this statement would have the same meaning regardless of what response he was discussing. This unit is also convenient for analyzing competition between responses, since knowing the $_sE_R$ for each response in standard deviation units also automatically tells how much their ranges of oscillation overlap and hence how often each will occur. Hull regarded the development of this scaling unit as one of the leading achievements of his life.

The evaluation of Hull's work by others has, however, been rather different from his own evaluation. It is just on the matter of quantitative rigor that he is most vulnerable to criticism. To some extent the reason is that his attempts at quantification were premature. The exact values in his equations, such as the $-.0305$ in the equation for habit strength, were typically based on the results of a single experiment. He made the suggestion, but never developed it, that the values in the equations might vary from individual to individual. Thus different people might have different equations for the development of habit strength, with the specific absolute value being greater than .0305 for fast learners and smaller for slow learners. Moreover, when Hull came to derive theorems from his postulates, he often used different values in his equations from the ones given in the postulates. For all of these reasons, it seems clear that these values were intended to be illustrative rather than literally correct. What Hull attempted to present in his books was the general outline of a rigorous theory together with some suggestions as to how the outline could be developed into a full-scale, quantitatively exact system. He was still a long way from actually having such a system when he died.

Even if we leave aside the matter of precise, quantitative values, the system does not live up to the ideals that Hull set for it. In a system such as Hull's, it should be possible, given the values of the independent variables, to compute the values of the intervening variables and from these the dependent variables. Even if the precise numbers needed to make the computations are not available, it should be possible to explain how the computations would be made. In many of Hull's cases, however, it is not possible, because a given topic is either covered by two or more contradictory postulates or is not covered at all. An example of the latter kind of problem is the definition of incentive motivation (K) when the drive is a painful stimulus, such as electric shock. Presumably in that case K would be determined by the amount of pain reduction that a response produced, perhaps specified by the difference in volts between the shock received before the response and the smaller shock received afterward. However, since K is defined by the weight of food or other nutriment consumed, it is impossible to apply Hull's equations to the situation where painful stimulation is the drive.

As an example of the former type of problem, in which the same question can logically be answered in different conflicting ways, let us consider the question of how to predict resistance to extinction. Suppose you want to know how many successive nonreinforced trials it will take to produce complete extinction. One approach would be to use Postulate 16, which translates excitatory potential directly into trials to extinction. A second approach would be to use Postulate 9 to calculate the amounts of reactive and conditioned inhibition and subtract them from excitatory potential. A third would be to note (Postulate 7) that when the amount of reward is zero, the value of K is also zero, which makes excitatory potential zero regardless of the values of the other intervening variables. It turns out that these three approaches, to the extent that they give precise answers at all, give conflicting ones. One could thus obtain three different answers to the question, depending on which postulates one decided to use in deriving one's "theorem" about extinction.

The fact that different approaches can give different quantitative answers is not necessarily a crucial problem, since we have seen that the particular numerical values Hull used were mainly illustrative. However, the lack of internal consistency which this illustration points up is a serious weakness in the system, probably more so than any other flaw. When a theory makes incorrect predictions, it can be modified, as Hull intended that his theory should be. When a theory does not deal with a given issue at all, we can accept this limitation in its scope and hope that some day it may be expanded to include the neglected topic. However, when a theory is internally inconsistent, so that it makes conflicting predictions about a given issue, its worth as a rigorous theory is seriously compromised. To some extent we can blame Hull's failure in this regard on the revisions in his theory. For example, when the intervening variable K was added to the system in a later revision, this change called for a number of adjustments in other postulates, but some of these were never made. Racing against time in the last years of his life, Hull considered it more important to show what could be done with parts of his system than to make the system as a whole complete and consistent. Nevertheless, we must recognize that the theoretical system Hull actually created falls far short of the standards he himself set for theories.

By the irony of history, it appears that Hull failed where he most wished to succeed and succeeded in the respect that interested him least. He wanted both to build a deductive theory, at once broad in scope and rigorous in detail, and to encourage others to carry on the same sort of theoretical work. We have seen how far he fell short of his first aspiration. Moreover, his failure may have discouraged others from attempting such a task. Many observers have noted a trend in learning theory away from the sort of all-encompassing theories that we have been discussing so far, toward theories of smaller scope designed to explain only certain kinds of learning. This trend may well reflect in part Hull's failure. For many years, psychologists have dreamed of doing for their field what Newton did for physics—developing a theory that would be at once vast in its scope, precise in its applications, and elegant in its simplicity, a theory that would pull together the loose ends of psychology into one master system. In pushing so far toward this goal and yet falling so far short of it, Hull convinced many psychologists that the day of such a master theory in psychology is still far off.

Yet in his failure, Hull also achieved striking success. His terms, his interests, and his ways of formulating psychological questions became more widespread than those of any other theorist of his time. A large number of experiments were inspired by his work. His interpretations of drive, reinforcement, extinction, and generalization became standard starting points for discussion of these topics. He was attacked, defended, and elaborated until to many people "learning theory" and "Hullian theory" became synonyms. Not until about two decades after his death did Hull's preeminence in learning theory pass to another system builder, B. F. Skinner. It is to Skinner's system that we now turn.

chapter 4

Skinner's Form of Behaviorism

During the period of Hull's greatest influence, and beginning several years before Hull published his *Principles of Behavior,* B. F. Skinner had been studying learning in his own distinctive way. He did not consider himself a theorist and had little use for the theories of others. Both the data he gathered and the pungent opinions he expressed soon brought him to general attention, but his distinctive research methods and his lack of interest in theories kept him outside the mainstream of learning theory for a long time. Yet by the same sort of irony that made Hull a great success even as he was failing in his dearest ambitions, Skinner has come to be the best-known learning theorist of the 1980s. Like Hull in a slightly earlier period, he is widely praised, condemned, and imitated, but rarely ignored, and many of his terms have become part of the standard vocabulary of learning.

Skinner was born in 1904 and received a Ph.D. in psychology from Harvard in 1931. After teaching at the Universities of Minnesota and Indiana, he returned to Harvard and has remained there ever since. His first book, *The Behavior of Organisms,* was published in 1938, three years after the first edition of Guthrie's *The Psychology of Learning* and five years before Hull's *Principles of Behavior.* Thereafter his influence increased gradually, until somewhere around 1970 he replaced Hull as the most talked about figure in the analysis of learning.

THE BASIC ELEMENTS OF SKINNER'S SYSTEM

Of the theorists we have considered so far, the one whom Skinner most resembles is Thorndike. The two are alike in being connectionist theorists (though Skinner emphasizes the connectionism less than Thorndike) who emphasize reinforcement as a basic factor in learning, who take a keen interest in problems of education, and who deemphasize theory. This lack of interest in high-level theorizing was only implicit in Thorndike's writings, but Skinner has made it quite explicit in his system. However, the fact that Skinner does not elaborate theorems, postulates, and intervening variables in the same formal way as Hull does not mean that Skinner is not a theorist at all. It does mean that his contributions as a theorist and as an experimenter are more closely intertwined than is the case with most of the system builders we have considered.

Two Kinds of Learning

In contrast to the other theorists we have discussed so far, Skinner recognizes two different kinds of learning. They are different because each involves a separate kind of behavior. *Respondent* behavior is elicited by specific stimuli. Given the stimulus, the response occurs automatically. The learning of respondent behavior follows the pattern that we have referred to earlier as classical conditioning. A new stimulus is paired with the one that already elicits the response, and after a number of such pairings the new stimulus comes to elicit the response. The presentation of the old (unconditioned) stimulus during training may be considered the reinforcer, since without it learning will not occur. Thus the learning of respondent behavior in Skinner's system is similar to the kind of learning that Watson assumed made up all learning.

Skinner maintains, however, that most behavior is of a different sort. This kind he refers to as *operant* behavior. Whereas the distinctive characteristic of respondent behavior is that it is in response to stimuli, the characteristic of operant behavior is that it operates on the environment to secure particular consequences. There is no specific stimulus that can be identified which will consistently elicit an operant response. Skinner speaks of operant behavior as being emitted by the organism rather than elicited by stimuli. Most behavior is of this sort; walking, talking, working, and playing are all made up of operant responses.

Skinner does not mean to say that operant behavior is not influenced by stimuli. Much of his analysis of behavior is concerned with ways in which operant behavior is brought under the control of stimuli. However, such control is only partial and conditional. The operant response of reaching for food is not simply elicited by the sight of food; it also depends on hunger, social circumstances, and a variety of other stimulus conditions. In these respects it is in contrast to the respondent jerking back of one's hand from a hot stove, which is regularly elicited almost without regard to other conditions. Because of this distinction, Skinner does not consider it useful to think of operant behavior as made up of specific stimulus-response connections in the sense that respondent behavior is. Whereas Guthrie analyzes every bit of behavior in terms of the stimuli that produce it, and Hull includes the S in $_SH_R$, Skinner prefers to think of most behavior (the operant kind) as emitted by the organism, without bothering to consider the multitude of stimuli that have something to do with its occurrence. The difference on this point is mainly one of emphasis and convenience rather than of direct disagreement. All three theorists agree that behavior depends on the total pattern of stimuli, external and internal, that are present when it occurs, but Guthrie and Hull prefer to emphasize this point for all responses, whereas Skinner prefers to ignore it in those cases where no one particular stimulus is crucial to the occurrence of the response.

The learning of operant behavior is also known as conditioning, but it is different from the conditioning of reflexes. Operant conditioning is the same sort of learning that Thorndike described. Because for Skinner this is by far the more important kind of learning, this topic is one on which he and Thorndike are close together. If an operant response (often called simply an operant) occurs and is followed by reinforcement, its probability of occurring again increases. Whereas for reflexes the reinforcer is an unconditioned stimulus, for operants it is a reward (or, as Thorndike would say, a satisfier). Thus we may say that reward following an operant makes that response more likely to occur again. (Even though the stimulus for an operant is unknown, Skinner still often refers to the operant behavior as a response.) This is the pattern of operant learning, which is to say, of most of the learning discussed by Skinner.

Whereas a respondent is usually a single bit of behavior, easy to identify separately, it is sometimes less clear where one operant stops and another starts. If a series of operants must occur in a particular sequence in order to obtain reinforcement, they become organized in a *chain*. The whole chain then comes to have some of the characteristics of a single operant, since the whole chain is the response unit that gets reinforced. In order to get a drink of water, for example, one may have to get up from a chair, walk into the kitchen, open a cupboard, take down a glass, turn on the faucet, fill the glass, raise it to one's mouth, and drink. Clearly this chain is made up of many operant responses, yet in another sense it functions as a single operant. If at any point the chain is broken —if there is no glass or if the faucet is broken or if there is some other obstruction —the whole chain up to that point will tend to undergo extinction. A large part of human behavior consists of such operant chains which function in some degree as units but can nevertheless be analyzed into their component parts.

Positive and Negative Reinforcers

Although Skinner is largely concerned with *positive reinforcers,* he also recognizes the existence of *negative reinforcers.* Negative reinforcers are aversive stimuli, ones that the individual commonly seeks to avoid. The *removal* of a negative reinforcer increases the probability of the preceding response, just as does the *presentation* of a positive reinforcer. Electric shock, for example, is a negative reinforcer because the termination of the shock is reinforcing. Thus a response can be reinforced either by presenting a positive reinforcer or by removing a negative one.

An important point about reinforcers, both positive and negative, is that they can be conditioned. If a stimulus occurs repeatedly with a positive reinforcer, it tends itself to acquire the capacity to reinforce behavior. It then is called a conditioned positive reinforcer. A sign reading "Restaurant" will serve as a conditioned positive reinforcer for a hungry person in a strange city, because such signs have been associated with food in the past. Similarly, a stimulus that occurs with a negative reinforcer tends to become a conditioned negative reinforcer, as in the familiar case of the burnt child who learns to avoid the stove even when it is cold.

The topic of negative reinforcement is obviously related to punishment, but the exact relation is not obvious. Negative reinforcement results from the removal of a negative reinforcer, whereas punishment involves the *presentation* of a negative reinforcer. (The reader should be warned that some other writers have used these same terms with somewhat different meanings, which can be confusing, but Skinner is not to blame for that.) What effects does punishment have, and how are these effects produced? Skinner points out that punishment is not a very reliable way of preventing responses from occurring. Reinforcement increases the probability of a response, but punishment does not necessarily reduce the probability. When it does, the reduction may result from any of three reasons.

First, the aversive stimulus used as punishment is likely to have emotional effects. These emotional effects are respondent behavior. In addition to whatever specific respondents an aversive stimulus may elicit (jerking back the hand that has just touched a hot stove, for example), it is likely also to elicit more general, emotional respondents. These respondents may include both observable, external responses, such as crying or trembling, and such less easily observable ones as a pounding heart and rapid respiration. These various emotional respondents are likely to be incompatible with the punished response, so that they reduce its probability of occurrence. For example, if scolding a child for eating forbidden candy makes her cry, it is likely also to stop her eating, since it is difficult to eat and cry at the same time. This effect, however, is temporary. When the aversive stimulus is removed the emotional effects soon dissipate. The punished behavior then occurs again, often at an even higher rate than before punishment. So, although this effect of punishment is often useful in temporarily stopping undesirable behavior, it is not useful in keeping it from happening again.

The second effect of punishment is an extension of the first. When a neutral stimulus is paired with an aversive stimulus that elicits a respondent, this is a conditioning situation. Whatever stimuli are present when punishment occurs thus have a chance to become conditioned stimuli for the emotional responses to punishment. These conditioned stimuli would then produce emotional respondents in the absence of the original punishment. As a result, the previously punished response would tend to be replaced by these competing responses, much as if punishment were still being presented. In our previous example, the child would tend to be frightened (make emotional responses) as soon as she touched the forbidden candy that had previously been paired with punishment. This fear would inhibit her eating responses. This effect of punishment, though basically similar to the first, is thus more lasting in its effects.

The third effect of punishment is an application of negative reinforcement based on the conditioned aversive stimuli from the second effect. When the individual turns away from the conditioned aversive stimuli, this act removes these stimuli and provides negative reinforcement. She is thus reinforced for making a response (turning away) that is incompatible with the punished response. As a result, she learns to turn away instead of making the punished response. Once stimuli from the forbidden candy became aversive to the child, she was reinforced for anything that got her away from these stimuli. Since getting away from these stimuli is incompatible with approaching them, she was learning not to eat the forbidden candy. This process, somewhat similar to Guthrie's interpretation of punishment, is what disciplinarians usually hope to accomplish by punishment. However, this effect, like the second one, lasts only until the conditioned aversiveness of the stimuli extinguishes. To maintain this effect, the disciplinarian must be prepared to give further punishments as needed to maintain the new behavior.

In general, Skinner regards punishment as a poor method of controlling behavior. For one thing, it is deceptive, since the first of its three effects often makes it appear dramatically successful when in fact it has produced only a temporary effect. For another thing, the emotional behavior it produces is likely to be undesirable from other points of view. Replacing misbehavior with crying or anger is seldom a good solution. Finally, the emotional responses may become conditioned to stimuli other than the ones the punisher wishes, including the stimuli of the punisher. For example, a child punished for some misbehavior in school may learn to respond with anger to the stimulus of the teacher or with avoidance to the whole school situation. For all of these reasons, punishment is both a rather unreliable technique for controlling behavior and one that is likely to have unfortunate side effects.

Nevertheless, Skinner would not claim that punishment is worthless as a device for changing behavior. When it is possible to arrange a situation so that punishment immediately follows the undesirable behavior, but does not occur at other times, it may be effective in suppressing undesirable behavior without producing harmful side effects. Under such conditions of very specific punishment, the individual learns emotional respondents and operant avoidance responses only to stimuli closely associated with the punished behavior. Since the person is exposed to all the other stimuli in the situation at other times when he is not being punished, whatever responses he learns to these other stimuli soon extinguish. However, such carefully arranged punishment situations are hard to maintain, and are a far cry from the haphazard and sometimes vengeful way that punishment is commonly used in everyday life. So in spite of some noteworthy exceptions, in general Skinner maintains that punishment is usually a poor method for modifying someone's behavior.

The Role of Stimuli

Although stimuli do not elicit operants in the sense that they elicit respondents, they may determine whether or not any given operant will occur. A stimulus acquires this influence through the process of discrimination. If an operant is reinforced in the presence of one stimulus but not reinforced when it occurs in the presence of a different stimulus, the tendency to respond when the second stimulus is present gradually becomes extinguished, and a discrimination is formed. The operant will then occur in the presence of the first stimulus but not of the second. Since the individual has learned to discriminate between the stimuli, they are referred to as discriminative stimuli. A positive discriminative stimulus is one which indicates that responding will be reinforced; a negative discriminative stimulus indicates that responding will not be reinforced. In some cases the main focus of interest is on the positive discriminative stimulus, as when the ringing of a phone indicates that someone is calling, and the negative stimulus is simply the absence of the ringing. In such cases the (positive) discriminative stimulus often is abbreviated S^D. In other cases the positive and negative stimuli are more symmetrical, as when the sign "OPEN" indicates that trying the restaurant door is likely to be reinforced and the sign "CLOSED" indicates that it is likely not to be reinforced. In such cases the positive and negative stimuli are likely to be labeled, respectively, as $S+$ and $S-$.

When one has learned a discrimination thoroughly, one may respond so rapidly to the onset of S^D that it looks almost as though the response were a respondent, elicited by S^D. It is not, however, since occurrence of the operant depends on factors other than the S^D. For example, a pigeon can be taught to peck a key when it is red $(S+)$ but not when it is green $(S-)$ by reinforcing with food the pecks of the red key but not those of the green key. However, the pigeon will show little tendency to peck the red key when completely satiated for food. The S^D is a major determinant of the operant pecking response, but it does not produce it in the automatic way in which a stimulus elicits a reflex. It sets the occasion for the occurrence of reinforcement. Under these conditions the operant is said to be under *stimulus control*.

The usual process of discrimination learning can be seen as a combination of acquisition and extinction. Responding in the presence of $S+$ is reinforced and therefore acquired. Because of generalization, the response also occurs in the presence of a similar stimulus, $S-$, but then it is not reinforced and therefore gradually extinguishes. In the process of learning the discrimination the learner makes many errors, that is, unreinforced responses to $S-$. However, it is also possible to teach someone a discrimination virtually without errors. First the learner acquires the response to $S+$, without $S-$ ever being presented. For example, a pigeon may learn to peck a green key for food reinforcement on some schedule (most often a variable interval). Then brief periods are introduced in which the key is completely dark. The dark key both looks considerably different from the green key, and in addition stands out much less against its background. As a result, the pigeon rarely pecks it in the few seconds it is available. Then a faint red light is projected on the key, so faint that there is again little likelihood of the pigeon pecking at it. Gradually the red is made brighter and the length of time it is visible is made longer. If the pigeon does peck at it, he is not reinforced, but the important point is that he rarely does peck it. Eventually bright red and bright green are alternating on the key, each present half the time, with the pigeon responding regularly to the green but almost never to the red. The gradual "fading in" of the red color made it possible for the pigeon to discriminate it from the green without going through the process of pecking red and being nonreinforced. He learned an *errorless discrimination* (Terrace 1963).

Whether a discrimination is learned with or without errors makes a considerable difference in the pigeon's later behavior. Various lines of evidence suggest that a pigeon that learned with errors dislikes the S— and is reinforced by its being turned off, over and above the reinforcement of getting back to the food-related S+. For example, it will learn a new response that turns off the S—, even though it neither turns on S+ nor provides food. A pigeon that learned without errors is much less likely to show this response (Terrace 1971). Moreover, if pigeons are now tested with a number of different colors, without reinforcement, pigeons that learned without errors will peck most often when the original green light is on the key. This is scarcely surprising, since green is the only color for which pecking has previously been reinforced. Those that learned with errors, however, peck most to a color somewhat bluer than the original green, in other words, to a color farther away from S— than the original S+. Their "favorite" color is now not green (the S+) but instead a different color farther away from red in the scale of colors (Hanson 1959). Both of these findings suggest that for pigeons that learned without errors, S— is neutral, neither liked nor disliked, but for those that learned with errors, the frustrating experience of repeatedly pecking S— without reinforcement has given them an active dislike of it.

Discussing these findings in terms of what the pigeon likes and dislikes is not a faithful rendering of the way Skinner would discuss them. He is interested in what the animals do, and in the independent variables that induce them to do it, not in how they feel or think about it. Nevertheless, it is easy to see similarities between the way pigeons that have learned with errors react to S— and the way humans sometimes react to stimuli in the presence of which they have experienced failure, frustration, and disappointment. As long as we keep the analogy at the level of behavior rather than of intervening variables such as pleasure or annoyance, Skinner is as glad as anyone to point such analogies out.

Skinner's rejection of theorizing is largely an objection to intervening variables, which he regards as useless at best, and often actually harmful, since they focus our attention on imaginary constructs instead of on reality. As a result, he is sometimes said to study the "empty organism"; not empty in fact, of course, but empty so far as Skinner's interpretations are concerned. As a result, though Skinner will talk about the tendency for a given operant to be emitted in the presence of a given discriminative stimulus, he will not talk about any habit or stimulus-response bond as being responsible for the tendency. Even in the cases of respondents, he will say only that the stimulus reliably elicits the response, not that there is a stimulus-response connection in the nervous system. Here he diverges not only from the arch-theorist, Hull, but even from Thorndike.

Skinner certainly gives a good deal of emphasis to stimuli, both as elicitors of respondents and as discriminative stimuli for operants. At the same time, he points out that stimuli are only one set of variables that influence the emission of operants; such factors as food deprivation must also be considered, and Skinner differs from Guthrie, Miller, and Hull in not interpreting food deprivation as a source of strong stimulation. Moreover, he prefers to speak of the rate at which an operant is emitted under a given set of conditions rather than of the probability that a given stimulus will be followed by a given operant, and completely rejects any reference to the strength of a stimulus-response bond. He is not, therefore, a connectionist in the same sense as the other theorists at which we have looked so far. The only stimulus-response connections he will discuss are relationships in behavior, not bonds in the nervous system, and at least so far as operant behavior is concerned, they are relationships that depend heavily on other factors as well. In a narrow sense of the term, therefore, we might say that Skinner is not really a connectionist at all.

Nevertheless, in a broader sense Skinner is still a connectionist. In contrast to the cognitive theorists, whom we will consider in the next chapter, but like the other connectionist theorists, he analyzes behavior in terms of responses and the stimuli that influence them. His concept of causation runs rather directly from independent to dependent variables, without discussing any system of beliefs or any pattern of mental activity that might occur between. Though the connections he studies between stimuli and responses are not interpreted as habits or bonds within the nervous system, they are connections nonetheless, and as direct connections as in any other theory. So, although he relates responses to stimuli somewhat differently from other connectionist theorists, it makes sense to include him as a connectionist. Indeed, at this point in the history of learning theory he is in a broad sense the best-known exemplar of the connectionist tradition.

THE EFFECTS OF REINFORCERS

Skinner's antitheoretical bias makes it difficult to discuss his system apart from his research and its applications (a fact of which Skinner would be proud). His research has been conducted almost entirely in one version or another of an apparatus that has become known as the *Skinner box.* This varies in size and form according to the organism being studied, but basically it is simply a box (or, from the subject's point of view, a room) containing a simple *manipulandum* (i.e., something the subject can manipulate) and a device for delivering reinforcers. The manipulandum may be a lever for rats to press, a key for pigeons to peck, a vending-machine plunger for humans to pull, or anything else appropriate for the kind of subject using it. The mechanism for providing reinforcers is typically some sort of feeder, delivering food pellets to rats, grain to pigeons, or candy bars to humans. Other sorts of reinforcers may be used, however, from drops of water for thirsty rats to peep shows for monkeys and humans. In some cases escape from electric shock to the feet is used as the reinforcer, in which case no separate reinforcement dispenser is required.

The basic principle on which the box operates is that responses to the manipulandum produce reinforcers. These responses are called *free operants,* since the subject is free to emit them at his own speed. The rate at which the free operant is emitted is the response measure. Whereas other experimenters may study speed of running, number of correct choices, or other aspects of operant behavior, Skinner and his followers study only the rate of emission of free operants. Whatever variable they manipulate, they study its effects in terms of this measure. However, as we have seen, there are many different free operants that can be studied. The important thing, says Skinner, is to find an appropriate operant for the kind of individual one wants to study, that is, an operant that the subject can emit conveniently and fairly rapidly. If this condition is met, the particular operant chosen makes little difference to the laws that will be found. We use levers for rats and keys for pigeons rather than *vice versa* because these manipulanda suit the response capacities of these animals, but we find similar laws for rats and for pigeons when each learns an operant appropriate for its own capacities.

Schedules of Reinforcement

The rate at which the free operant is emitted (the dependent variable) can be related to a great variety of independent variables. In practice, however, Skinner and his followers have concentrated largely on one independent variable, the *schedule of reinforcement.* This term refers to the particular pattern according to which reinforcers follow responses. The simplest schedule is *continuous reinforcement,* in which a reinforcer is given for every response to the manipulandum. This schedule generally is used when the subject is first being trained to use the manipulandum. After the response is learned, the schedule usually is shifted to some form of *intermittent reinforcement,* in which only some of the responses are followed by reinforcement. Skinner has collaborated with Charles Ferster on a book, *Schedules of Reinforcement* (Ferster & Skinner 1957), describing a great many different schedules of intermittent reinforcement and their effects, but fortunately for the student they tend to represent variations on two basic patterns. If the frequency with which reinforcers are presented depends on the rate at which responses are emitted, this is called a *ratio* schedule; if it depends simply on the passage of time, it is called an *interval* schedule. In addition, each of these two kinds of schedules may be either *fixed* or *variable.* Combining these two bases of classification gives four main kinds of schedules.

In a *fixed-ratio* schedule, the subject is reinforced after every so many responses. Thus a reinforcer may be delivered after every fourth or every tenth or every twentieth response. A *variable-ratio* schedule differs from a fixed-ratio schedule in that the reinforcer, instead of being presented consistently after every so many responses, is presented after a different number of responses on different occasions. In this case the ratio is the average number of responses per reinforcer. Thus on a variable-ratio five schedule, reinforcers are delivered on the average after every five responses, but on one occasion two successive responses might be reinforced, while on another occasion the individual might have to make as many as ten responses after getting one reinforcer before getting another.

On a *fixed-interval* schedule, a fixed interval of time has to elapse after one reinforcer is delivered before another can be obtained. Once this interval has elapsed, the first response will be reinforced. Thus on a fixed-interval one-minute schedule, the subject cannot obtain reinforcers more often than one a minute regardless of how fast he responds. He can obtain one each minute equally well by responding rapidly all the time or by responding only once a minute. If he waits for awhile after the minute has elapsed before making the response, the reinforcement will be correspondingly delayed. A *variable-interval* schedule makes it possible to obtain a reinforcer sometimes sooner and sometimes longer after the previous one. Thus on a variable-interval two-minute schedule, the average time after presentation of one reinforcer when another would become available would be two minutes, but on any particular occasion the interval might be considerably shorter or longer. Hence the only way to be sure of getting all available reinforcers as soon as possible would be to respond continuously.

How do these schedules differ in the patterns of responding that they produce? First, ratio schedules typically give higher rates of responding than interval schedules. This difference is not surprising, since fast responding on a ratio schedule increases the number of reinforcements in a given period of time, whereas fast responding on an interval schedule only serves to obtain each reinforcement a little sooner. Second, on both kinds of fixed schedule there is a tendency for responding to be slowest immediately after reinforcement (more so than can be explained simply by the time required to consume the reinforcer). The reason is that responses immediately after reinforcement are never reinforced. Intuitively this effect is easier to appreciate in the fixed-interval schedule, since the individual has nothing to gain from responses during the interval. On a fixed-interval schedule, the resulting pattern is a gradual increase in rate of responding from just after one reinforcement to just before the next. Because it looks on a graph like the edge of the familiar sea shell, this effect is known as *scalloping*. The fact that there is a gradual increase in rate during the interval rather than a sudden burst of responding just when the next reinforcer is due reflects the subject's inability to discriminate time perfectly.

On a fixed-ratio schedule we might expect the individual to respond just as rapidly after a reinforcement as at any other time, since he has to make a certain number of responses before the next reinforcement regardless of when he makes them. This expectation, however, reflects a view of the organism as figuring out the most profitable strategy and acting accordingly. According to Skinner, we must simply look at the reinforcement contingencies. On a fixed-ratio schedule, the first responses after a reinforcement are never reinforced as quickly as the later ones, hence they occur at a slower rate. However, this makes a difference only when the ratio is high enough so that the subject cannot make all the necessary responses quickly and get almost immediate reinforcement. Consequently, low fixed-ratio schedules show very little drop in responding after reinforcement, while high fixed ratios show a sometimes lengthy pause after reinforcement. This pause tends to be a total cessation of responding for some period of time, after which responses are emitted at a fairly constant rate until the next reinforcement. This pattern is therefore slightly different from the scalloping on a fixed-interval schedule, in which responding gradually increases during the interval, from a very low rate immediately after one reinforcement to a fairly high rate just before the next.

Finally, these variations in response rate during the interval between successive reinforcements are found only in fixed schedules, not in variable ones. Since all responses, early or late, have a chance of being reinforced on a variable schedule, responding is at a constant rate except for the brief period that may be required for actually consuming the reinforcer. Typical patterns of responding on these four kinds of schedules are shown in Figure 4.1.

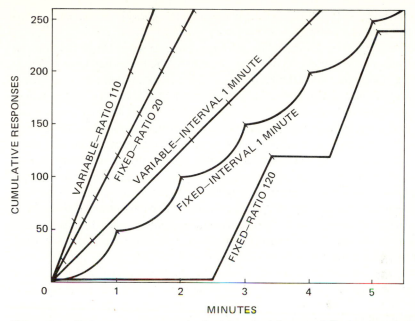

Figure 4.1 *Performance on several schedules of reinforcement.* Each curve represents the behavior of a single pigeon pecking a key on the designated schedule, plotted in the usual Skinnerian style. The vertical axis gives the number of responses emitted since the beginning of the time interval, so steeper curves indicate faster responding and a horizontal line indicates a period of no responding. The delivery of each reinforcer is indicated by a short diagonal mark intersecting the cumulative response curve.

Organisms will make more responses per reinforcer on most kinds of intermittent schedules than on continuous reinforcement. If reinforcement finally is terminated altogether, resistance to extinction is also greater after intermittent than after continuous reinforcement. To obtain rapid steady responding and high resistance to extinction, the variable-ratio schedule is most effective. It is possible, in fact, to get animals to work for food reinforcement on ratios so high that they are actually operating at a biological loss: the energy expended in operating the manipulandum is greater than that obtained from the occasional food reward, so that an animal can literally work itself to death.

These schedules differ in their sensitivity to various disrupting factors. This fact has been of particular interest in connection with the effects of various drugs, and pharmaceutical companies have found it useful to test new drugs on animals responding to different schedules of reinforcement. One generalization which emerges from many studies is that interval schedules are more easily disrupted by a variety of drugs than are ratio schedules. Doses that will make responding on an interval schedule quite erratic will leave a ratio schedule largely unaffected. Apparently the rat's counting mechanism is more stable or less vulnerable than its timing mechanism. Though Skinner is pleased that his experimental techniques have been found useful for studying drugs, it is characteristic of his approach that he makes no attempt to draw inferences about what these drugs are doing to the animal's body. There is a lawful relationship between what drug goes into the body and what behavior comes out; what goes on between these two is no concern of Skinner's.

Responding to a given schedule of reinforcement depends not only on the characteristics of that schedule but also on other schedules that have recently come before. One example is the greater resistance to extinction following intermittent rather than continuous reinforcement, mentioned above. In that instance, behavior on a no-reinforcement (extinction) schedule varies markedly as a function of the prior schedule. Another example is seen in the phenomenon known as *behavioral contrast.* This occurs when a subject is alternated between two different schedules, one of which makes possible a much higher rate of reinforcement than the other. Two distinctive stimuli (S+ and S−) tell the subject which schedule is in effect at the moment: for pigeons, these stimuli usually are colored lights projected on the key that the pigeon pecks. Any two schedules may be used to demonstrate behavioral contrast, so long as they differ in the rate of reinforcement that they provide, but it is most common for the more favorable schedule to be some variable-interval schedule, and for the less favorable to be extinction. Behavioral contrast is demonstrated by the fact that the subject responds faster to the more favorable schedule under these conditions than if that same schedule were the only one the subject experienced. The contrast between the two schedules somehow makes the subject respond to the more favorable of the two as if it were even more favorable than it is.

It should be noted that studies of different schedules of reinforcement are not concerned with how the response is originally learned. Ordinarily the subject is well trained to use the manipulandum before any form of intermittent reinforcement is introduced. Thereafter a given indiviual can adapt fairly readily to one schedule after another, changing behavior to suit each new schedule. Thus Skinner's formal research has been largely concerned with a short-run aspect of learning, the rapid shifts in performance level to match shifts in reinforcement conditions. (Some writers, in fact, consider such shifts too short-run to be called learning at all, and refer to them simply as changes in performance.) These studies are concerned not with an individual's learning how to respond, but rather with learning how rapidly to respond under a new set of reward conditions.

Shaping

We should not conclude from this emphasis, however, that Skinner has been uninterested in the process of learning how to perform complex tasks. Much of his less formal work has been concerned with this problem, and he has given striking demonstrations of training techniques. Though many experimental psychologists study animal learning, Skinner and his followers are almost unique in their concern with animal training. The technique by which they train animals to perform complex acts that are outside their normal range of behavior is known as *shaping.* The behavior is shaped through a series of successive approximations to the desired behavior, each made possible by selectively reinforcing certain responses and not others. Thus behavior gradually is brought closer and closer to the desired pattern.

Suppose you want to train a pigeon to bowl in a miniature alley with a wooden ball and toy pins (as Skinner has done). If left to its own devices, the pigeon might occasionally move the ball around, but would quite possibly never do so in a way that would get the ball down the alley and knock over any pins. If you waited to reinforce a full bowling response, therefore, you would have a quite impractically long wait, and even if the response finally did occur spontaneously, and you reinforced it, it would probably be another long wait before it occurred again. Yet this is not a particularly hard game for a pigeon to learn to play, given proper training.

To teach the pigeon to bowl, Skinner began, of course, by depriving it of food. Next, he trained it to eat from the food magazine. The operation of the food magazine made a distinctive sound, which, since it always signaled the availability of food, became a conditioned positive reinforcer. This conditioned reinforcer was a critical feature of the shaping process. If the food magazine had been silent, some of Skinner's attempts to provide immediate reinforcement would probably have failed, since it would have taken the pigeon some time to notice that the magazine was open. With the sound, however, Skinner could be sure that the opening of the food magazine would have an immediate reinforcing effect on the pigeon.

Given this means of reliably producing immediate reinforcement whenever he wished, Skinner then proceeded to reinforce behavior that approximated the desired final performance: the pigeon's striking the ball in such a way that it would go down the alley and knock over some pins. First he reinforced merely being near and facing toward the ball. When that behavior had been reinforced often enough so that it was occurring much of the time, he changed to giving reinforcers only when the pigeon pecked close to the ball. When that response had become common, he moved on to reinforcing only pecks that moved the ball. From there he narrowed the range of reinforced responses even further until the pigeon was sending the ball down the alley against the pins as reliably as a (novice) human bowler (Skinner 1958).

Though shaping is an application of the scientific principle of reinforcement, it involves a good deal of art. If the trainer proceeds too fast in narrowing down the range of responses that will be reinforced, the behavior already shaped will begin to extinguish. If the trainer proceeds too slowly, the training will take excessively long to complete. The trainer must therefore be constantly alert to the effect of his behavior on the learner's behavior and constantly ready to change it as needed in order to achieve the most effective shaping.

Given skillful application of the basic principle of shaping, striking results can be obtained. Skinner has not only trained one pigeon to bowl, but he trained two pigeons to cooperate (as well as compete) in a modified version of ping pong. Rats have been trained to go through whole sequences of unratlike operations worthy of Rube Goldberg, such as pulling a string to obtain a marble, carrying the marble in its paws to a tube projecting above the floor, and dropping the marble into the tube. Pigs have learned to dance and play the piano (not well enough for the concert stage, but well enough for county fairs!). Some of Skinner's followers have found a considerable market for their talents in training animals for fairs and movies, as well as for more "serious" purposes.

Even though rapid and effective shaping requires a good deal of skill, the most striking significance of shaping is the impressive effects that can be obtained by applying the simple principle of reinforcement. Not all of the demonstrations have been with animals. A technique for showing the automatic effects of reinforcement on human behavior is called *verbal conditioning.* In the first experiment of this sort (Greenspoon 1955), the subject was instructed simply to say words. The experimenter gave the subject no clue in the instructions as to what sorts of words were desired. However, whenever the subject said a noun in the plural form, the experimenter said "mmhm." There was an increase during the session in the frequency with which subjects said plural nouns. This increase occurred in spite of the fact that many subjects were quite unaware, so far as could be determined by questioning, either of the fact that they were saying more plural nouns or of any relation between the experimenter's behavior and their own. When the "mmhm" was discontinued, frequency of plural nouns declined (extinction).

In another less formal experiment (Verplanck 1955) subjects were simply engaged in conversation without even being told that this was an experiment. The experimenter (who in this case might better be called the interviewer) expressed interest in and agreement with any of the subject's remarks that were presented as expressions of opinion (i.e., "I think . . .," or "It seems to me . . ."). Other kinds of remarks produced no reaction from the interviewer. Expressions of opinion became more and more frequent during the conversation. In both of these verbal-conditioning studies, verbal behavior was modified by reinforcing a given kind of verbal response and no other. Like any technique of operant training, this one depends on finding a reinforcer that will be effective for the particular kind of individual being studied, but once one is found the principle of reinforcement seems to apply as well here as elsewhere.

However, the "automatic" nature of these effects has been subjected to a good deal of question. In studies of animals, no problem arises: one need only note the systematic ways that behavior is influenced by reinforcement, and whether or not one calls the effects automatic is pretty much irrelevant. With humans, however, one can ask them what they thought about the whole procedure and thus try to determine whether they reacted automatically and largely unconsciously to the reinforcement or whether they noticed what kinds of responses were being reinforced and then decided whether or not to work for reinforcers. From Skinner's point of view, the person's awareness is not a particularly important issue—the important question is whether the reinforcement influences the behavior, not whether the person can accurately describe what is going on or whether he feels that he is making a free choice. However, the issue of awareness in verbal conditioning has aroused considerable interest among other psychologists. Although the issue is far from settled, the weight of current evidence suggests that humans who are influenced by verbal reinforcement are usually at least partly aware of what is going on and have some sense of choosing how they will react to it (see, e.g., Spielberger & DeNike 1966). On the other hand, when a person is busy concentrating on one aspect of his own behavior, it may be possible to condition some other aspect of his behavior without his being aware of it (Rosenfeld & Baer 1969). Probably the best conclusion is that reinforcement sometimes works automatically, without the learner being aware of what is going on, but that such events are the exception rather than the rule.

An interesting sidelight on the shaping of behavior is the way in which reinforcement can produce not only behavior that the experimenters intend but also behavior of which they have no advance idea. Suppose a timer is arranged to deliver a reinforcer every 30 seconds regardless of what the subject does. (This schedule is not the same as a fixed-interval schedule, where the subject has to make a particular response after the interval is up in order to be reinforced.) Whatever the individual is doing when the reinforcement comes is more likely to occur again the next time. Purely on the basis of chance, he is more likely to be doing something at that moment that he commonly does than something that he does more rarely. Given the fact that this behavior occurs commonly to start with, plus the fact that it has now just been reinforced, it is all the more likely to be occurring when the next reinforcer is delivered. This reinforcement will strengthen it some more and make it even more likely to occur at the right time to receive the third reinforcement. Thus this particular behavior becomes more and more likely to occur because it is reinforced, even though the experimenter did not deliberately reinforce that response rather than others. Rather, the learning was the result of a vicious circle: because the response occurred frequently, it was reinforced, and because it was reinforced, it occurred more frequently. The experimenter did not know in advance which of the various responses that the individual made frequently would be learned in this way; that selection depended on chance. There might be a period during which several different responses were reinforced before any one gained enough of a lead to start the vicious circle going. Behavior might be too variable for any one response ever to get the necessary head start. However, when it occurs, this unplanned reinforcing effect is an impressive demonstration of the automatic operation of reinforcement.

Skinner refers to this kind of unplanned learning through "accidental" reinforcement as *superstitious* behavior. The justification for this term is that the subject acts as though a certain behavior produced reinforcement, when in fact there is no necessary connection between the behavior and the reinforcement. The response is commonly followed by reinforcement only because both behavior and reinforcement occur frequently and hence often occur at the same time. The most successful experimental demonstrations of superstitious behavior have been with pigeons, but applications to human learning are not difficult to see. If a student carries a rabbit's foot into an examination for good luck, and does well, this experience will make him more likely to carry it into the next examination. Repeated successes while carrying the rabbit's foot will make his adherence to the foot as a source of luck stronger and stronger, even though it contributed nothing to his success and he would have done just as well without it. (We overlook the possibility that the confidence the talisman gave the student may have increased his effectiveness in taking the examination.) Many of our beliefs, not only in charms and magic, but also in medicine, mechanical skills, and administrative techniques probably depend on such superstitious learning. A public speaker who thinks he is successful because he knocks three times on the podium before starting to speak is generally recognized as superstitious, but a speaker who thinks he is successful because he starts each lecture with a funny story may be equally superstitious by Skinner's definition. In humans, such superstitions are probably more often learned in the first place from other people than from chance occurrences. However, when people claim that their faith has been validated by experience, this experience probably often follows the learning pattern that Skinner has described and illustrated.

APPLICATIONS AND IMPLICATIONS OF SKINNER'S SYSTEM

As the reader has probably already guessed, Skinner has shown much interest in the application of learning principles to complex practical situations. Many of these applications are at the level either of philosophical principles or of speculation about what might work. Two, however, have been extensively tested. In the treatment of behavior disorders, and in education, Skinner's ideas have not only demonstrated their validity outside the laboratory but they also have had major practical effects on psychotherapy and on schooling.

Behavior Modification

The heading of "behavior disorder" covers a wide range of problems from those mildly irritating behaviors that we all notice in each other (and sometimes even in ourselves!) through delinquency and neurosis to severe psychosis. Whether the problem is minor misbehavior on the part of a relatively normal child or a psychosis that has kept a patient hospitalized for many years, Skinner's approach to treatment is quite straightforward. Rather than focusing on early childhood, current psychodynamics, or possible organic abnormality, Skinner simply asks what this person is doing that we do not like and what we would like to have the person do instead. Once we have decided this, we can proceed to extinguish the undesirable behaviors and reinforce desirable ones. In other words, we can change the *contingencies of reinforcement,* the specific relationships according to which reinforcement is contingent on one or another behavior. This approach, basically similar to Guthrie's but with the additional element of reinforcement, forms the basis of various *behavior-modification* techniques of psychotherapy.

The behavior-modification approach may be illustrated by a case in which two nursery-school children were cured of excessive crying (Hart, et al. 1964). The therapists (experimenters? educators?), like true Skinnerians, began by differentiating the child's crying into respondent (usually produced by physical pain and not influenced by the social situation) and operant (less directly influenced by specific stimulation, but occurring when an adult was nearby and involving frequent glances at the adult, apparently to see the adult's reaction). No attempt was made to modify the respondent crying, but all the nursery-school teachers were trained to recognize and to ignore the operant crying. The attention from teachers that had previously reinforced the operant crying was thus removed, and extinction began. That the reduction in operant crying was really the result of the extinction procedure is indicated by what happened when the teachers were instructed to begin again paying attention to the children when they cried—there was rapid relearning of the crying. A second extinction was then begun, and the operant crying was virtually eliminated.

Similar techniques have been used in mental hospitals and in a variety of other settings to deal with such diverse behaviors as over- and undereating, hoarding of towels (by a mental patient), inattention in school, and the extreme social withdrawal of autistic children and of many psychotics. Sometimes the awarding of reinforcers for certain behaviors has been organized and formalized in the form of *token economies.* In a token economy, the people in an institution (students, patients, prisoners, or whatever) can earn tokens by engaging in certain behaviors or by not engaging in others, and can then exchange these tokens (which become conditioned reinforcers) for primary reinforcers of their choice. It is easy to belittle token economies by saying that what they show is that modern behavioral science has finally invented money! However, when the use of a token economy changes people from disruptive to constructive and cooperative behavior, and does it without the use of aversive stimulation, the fact that the basic idea is nothing new should not detract from the ingenuity of those who figured out when and how to apply it.

Its supporters regard behavior modification as the most significant innovation in psychotherapy at least since the advent of psychoanalysis. In support of this view, they point out its many dramatic successes, beneficial changes in behavior which, though sometimes slow in absolute terms, are still usually a good deal faster than traditional psychotherapies. Moreover, the same techniques can be used in a wide variety of settings to produce many different kinds of behavior change. Further details about the many uses of behavior modification (or behavior mod, as it is commonly abbreviated) can be found in Bootzin (1975), and evidence of its effectiveness relative to other psychotherapies in a study by Smith and Glass (1977).

Critics of behavior mod have not hesitated to point out its difficulties. Interestingly, it has been attacked from two opposite directions. On the one hand, it has been criticized as producing only temporary and superficial changes. That the changes are often temporary is to be expected, since Skinner would not expect changes in behavior to last unless the changes in the contingencies of reinforcement also last. In some cases, behavior modifiers are satisfied if, by arranging proper contingencies of reinforcement, they can get students to study harder or mental patients to behave in more "normal" ways in the hospital, without worrying about anything further. In other cases they hope to produce more lasting changes, but they expect success only if they can bring about lasting changes in the contingencies of reinforcement. If a school child who has acquired good studying behavior as a result of a token economy in the classroom continues to show that changed behavior after the token economy is gone, it will be because other reinforcers have taken over, whether they are the fun of learning, the usefulness of the knowledge, or the satisfaction of pleasing the teacher. If none of these reinforcers is strong enough to keep the child studying, perhaps the problem is neither in the child nor in the token economy but in the curriculum!

The importance of maintaining the contingencies of reinforcement is shown in a follow-up of 13 autistic children who had received behavior mod treatment (Lovaas, et al. 1973). All of these children showed severe abnormalities of speech and social behaviors such as flapping their arms or holding the head cocked in a fixed position for long periods of time. Treatment varied from child to child, but in general involved a combination of shaping normal responses through positive reinforcement, mildly punishing abnormal responses, and trying to bring the child's behavior increasingly under the control of stimuli from other people. All the children showed increases in normal and decreases in abnormal behavior. A follow-up compared the four children who then went to live in an ordinary institutional setting, without behavior mod, with the nine who lived with their parents, who had received training in behavior mod. The nine who lived at home maintained their improvement much more than did the four who were institutionalized, a difference that could not be explained by any difference in the seriousness of their symptoms either before or just after treatment. It looked, therefore, as though the effects of treatment would continue if and only if at least part of the treatment was also continued, as was the case in the homes but not in the institutions.

However, there are other differences between living at home and living in an institution that might possibly explain the difference between the two groups. To obtain further evidence as to whether the contingencies of reinforcement were what made the difference, the therapists tried bringing two of the institutionalized children back for further treatment. The improvement in the behavior of these two children was rapid, as soon as the behavior mod contingencies were reinstated. It was evident that they had not forgotten what they had learned, but rather that the new behavior had been extinguished in the institutional setting. If these had been more normal children, the ordinary reinforcers of everyday life might have been enough to sustain the new behavior they learned through behavior mod, but for these autistic children only deliberate continued use of the original reinforcers could do so.

The opposite criticism of behavior mod is that, far from being too weak and trivial, it is too dangerously powerful. The worry these critics have is that someone exposed to planned contingencies of reinforcement loses freedom and comes under the control of the person who controls the reinforcers. Skinner's reply to this challenge is that we are all controlled by many contingencies, some deliberate, some accidental. If the contingencies of positive reinforcement used by behavior modifiers are more effective than others, and at the same time more pleasant for the learner and more beneficial in their effects, why is that a criticism? Isn't it better, says Skinner, to be controlled pleasantly by a beneficient controller than to be subjected to all the conflicting, selfish, and often aversive attempts at control that so often occur? Not necessarily, say his critics: the worst enemy of freedom may be a gentle, beneficent dictator. To pursue the argument further would take us too far afield, but at least these latter critics do behavior mod the honor, however dubious, of being afraid of it.

Teaching Machines

As the above discussion indicates, behavior modification is as much an educational as a psychotherapeutic technique. It is therefore not surprising that the other of Skinner's applications that has had important practical effects is in the field of education. This is the study of programmed learning, first popularized through its use in teaching machines. Though Skinner was not the first to suggest this approach to teaching (Sidney L. Pressey is generally credited with making the first teaching machine), he gave the idea much of its early impetus. His object was to treat classroom learning like any other situation in which certain behavior, in this case largely verbal behavior, is to be shaped. The student must progress gradually from familiar to unfamiliar material, must be given an opportunity to learn the necessary discriminations, and must be reinforced. The classroom situation has many disadvantages from this point of view. A rate of progress appropriate for one student is too fast or too slow for another. Opportunities for each individual to make the required responses are limited, and reinforcement is often greatly delayed. Individual tutoring could solve all of these problems, but in most cases this is out of the question except perhaps for occasional supplementary work. What, then, can be done to give students in school the same advantages that pigeons in boxes have? Skinner's answer to this question was the teaching machine.

The basic component of the machine is the program. This is a series of combined teaching and test items that carries the student gradually through the material to be learned. An item may or may not convey new information to the student, but in any case it calls for him to fill in a blank in a statement. He can then look at the correct answer. If it agrees with his answer, this agreement constitutes the reinforcement. If not, he can study the correct answer so as to increase his chance of being reinforced next time. However, Skinner prefers to make the learning requirements so gradual that the learner rarely if ever does make mistakes. If this effort is successful, then on every item the student makes a correct response and is reinforced, which in Skinner's view is the best possible arrangement for learning. Individual differences then are reflected in the rate at which the student proceeds through the program. (For a discussion of the logic and the advantages of this approach to teaching, see Skinner 1962.)

At this point the reader may be wondering, "Where does the machine come in? This is just the old, familiar workbook method." To some extent this is a valid point. Much current programmed instruction is in workbook rather than machine form. The student fills in a blank, then turns to another page to check the answer. However, these programmed workbooks differ from the more familiar type of workbook in that they do all teaching through the items in the program, rather than serving to supplement lectures and textbooks. The same series of items that calls forth the student's responses also provides the information necessary for making the responses. This arrangement, in turn, forces the author of the program to plan the sequence of items very carefully in terms of just what the student needs to learn and just how it can best be presented. Whether the program is in a workbook or in a machine is of secondary importance. Machines have some advantages in speeding up the reinforcement and reducing the likelihood of cheating by the student. It is probable, however, that much of Skinner's preference for machine presentation results from two factors: (1) the novelty effect of the machine, which very likely makes its use more reinforcing to the student, and (2) Skinner's personal liking for mechanized procedures. Although the machine itself has sometimes been a bone of contention between those who favor increased classroom efficiency and those who fear the loss of more personal values in education, this is a misplaced emphasis. The pertinent question is about the value of programmed methods of instruction in whatever form, not about teaching machines as such.

It is too soon to judge how valuable programmed teaching, by machine or otherwise, will prove in the whole context of education. Many factors besides efficiency as a specific teaching device are involved. Moreover, the increasing availability of computers provides for more varied forms of presentation than either workbook programs or the original form of teaching machine. Although Skinner favors *linear programs,* in which every learner goes through the same sequence of steps, which are easy enough so that mistakes are rare, computers have increased the use of *branching programs,* in which the learner's answers determine what material will be received next. In some computer teaching programs, the learner and the computer carry on quite a spirited dialogue, including both praise and sharp admonishments from the computer as it responds to a great variety of possible behaviors by the learner. The computer can decide how lavishly to praise or how strongly to reprove the learner, as well as what material to present next, not just on the basis of the learner's last response, but on the basis of the learner's whole record of performance. Though the computer usually communicates in writing on a cathode-ray tube, it can also be designed to speak. Both of these capabilities are illustrated in a program teaching children to read (Atkinson 1974).

As a result of the computer's great flexibility, computer-aided instruction (CAI) is rapidly replacing programmed instruction as an active topic of research and an expanding area of education. The technology of programmed instruction has now gone far beyond Skinner's initial contribution, but it continues to provide striking evidence that Skinner's applications are not restricted to tricks of animal training and to speculations about the organization of society.

Other Applications

In addition to behavior mod and programmed instruction, both of which have given rise to much research and development, Skinner has presented a number of other logical applications that are still largely at the level of talk. One (appropriately enough) is the analysis of language. In his book, *Verbal Behavior,* Skinner (1957*b*) analyzes language as a system of operants. He notes that all of us live in a *verbal community,* a group of people who share a common language and who shape our own language by reinforcing correct usage and extinguishing incorrect usage. This shaping process is most noticeable with children, who must learn the language from scratch, but it continues to operate in adults as they learn new words and as they are either reinforced or not for the various spicy elements they include in their speech. Some utterances, such as requests and demands, are reinforced by another person's compliance; these utterances are called *mands*. Other utterances, which include most conversations, are reinforced in subtler ways by signs of understanding, such as smiling or answering appropriately. Utterances of that sort are called *tacts*. It is easiest to learn correct speech when the events that the speech refers to are external ones that everyone in the linguistic community can observe. When the events are unobservable, as in discussing one's own or someone else's feelings, it is much harder to decide whether a tact is correct or not. A child learns to describe his own feelings correctly only to the extent that others can infer those feelings from other evidence and reinforce the child's descriptions when they are accurate. No wonder our vocabularies for describing feelings lack the precision of science!

A second area of interest is the application of Skinnerian principles to complex social behaviors. Any social interaction is a situation in which two or more people are providing one another with stimuli and with reinforcers, and perhaps also failing to reinforce one another in some critical ways. Whether the interaction is formal or casual, friendly or hostile, dominant or egalitarian, it can be analyzed in these basic terms. For example, a factory worker who is paid on piecework (pay proportional to the amount produced) is being reinforced by his employer on a form of fixed-ratio schedule. For a quite different example, a mental patient diagnosed as depressive may be on a schedule where almost nothing he can do is reinforced, so that he complains of feeling helpless, hopeless, and worthless. Once familiar with Skinner's thinking (or should we say with his verbal behavior?), the reader can probably predict some of Skinner's comments on the mutually reinforcing or nonreinforcing contingencies in politics, business, religion, and the family.

Finally, Skinner has devised a utopian community called Walden Two (in honor of Thoreau, who might or might not feel honored), in which the principles of learning are used to create a more ideal form of social organization (Skinner 1948). In contrast to such negative utopias as those of Huxley's *Brave New World* (1932) and Orwell's *1984* (1949), *Walden Two* describes what Skinner believes would be a desirable community, one in which principles of behavioral engineering would be used to create a more fulfilling environment for all the residents. Many of the details of this imaginary community run sharply counter to what we are used to considering appropriate. The economy is socialized; government is by self-perpetuating committees instead of by elected representatives; children are reared primarily by child-rearing professionals, rather than by their parents, and the child-rearing practices include some that are deliberately designed to frustrate the children so as to build up their tolerance for frustration.

It is not at all clear that these particular ways of doing things follow from any of his data as a researcher. How did he happen to select them for his utopian community? One possibility is that the particular suggestions were intended for their shock value in showing how different a behaviorally engineered community might be from what we would at first think desirable. In the second volume of his autobiography, Skinner leaves this possibility open by saying: "I let Frazier (the founder of the fictional community) say things that I myself was not yet ready to say to anyone" [1979, p. 296]. He adds, however, "Eventually I became a devout Frazierian" [ibid., p. 298].

Another possibility, not necessarily contradicting the first, is that Skinner made Walden Two the kind of community that reflected his own felt needs at that point in his life. He remembered as the worst year of his life the one immediately after college when he was trying to become a novelist while his parents urged him to settle down to a more conventional career. Is that why he designed Walden Two as a community in which children are largely freed from family pressures, and in which it is easy to combine artistic creativity with "honest toil"? Later, when writing the book, he was faced with problems and disruptions in both family and professional life. Is that why Walden Two sometimes impresses readers as a fine community for an overburdened person to retreat to but not much of a place for the restless or the ambitious? Is such a community one that Skinner desired only at that point in his career? Elms (1981) thinks so, and further speculates that writing the book may have been the therapy Skinner needed, since he made no effort to put his ideas into practice.

Nevertheless, several attempts have been made to establish real-life communities based on his book. For the most part these attempts have had no better success than the many other utopian communities that have been tried over the years, but one, known as Twin Oaks, has lasted for some years and achieved at least a modest degree of success. The first five years of Twin Oaks have been described by one of its founders (Kat Kinkade 1973). The problems that the community struggled with sound much like those that would face any commune, irrespective of any special behavioral principles. Turnover in membership was high, and during that period no children stayed long enough for any of Skinner's suggestions about child rearing to have a chance to be effective. As for Twin Oaks's organization, Kinkade writes: "The debt we owe Dr. Skinner is enormous, but there is nothing sacred about the institutions we derived from his book. All of our systems are subject to change, and most of them have changed even over the few years that we have been a community" [p. 57]. This, presumably, is what Skinner would have expected and wanted.

Skinner's Relation to Other Psychologists

For many years, Skinner and his followers formed a small in-group within the psychology of learning. Whereas the followers of other theorists argued with each other and tried to best one another in experimental tests of their respective theories, the Skinnerians remained aloof and went their own way. They published their own journal, held separate meetings at psychological conventions, and eventually established a separate Division on the Experimental Analysis of Behavior within the American Psychological Association. As Skinner's research techniques and his ideas have become increasingly prominent, much of this separatism has disappeared, but much also still remains. What are the differences between Skinner and other psychologists of learning that account for it, and what factors have made him, in spite of it, such an important spokesman for the field?

It is hard at first to see what differences could account for this historical schism between Skinner and other learning theorists. We have already noted his similarity to Thorndike. Though he differs from both Watson and Guthrie in placing heavy emphasis on reinforcement, he resembles both of them in his practical emphasis. In analyzing a response, Guthrie's first question was, "What stimuli evoke it?" while Skinner's is, "What reinforcer sustains it?" Both of these, however, focus the emphasis on a specific, manipulable detail of the situation. Guthrie went farther in relating specific situations to a general statement of what learning is, while Skinner has gone farther in actually experimenting with the situations he analyzes. Their differences are substantial, but their similarities are nonetheless noteworthy.

As for Watson, he and Skinner have in common a missionary zeal about what psychology should be and what it should contribute to human affairs. Both react vigorously against what they regard as vague, overtheoretical interpretations of human nature and in favor of strictly scientific study of behavior. Both present systems that their friends regard as highly useful and their foes regard as highly oversimplified. (Both judgments may, of course, be valid, for oversimplifications can be useful for many purposes.) Both theorists appear as prophets, seeking to purge the errors from psychology as it is and to proclaim the glories of psychology as it should be. Both have a vision of what humankind can become if guided by proper application of the principles of learning.

On the issue of reinforcement, Skinner is closer to Hull and Miller than any of the three of them are to Watson or Guthrie. Indeed, though Skinner rejects Miller's suggestion that all reinforcement results from drive reduction, the two are otherwise not very far apart in their relatively straightforward interpretations of learning processes. Skinner's views of social influence and of behavior disorders are rather similar to those already described for Miller and Dollard.

Skinner's difference from Hull is sharper, since Hull was "Mr. Theorist" *par excellence,* while Skinner scorned theory building. Even so, the difference is not as fundamental as it might at first appear. There are two aspects to Hull's theorizing: postulating intervening variables, and deducing theorems from postulates. Certainly Skinner does not do either of these in anything like the formal way that Hull did, but then neither do the majority of other learning theorists. Skinner, however, does do things that bear a certain resemblance to both of these activities of Hull's. As regards intervening variables, Skinner has no such concept as excitatory potential, but he does speak of the strength of a response, even though the strength may be measured in different situations by size, or rate, or probability, or resistance to extinction. Is "the strength of a response" then so different from "excitatory potential"? Also, though he scorns completely unobservable entities, Skinner does not mind talking about ones that are merely hard to observe, like the many different emotional respondents that can interfere with making a punished response.

As for deducing theorems from postulates, Skinner often does something one step removed from that: expressing one law of behavior in terms of another. For example, why do subjects on a fixed-interval schedule respond later in the interval rather than early? Skinner replies that they have formed a discrimination, since responding in the early part is never reinforced while responding in the later part sometimes is reinforced. In other words, he starts with the law that subjects can learn to discriminate between two specific stimuli, S+ and S−, and then applies that law to a new and somewhat different case, where the discrimination is not between two observable stimuli but rather between whatever stimuli there may be to distinguish the first part of an interval from the last part. To Skinner, this line of reasoning is simply a matter of showing that a scientific law applies in a new situation, but it does not seem so terribly far removed from Hull's more formal deductions.

Given that Skinner's differences from the other theorists we have considered are not much greater than their differences from one another, why has there been such a schism between him and them? Part of the impetus for the separation has come from Skinner's conviction that he has a whole new approach, one that makes nearly all previous theorizing and a large part of previous research obsolete. Whether or not it is correct, his expression of this opinion in his publications (more so, be it noted, in earlier years than recently) has naturally tended to keep him and his followers aloof from other psychologists of learning. The rest of the impetus has come from objections by other psychologists to the research methods Skinner uses. Though he puts great emphasis on the scientific character of his work, many others have felt that his methods were untrustworthy as sources of scientific data.

The main objection to Skinner's research methods is that his experiments have typically been conducted on one or a very few subjects. Skinner believes that only by looking at the behavior of a single individual can one find the lawfulness in behavior. Many psychologists, however, take the contrary view: that stable, general laws can be obtained only by averaging the behavior of many individuals. Only thus, they say, can individual differences and accidental fluctuations be ruled out so that the widely applicable, general laws remain. The arguments on both sides of this question are too complex to consider here. Whatever the rights and wrongs of the argument, for a number of years journal editors and convention program committees often rejected Skinnerian research on these bases, thus forcing Skinnerians to find their own publication outlets and further isolating them from other researchers in learning.

Given this division, how is it possible that Skinner has come to be such a dominant figure in the psychology of learning? To some extent it is due to the very methodological factors that so long isolated him. The Skinner box has proved a very valuable research tool, and Skinnerians have had enough success in demonstrating lawfulness with single individuals to impress other researchers. This success in dealing with individual cases has made Skinnerians strikingly successful in their applications of psychology, which we have already discussed, and thus given them extra credibility with practical-minded observers. Finally, Skinner has been a tireless popularizer of the ideas about psychology that many non-Skinnerians share. He has preached the gospel of objective research on learning and its practical applications, presented in a relatively simple, no-non-sense way, more vigorously and persistently than anyone else since Watson. As a result, more outsiders have heard of him and more insiders have had reason to be proud of him. As the psychology of learning has moved into more complex channels of research and theory (some of which we will see in later chapters), Skinner has stood as the most conspicuous spokesman for those simple, tradi-tional ideas that Thorndike, Watson, Guthrie, Miller, Hull, and Skinner himself, whatever their differences, have all shared.

In this role as spokesman for a point of view about human behavior, Skinner has again been the focus both of enthusiastic support and of angry criticism. Supporters see his views as marking the way to a new era of scientifically based human improvement; critics see them as the mechanization and enslavement of the human spirit. He threw additional fuel on these fires of controversy in *Beyond Freedom and Dignity* (Skinner 1971). Answering those critics who claim that his system deprives people of freedom and of dignity, he argues that freedom and dignity are merely the terms we apply to behavior when we cannot detect the reinforcers that control it. All behavior, he insists, is under the control of contin-gencies of reinforcement, planned or unplanned. The fact that in some cases we have trouble determining what the contingencies are does not make the behavior any more desirable. We should give up pursuing these shadowy goals of freedom and dignity and instead work on building a society in which well-planned contin-gencies of reinforcement give rise to desirable behavior.

In spite of the sometimes sharp differences between Skinner and the other theorists we have considered, he is now the outstanding exponent of the connec-tionist tradition. Watson, Guthrie, Thorndike, and Hull are dead; Miller's inter-ests have changed; Skinner remains as the current spokesman for those ap-proaches to psychology which they all held in common. A look at Skinner is both a look backward at this tradition and a look forward at the direction in which Skinner thinks psychology is and should be headed. Others disagree about this direction, and it is to this considerably different set of viewpoints that we next turn.

chapter 5

Cognitive Theories in the European Tradition

One year before Watson published his first challenge to American psychology, Max Wertheimer (1880–1943) published a challenge to the established psychology of Germany. The orthodoxies against which these two revolts were directed were, as we noted in Chapter 2, much alike. Both the American and the German versions were largely concerned with the structure of the mind. They tried to analyze conscious thought into its fundamental units, such as sensations, images, and ideas. Particularly in America, there was some trend toward studying behavior for its own sake, but psychology was still regarded as primarily the study of conscious experience. Experimentation was directed toward a more complete analysis of the contents of consciousness.

The forms which these two revolts took, however, were strikingly different. Watson's objection was that psychology should not be concerned with consciousness, but with behavior. He wanted to abolish the discussion of images and ideas in favor of a discussion of stimuli and responses. He still agreed with the earlier position, however, in being interested in analysis. He still wanted to work with fundamental units, though they were now to be units of behavior instead of units of consciousness.

Wertheimer, on the other hand, objected to the concern with analysis. It seemed to him that breaking consciousness into its parts destroyed what was most meaningful about it. He had none of Watson's objection to the study of consciousness; indeed consciousness was his main concern. What he wanted to do was to study consciousness as it appears, rather than break it down into parts. To the traditional psychology, anything we look at is a mosaic of tiny patches of color. Only as all of these tiny patches are put together do they make up the scene we observe. Wertheimer challenged this view. We actually see the scene, he insisted, as a meaningful whole. Only by a very artificial process of analysis can we break down this whole into patches of different colors and shades. The same applies to thinking. The traditional psychology regarded all our thoughts as made up of images connected by a process of association. This breakdown, too, Wertheimer rejected. Our thoughts are whole meaningful perceptions, not associated collections of images.

Wertheimer's first publication in this revolt against analysis was concerned with the phenomenon of apparent movement. It is well known that we see a light as moving from one place to another when in fact what has happened is that a light in one place was turned off and one in another place immediately turned on. This illusion is the basis of the apparent movement in lighted advertising signs. Prior to Wertheimer, this phenomenon had been regarded as a minor curiosity of no theoretical importance. To Wertheimer, however, it was striking evidence of the futility of analyzing a whole into its parts. The components were two separate lights going on and off, but the resulting whole was an impression of movement. The observer does not see the two lights flashing and infer that something is moving; the impression of movement is immediate and direct. This phenomenon of apparent movement so impressed Wertheimer that he named it the *phi phenomenon* and began a series of studies on it.

EARLY GESTALT PSYCHOLOGY

The phi phenomenon was only the starting point of an intellectual movement within German psychology. This movement was primarily concerned with perception, but came to include learning and other topics as well, treated according to the same principles as were used to study perception. Its emphasis was on whole systems in which the parts are dynamically interrelated in such a way that the whole cannot be inferred from the parts taken separately. Wertheimer applied the German word *Gestalt,* which may be roughly translated as "form" or "pattern" or "configuration," to these dynamic wholes. Such gestalts (treating "gestalt" now as an English rather than a German word) are of many sorts, and they occur in physics as well as in psychology. We have already considered the phi phenomenon as one example. A melody is another, since it depends on the relation between the notes rather than the notes themselves. "Die Lorelei" (to take an appropriately German example) is still the same tune when transposed into another key so that every note is different. A whirlpool is a third example, since it is a whirlpool not because of the particular drops of water it contains but because of the way the motion of the water is patterned. Because of this concern with gestalts, the movement that Wertheimer started came to be known as *gestalt psychology.*

The emphasis of the gestalt psychologists on unified wholes does not mean that they never recognized separateness. Indeed, a gestalt may be referred to as a segregated whole. Of particular interest was the way that gestalts come to stand out as distinct entities separate from the background against which they appear. This interest was expressed in the concepts of figure and ground. The *figure* in any perception is the gestalt, the entity that stands out, the "thing" we perceive. The *ground* is the largely undifferentiated background against which the figure appears. A melody, for example, is a figure against a ground that includes many other sounds. What appears as figure at one moment may not at another. If the listener stops paying attention to the melody in order to hear what a friend is saying, the friend's speech becomes figure and the melody becomes part of the ground. Such changes in figure-ground relationships play a part not only in perception but in learning and thinking as well.

It is of course possible to analyze a gestalt figure into component parts. The fact that three black dots on a white page appear as a triangle does not keep them from still being three dots. However, the important thing to a gestalt psychologist is that what we see immediately is a triangle. Afterward we can analyze the triangle into three dots and study what it is that makes these three dots appear as a triangle when another three, differently placed, do not. We cannot say, however, that the triangle is nothing but three dots. The triangularity, which depends on the pattern of the dots rather than on the dots themselves, is the most essential aspect of what we see. The gestalt figure is more than just the sum of three dots. This relationship is the basis of an expression often applied to gestalt psychology: "the whole is more than the sum of its parts."

It is evident that Wertheimer and Watson, though rebels against similar traditions at the same time, were moving in opposite directions. Each may be considered both a pioneer and an extreme prototype of a certain approach to psychology. Watson's was the mechanistic approach, concerned with the components of behavior and the connections between them. Wertheimer's was the dynamic approach, concerned with unified patterns in consciousness. Without judging their importance relative to that of other theorists, we can say that in terms of conspicuous intellectual movements, Watson was the outstanding pioneer of connectionist theory and Wertheimer the outstanding pioneer of cognitive theory.

From the first, however, Wertheimer shared the spotlight with two of his colleagues, Wolfgang Köhler (1887–1967) and Kurt Koffka (1886–1941), both of whom eventually surpassed Wertheimer as publicists for the new movement. These two men wrote a number of books on different aspects of gestalt theory. Together with Wertheimer, they formed the nucleus of a group that became known as the Berlin school. All three, however, eventually moved to the United States. Perception remained their primary interest, but learning was by no means neglected. Throughout, the emphasis was on organized wholes, separated from other wholes but united within themselves by their dynamic patterning.

The interpretations of learning presented by Wertheimer, Köhler, and Koffka tend to be presented in the terminology of perception. Instead of asking, "What has the individual learned to do?" the gestalt psychologist is likely to ask, "How has the individual learned to perceive the situation?" Gestalt interpretations thus make an interesting contrast with the connectionist interpretations we have discussed earlier. It is true that gestalt theorists speak of memory traces, which are the effects that experiences leave in the nervous system. However, these are different from the stimulus-response bonds discussed by connectionist theorists. The memory traces of the gestalt psychologists are not isolated elements, but organized wholes—in other words, gestalts. Consequently, learning is not primarily a matter of adding new traces and subtracting old ones, but of changing one gestalt into another. This change may occur through new experience, but it may also occur through thinking or through the mere passage of time. The way in which these restructurings occur is the concern of gestalt learning theory.

Studies of Insight

The most important contribution of gestalt theory to our understanding of learning is in the study of *insight*. Often learning occurs suddenly with a feeling that now one really understands. Such learning is likely to be especially resistant to forgetting and especially easy to transfer to new situations. We speak of such learning as involving insight. In such cases the gestalt language of perceptual reorganization is particularly applicable. The learner who has insight sees the whole situation in a new way, a way which includes understanding of logical relationships or perception of the connections between means and ends.

Such insight is by no means restricted to humans. During World War I Köhler, technically interned in the Canary Islands, did extensive studies of insightful problem solving in apes. These are described in his book *The Mentality of Apes* (1925). He presented apes with problems in which bananas were displayed out of reach and could be obtained only by using techniques new in the apes' experience. For example, a banana might be hung from the top of the animal's cage, with boxes elsewhere in the cage which could be piled under the banana so that the ape could climb up and get it. Or a banana might be outside the cage, far enough away so that it could be obtained only by pulling it in with a stick. Such arrangements had the advantage, from the gestalt point of view, of making all the necessary elements of the solution visible to the animal, which is not the case in a puzzle box or maze. He found that these problems not only were often solved suddenly, but frequently were solved immediately after a period of time during which the ape was not actively trying to reach the banana. Sometimes it appeared that the animal, having failed to obtain the banana by familiar methods, sat and thought about the problem and then suddenly saw the solution. Such incidents are well suited to a description in terms of perceptual restructuring. Köhler could say that an ape suddenly saw the boxes, for example, not as playthings to be tossed around but as supports to be climbed on. It saw the relationship between the boxes and the bananas. During the time that it was not actively doing anything about the problem, the ape was undergoing a process of restructuring which, when complete, made an immediate solution possible.

It should not be supposed, however, that only such dramatic examples of sudden and complete insight can be explained in gestalt terms. Gradual learning by trial and error can be interpreted as a series of small, partial insights. Köhler's problems were so arranged that the ape could see all the necessary elements of the solution at once. All that was necessary was for these parts to become organized into an appropriate gestalt. A rat in a maze, on the other hand, cannot see any relation between the pattern of turns and the food at the end until this relation has been discovered by experience. The rat's restructuring must therefore be gradual and piecemeal, since the situation permits no other kind. Nevertheless, the discovery that a certain pattern of turns is the way to food is no less a cognitive restructuring than the discovery that boxes piled on one another are the way to food. The suddenness of the restructuring depends on the problem and the way it is presented to the subject, but the principle is the same.

Gestalt Laws of Learning and Forgetting

Insight requires that certain aspects of a situation be seen in relation to one another, that they appear as a single gestalt. What factors determine whether this event will occur? In one book, *Principles of Gestalt Psychology,* Koffka (1935) pointed out that the same principles could be used to answer this question both in complex problem-solving situations and in very simple perceptual situations. He suggested, therefore, that certain laws of perception proposed by Wertheimer should also be taken as laws of learning. We will consider two of these: the law of proximity and the law of closure.

The *law of proximity,* as applied to perception, refers to the way in which items tend to form groups according to the way they are spaced, with the nearer ones being grouped together. For example, if a number of parallel lines are drawn on a sheet of paper, with alternate wide and narrow spaces between them, the pairs with narrow spaces between will be seen as groups of two (see Figure 5.1, part A). It is these that are seen together, rather than the pairs with wide spaces between, because of their closer proximity to one another. This law also applies to spacing in time. Sounds close together tend to be heard as units. International Morse Code takes advantage of this principle by using intervals of silence of different lengths to separate letters and words, thus making these groups of sounds stand out as units. As applied to learning, the law of proximity may again refer to closeness either in space or in time. In reference to space, it would explain why it is easier for an ape to discover that he can reach a banana with a stick if the stick and the banana are on the same side of the cage. (The reader may think that this is really an example from perception rather than learning, since the ape sees stick and banana as going together. If so, the reader has grasped part of the spirit of gestalt theory, in which perception and learning are inextricably tied up together.) In reference to time, it would explain why it is easier to remember recent events, which are closer to the present and hence more easily joined with the interests of the present in a common gestalt.

The *law of closure* states that closed areas more readily form units. Applied to perception, this fact can be seen by referring to the previous example of parallel lines. It is possible to change the grouping and make the more widely separated pairs of lines appear as groups. This change may be accomplished by connecting the ends of these lines so that they form two sides of a box. The connecting lines need not be complete; so long as the more widely separated pairs of lines appear to be parts of a figure that enclose space, they tend to be seen together (Figure 5.1, part B). Applied to learning, the law of closure plays the same role in a cognitive theory of learning that reinforcement plays in a connectionist theory.

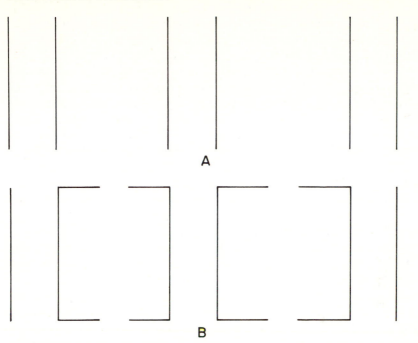

Figure 5.1 *The laws of proximity and closure.* The parallel lines in part A form three sets of two because of their proximity. In part B they form two sets of two with an extra one on each end because of the closed figures formed by the middle pairs of lines.

As long as an individual is struggling with a problem, his perception of the situation is incomplete. A reward brings the hitherto separate parts of the situation together into a closed perceptual figure, consisting of the problem, the goal, and the means of obtaining the goal (Koffka 1925). The emphasis is not on obtaining a reward but on completing an activity and bringing a number of parts into relation with one another. Thus this explanation is most convincing when applied to adult humans consciously working toward certain goals. The term "closure" has indeed been adopted informally by many nongestalt psychologists to refer to the sense of completion when a task is finished or a mystery solved. However, the relation between closure in this sense and closure of a geometric figure may seem a bit forced. There is some question as to whether we should say that Koffka discovered the law of closure in perception and applied it to the study of learning, or whether he called two somewhat related principles, one in perception and one in learning, by the same name.

It is interesting to note that, for all the enormous difference between Guthrie's interpretation of learning and that of the gestalt psychologists, there is a certain similarity between Guthrie's primary law of conditioning and the gestalt psychologists' law of closure. Both regard reward as producing its effect by the way that it changes the situation for the learner. For Guthrie, the reward changes the situation so that the last response which occurred remains conditioned to the stimuli of the situation. For the gestalt theorists, reward changes the individual's perception of the situation so that the stimuli, the response, and the reward form a gestalt. From the point of view of a reinforcement theorist, this feature would justify classifying Guthrie's theory and gestalt theory together as continuity (as opposed to reinforcement) theories.

The gestalt interpretation of forgetting, like that of learning, is concerned with perceptual changes. The memory trace tends to change spontaneously with time into a "better gestalt." The concept of a good gestalt is a rather difficult one to explain. It is the pattern of organization which a system tends to adopt, whether the system is a soap bubble or a perception. Thus, a soap bubble tends to adopt the form of a sphere; if forced into a different form without breaking, it will tend to become a sphere as soon as the force is removed. Similarly, perceptions tend to adopt certain forms as closely as the conditions of stimulation permit. Good gestalts tend to be simple and regular. In the case of physical gestalts, it is often possible to describe the characteristics of a good gestalt quite precisely with mathematical equations (for example, the formula for a sphere as applied to the soap bubble). As we move into the realm of perception, previous experience begins to play a part in determining what is a good gestalt. Familiar, meaningful forms tend to be better gestalts than unfamiliar, meaningless ones. Innate factors are still of major importance, however, in determining what constitutes a good perceptual gestalt. When we consider the topic of learning, we find experience still more important, but innate perceptual criteria still apply.

It is not surprising, in view of this interpretation, that the most famous study of forgetting by a gestalt psychologist (Wulf 1922) was concerned with the forgetting of visual figures—simple line drawings. The subjects in this experiment were asked to look at the drawings and try to remember them, and then at various later times they were asked to draw them from memory. Many differences appeared between the original drawings and the reproductions. In some cases the reproduction was simpler and more regular than the original; in other cases some salient detail of the original was accentuated in the reproduction; in still other cases the reproduction was more like some familiar object than the original had been. (None of the original drawings was clearly a picture of anything, but subjects saw many resemblances to familiar objects or patterns.) In all of these different kinds of changes, however, the experimenter saw a trend toward a clearer or more consistent figure, at least as it appeared to the particular person —in other words, a trend toward a better gestalt. In trying to remember the original figure accurately, the subjects actually succeeded in remembering an "improved" version of it. Forgetting was thus not simply a loss of detail, but rather a distortion of what was physically present in the original drawing into something else that constituted a better gestalt.

Insight in Education

Wertheimer's most noted contribution to the development of Gestalt psychology, once the enterprise that he started was under way, was in applications to education. He was concerned with insightful learning in school children. Whereas Köhler studied insight in apes for theoretical reasons, Wertheimer also had a very practical interest in the topic in school children. It seemed to him that teachers put far too much emphasis on rote memorizing at the expense of understanding. He therefore directed his studies toward finding ways in which learning could take place with greater insight on the part of the learner.

In his book, *Productive Thinking,* Wertheimer (1945) makes a distinction between two types of attempted solutions to problems. Solutions of type A are those in which there is originality and insight; solutions of type B are those in which old rules are inappropriately applied, and hence are not really solutions at all. This distinction does not imply that B solutions depend on previous experience and A solutions do not. Both depend on previous experience; the difference lies in the original organization that characterizes A solutions.

Wertheimer found geometry an especially useful area in which to study different approaches to problems. One of his problems, which he presented to adults as well as children, required the subject to find the area of a parallelogram. Wertheimer would begin by showing the subject how to find the area of a rectangle, not simply the formula of length times height, but the reason why the formula works. He did so by dividing the rectangle up into small squares (Figure 5.2, part A) and showing that the area was the number of squares in a row times the number of rows. He then presented the subjects with a parallelogram cut out of paper (Figure 5.2, part B) and the instruction to find its area. Some people replied that this was a new problem and they could not be expected to solve it without being told how. Some blindly repeated the now incorrect formula of multiplying one side times the other: a B type of solution. Other people attempted to find an original solution, but were unable to see the essential relationships. A few, however, came up with genuine A solutions. One child, noting that the two projecting ends were what made the problem difficult, asked for scissors, cut off one end, and fitted it against the other end, thus converting the parallelogram into a rectangle (Figure 5.2, part C). Another subject achieved the same goal by bending the parallelogram into a ring, so that the two ends fitted together, and then cutting the ring vertically to convert it into a rectangle. These two individuals showed a genuine understanding of the situation that made possible correct, original solutions.

If these individuals had applied the rule "base times *height,*" which for rectangles is equivalent to the rule "one *side* times the other," the computation would have been correct, but nevertheless would have demonstrated no understanding. Thus it would have been much like a B solution, even though it would have happened to be correct. What they did, however, was to find an original way of converting this new problem into a familiar one, one that they knew how to solve. The final solution depended very much on previous experience, but it was previous experience organized in a novel way. The important thing about the solutions was the insight by which the new problem situation was restructured. From the solvers' point of view, they converted the parallelogram into a better gestalt, a rectangle.

Even when a solution is correct, it is important to distinguish whether or not real understanding is involved. Understanding is not the same as logic. Both the inductive and the deductive methods of logic may be applied blindly. The inductive method, in which one reasons from particular instances to a general

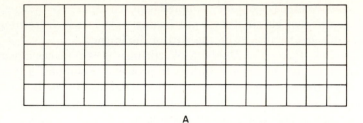

A

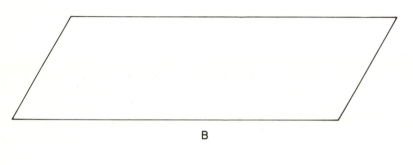

B

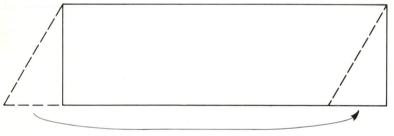

C

Figure 5.2 *Wertheimer's parallelogram problem.* Part A shows Wertheimer's way of explaining why the area of a rectangle equals the product of length times width, in this case 16 by 5. Part B shows the parallelogram for which he asked subjects to find the area. Part C shows one person's solution to this problem by cutting off one end, moving it to the other end, and thus converting the parallelogram into a rectangle.

conclusion, is really just trial and error. Another person might have tried various possible formulas for the area of a parallelogram, found that base times altitude gave the same answer as the book in several cases, and concluded that this was the correct formula but without having any idea why. Though adequate for practical purposes, this would be a solution without understanding. Wertheimer enjoys giving examples of cases where such blind induction leads to absurdly wrong conclusions. The deductive method, in which one reasons logically from one principle to another, can also be applied blindly. A student may fumble around algebraically until he finds a valid proof that a certain equation is correct, but he may still not understand the equation in the sense that Wertheimer means. Understanding implies not merely logical correctness but a perception of the problem as an integrated whole, of the ways in which the means lead to the end.

In going through an algebraic proof, for example, one should ask at each step not only "How does this follow logically from the previous step?" but also "How does this lead toward the solution I am looking for?" In Wertheimer's opinion, education should make such understanding, or perception of whole gestalts, its primary goal.

The value of creative problem solving is not restricted to such "purely intellectual" situations as the above. Wertheimer illustrates its value in social situations with an anecdote about two boys playing badminton. The older boy was so much better at the game than the younger that he won nearly every point, and the frustrated younger boy finally refused to play any more. Since this spoiled the fun for the older boy, it posed a problem for him. How could he get the younger boy to go on playing with him? He might have exhorted him to be a sport (probably in vain), or he might have offered a handicap (a better approach, but still not an answer to the fundamental problem posed by the one-sided competition). Seeing the competition as the crux of the problem, the older boy was able to propose a constructive solution. The competitive game of winning points was replaced by a cooperative game of seeing how long the two together could keep the bird going back and forth, and both were then able to enjoy playing. Again, understanding of the situation led to an insightful solution.

This book of Wertheimer's, set beside Guthrie's *Psychology of Learning,* points up the contrast between cognitive and connectionist views of learning in their extreme forms. Both books show a keen interest in the applied psychology of learning, especially as applied to children. Guthrie's emphasis is on training the child to make the right responses to the right stimuli. His question is always "What does the child do?" Wertheimer, on the other hand, is concerned with educating the child to have insights into the material. His question is "What does the child understand?" The difference is not irreconcilable, since Wertheimer is concerned with the ability to solve problems effectively and since Guthrie can talk about understanding in terms of movement-produced stimuli. Nevertheless, the difference in emphasis is tremendous. This emphasis on understanding, on the perception of relationships within an organized whole, is the great contribution of gestalt psychology to the interpretation of learning.

LEWIN'S SYSTEM

Among the gestalt psychologists who worked with Wertheimer, Köhler, and Koffka in Berlin was Kurt Lewin (1890–1947). Like the other leading gestalt psychologists, he eventually settled in the United States. His interests were different from theirs in a number of respects. Whereas they were mainly concerned with rather technical problems in perception, learning, and thinking, he was interested in motivation, personality, and social psychology. Gestalt psychology, in dealing with learning, tended to take the desire for certain goals for granted and to concentrate on the way the goals are obtained through cognitive restructuring. Lewin wanted to concentrate on the desires and the goals themselves, studying them in relation to the personality. The system he developed for conducting this study is not primarily a theory of learning, but it is a system of description within which learning, motivation, personality, and social behavior can all be discussed.

The Life Space

What Lewin wanted was a theoretical system for predicting the motivated behavior of a single individual. He found the answer in the concept of *life space*. This may be defined as the totality of facts which determine the behavior of a given individual at a given time. It is represented conceptually as a two-dimensional space in which the individual moves. This space contains the person himself, the goals he is seeking, the negative "goals" he is trying to avoid, the barriers that restrict his movements, and the paths he must follow to get what he wants.

This concept of life space is more complicated than is at first apparent. For one thing, it must not be confused with physical or geographical space. This is not the world of physical objects and real other people, but the world as it affects the individual. Hence an object of which he is unaware and which does not influence him would not appear in his life space, even though physically it may be close to him. Similarly, something he thinks is there and reacts to as if it were there is present in his life space even though physically absent. If a child thinks there is a tiger under his bed, the tiger is part of the child's life space, even if everyone else insists that the tiger is purely imaginary.

Can we say, then, that the life space is the person's environment as he himself perceives it? This is a hard question to answer, since it depends on just what we mean by "perceive." We cannot say that the life space is made up only of the things of which the person is consciously aware. An individual may be influenced by factors of which he is unconscious. For example, a certain high school teacher would like to take an administrative position, and feels quite able to do so. Nevertheless, whenever an opportunity to apply for such a position comes along, he finds some excuse not to apply. After this has happened several times, his friends suspect that something is holding him back from seeking an administrative position, perhaps some deep-seated lack of confidence in his own ability. In Lewin's terms, there is a barrier in his life space between him and the goal of an administrative job. Yet he insists that he wants such a job and is going to apply as soon as just the right opportunity comes along. If we go by what he says, we would conclude that he does not perceive any important barrier between himself and the goal of an administrative job. If we go by what he does, we would conclude that he does perceive such a barrier, since he acts as if one is there. Which does he *really* perceive? This is a question we cannot answer, but fortunately we do not need to answer it. If he acts as if the barrier is there, then it is in his life space. It is from the way a person behaves that we know what is present in his life space. It is often convenient to speak of the life space as "the environment as the person views it," but we must keep in mind that what we really mean is "the environment as it affects his behavior."

The life space includes the person himself and his behavioral environment, which consists of everything that influences his behavior. Of particular importance in the life space are the goals the person is seeking, the things or situations he is trying to avoid, and the barriers that restrict his movement toward or away from them. Lewin represents the life space by two-dimensional diagrams (see Figure 5.3). Any place, object, or situation that the individual wants to approach (strictly speaking, *acts as if* he wants to approach) is said to have *positive valence,* and is represented in the diagram by a plus sign. Any that the individual wants to avoid is said to have *negative valence* and is represented in the diagram by a minus sign. Barriers are represented by heavy lines separating one part of the life space from another.

These diagrams are, of course, highly schematic. They usually do not correspond to physical space. For example, a politician's life space might include the state governorship as a positive valence and the election as a barrier. The distances in the diagram between the politician, the election, and the governorship have no particular meaning in the life space that the diagram represents. What is important in the life space is the regions through which the politician must pass to reach the goal and the difficulties of getting from one region to another (i.e., the barriers). These considerations led Lewin to decide that the ordinary geometry of distances was not appropriate for picturing the life space. He therefore turned to the special kind of geometry known as *topology.* Topology sometimes is called "rubber-sheet geometry," since topological space can be stretched in any direction without making any difference. Topology is concerned only with the boundaries between regions, not with the sizes or shapes of the regions or the distances from one place to another. When an area is divided up topologically, all that matters is what regions separate one point from another. Such topological space was much more convenient for Lewin's purposes than the space of ordinary geometry.

Whereas it is meaningless to ask the distance, in inches or miles, between a politician and the goal of being governor, it is meaningful to ask what regions one must pass through to get to the goal. Certainly the final region before the region of being governor is that of being a candidate. Before that there may be alternative paths—perhaps one by way of the mayoralty of a large city and

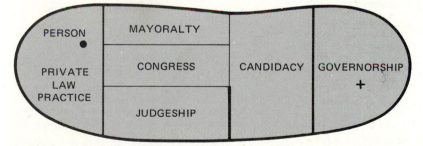

Figure 5.3 *A topological diagram of a politician's life space.* At present the individual is practicing law. He sees three other regions available to him. From the mayoralty or from Congress, he could become a candidate for governor, but the boundary between the judgeship and candidacy appears to be impenetrable. The boundary between the region of candidacy and the positively valenced region of the governorship also forms a barrier, indicating serious doubts as to whether he could win this election. Note that the sizes and shapes of the regions could be greatly changed without changing the meaning of the diagram, so long as the boundary relationships remained the same.

another by way of Congress. These regions are not, of course, particular places in physical space, but they are meaningful parts of the life space. They are positions that the individual can occupy. Positive and negative valences are attributes of certain regions, as with the positive valence of the governorship. Barriers are boundaries between regions that are especially hard to penetrate. The barrier formed by the gubernatorial election, for example, is the boundary between the region of candidacy and the region of governorship. If a barrier is impenetrable for the person in question, that person cannot enter the next region, and any path going to or through that region is blocked.

These topological diagrams can be used to represent all the significant elements in any life situation. Positive valences may be attached to regions as specific as "eating candy" or as vague as "maintaining social status." Negative valences may apply to situations as diverse as spanking for a child and guilt feelings for a criminal. Barriers may be physical (e.g., a locked door), intellectual (e.g., a difficult examination), or social (e.g., the exclusiveness of a positively valenced club). The regions through which a person must pass may be places, social statuses (e.g., child, adolescent, adult), activities (e.g., practicing tennis before becoming a star), or any other situations that necessarily occur to the individual as sequences. The diagrams of the life space can apply equally well to a child prevented from getting a cookie (positive valence) by a high cupboard (barrier) or to a student who must pass through the regions of college, medical school, and internship in order to become a doctor. In all of these cases we must remember that it is the situation as it influences the person, not the "objective" situation, with which we are concerned. If the politician felt sure to lose the election and thus declined to become a candidate, then the election would be an impenetrable barrier in the person's life space, even though this pessimism might actually be quite unjustified. (For a politician, such unjustified pessimism probably makes the example quite unrealistic!) In any case, it is subjective rather than objective reality that makes up the life space.

Predicting Behavior

The topological regions in a person's life space and the barriers between them indicate what paths it is (subjectively) possible to follow. The positive and negative valences of various regions suggest which of the possible paths one is actually likely to follow. However, Lewin also wanted to be able to indicate the relative strengths of tendencies to approach or to avoid different points in the life space. There are often a number of positive valences in the life space at a given time—which one will be approached? To answer this question, Lewin added *vectors* to his system. A vector is a force operating in a certain direction. It is represented by an arrow, with the direction of the arrow indicating the direction of the force and the length of the arrow indicating the strength of the force. Vector analysis has been most prominent in physics, where forces of different magnitudes operating in different directions play an important part. Lewin adopted only the idea of vectors, not the mathematical analysis that usually goes with them. In his diagrams, he indicated the tendency to approach a positive valence with a vector pointing from the person toward the valence, and the tendency to avoid a negative valence by a vector pointing from the person away from the valence. The length of the arrow indicates the strength of the tendency. This makes it possible to show which of the forces acting on an individual is the strongest.

Although the description of the life space provides a considerable basis for predicting an individual's behavior, a number of questions remain unanswered. When two or more paths toward a goal are available, which will be followed? When two or more vectors operate on an individual, will only the stronger be effective or will some compromise occur? If a barrier proves insurmountable, will some other goal be substituted for the inaccessible one? Lewin's reply is that topological psychology determines what behaviors are possible and what ones are impossible. It does not tell us which one definitely will occur. However, the more we know about the details of a person's life space, the more we can narrow down the range of possibilities that are open to him. Thus more and more information will make our predictions better and better, until perhaps eventually they will become almost perfect.

Let us consider, as an example, a student who has a strong vector toward the region of being a teacher, and also a moderately strong vector toward the region of being well-to-do. We may suspect that this situation will lead to problems. However, if we know nothing about the topology of his life space, we cannot predict his behavior. If we know that in his life space these two positively valenced regions overlap (i.e., he perceives teachers as well-to-do), then there is no problem (regardless of what the objective situation may be). He will simply approach this goal of being a well-to-do teacher. If, instead, we know that in his life space the two regions are separate (i.e., teachers are not well-to-do), we are again unable to predict. He may simply react to the stronger vector, or he may find some compromise, or he may investigate the matter further and perhaps as a result restructure his life space (as by finding out that some teachers actually are well paid), which would make the two regions move together and overlap. However, if we can find out more about his life space, our chance of predicting successfully which of these things he will do will increase. If the region of being well-to-do includes a subregion similar to teaching (such as industrial training or school administration), this fact makes him more likely to approach that subregion as a compromise. If he has a vector toward further investigation of the possibilities, this increases the chance that he will get new information leading to a restructuring of the life space. As our knowledge of his life space increases, our ability to predict his behavior also increases.

As we include more of these complexities, the task of diagraming the life space becomes more difficult. Lewin tried hard to make his system complete enough to handle the great variety of human situations. He discussed the problems of regions, subregions, and boundaries. He searched for the best way to represent looking at something as distinguished from going to it. He extended his diagrams into additional dimensions in order to deal with plans for the future and with fantasies. As a result, his complete topological and vector analysis is rather complicated. Most of these technical details are treated in his book, *Principles of Topological Psychology* (Lewin 1936). In addition, much of the research which he and his (often devoted) students carried on was concerned with clarifying these problems: What effect do barriers have on valences? What determines whether a substitute goal will be acceptable to the person? These are the sorts of questions to which Lewin's research made important contributions.

In addition to his work on the life space, Lewin also developed theoretical interpretations of personality structure. These interpretations led to many experiments and applications, some of which are discussed in another of his books, *Dynamic Theory of Personality* (1935). The only one of these that needs to be mentioned here is his concept of *tension*. Vectors result from tensions within the person. These tensions may be very similar to what Miller (and many others) refer to as drives. They may also, however, be of a less biological and more cognitive sort, such as the tension to complete a task once it is started.

Lewin's theoretical analyses of the person and the life space, along with the many experimental studies that he based on these analyses, made him famous as a psychologist of personality and of social behavior. He was always interested in the application of psychology to these areas. The organization of groups, the causes and cures of prejudice, and the effects of frustration are among the topics to which he made important contributions.

Lewin's Weakness in Predicting Learning

From the point of view of the psychology of learning, however, all of the above interests are pretty much beside the point. Lewin provided us with a system for describing and to some degree predicting behavior, but he did not give us a theory of learning. Much of the value of studying his system in this book lies in understanding why he did not. A knowledge of the life space as described by Lewin enables us to predict reasonably well what the individual will do. But how do we determine the structure of the life space? We do so by observing the individual's behavior and inferring from it what the structure must be. Having observed someone's behavior, we figure out the structure of his life space. From this structure we predict what his behavior in the future will be. In order for this method to work, his life space must remain the same except for his own position in it. learning, however, involves a change in the life space. How can we predict when and how such changes will occur? In some cases a knowledge of the life space (and the person in it) is enough, as for example when we predict that long exposure to a region of positive valence will produce satiation and make the valence less strongly positive. In most cases, however, we must take into account external, physical reality. If an individual comes to a door that he thought was unlocked, tries to open it, and finds it locked, the door changes in his life space from a permeable boundary to a barrier. How could we have predicted this change in the life space? We could have only by knowing that the door was, in fact, locked. But such questions of physical reality do not really enter into Lewin's system.

Lewin was, of course, aware of this problem, and he discussed the ways in which external events can produce changes in the life space. However, this part of his theory is very minor, and he never developed it in detail. In his research he showed a lively interest in finding out how best to change attitudes, but little of this practical interest found its way into his formal theorizing. In his theoretical work, for the most part, he was too busy examining the structure of the life space, the organization of the person, and the way these influence behavior to be concerned with the ways in which they are themselves changed by external events. As a result, his theoretical system is useful for stating the results of certain kinds of learning, but of little value in predicting what learning will occur under what conditions.

This lack of concern with learning as such reflects Lewin's philosophical view of science. He sees most psychologists as looking for statistical laws that apply more or less to people (or animals) in general, but not specifically to any given individual. To apply these laws accurately to a given person, you need to know a lot about that individual. In principle you might be able to find out enough about the individual by a detailed study of his ancestry and previous history of learning, but in practice such an approach would be enormously cumbersome, since each experience in the person's life may have affected how each future experience would be perceived. Consequently Lewin rejects that approach and seeks instead to find out about each individual's life space at the present time, without regard to how it got that way. With this bias, it is understandable that Lewin did not want to concentrate on problems of learning. However, in not doing so, he left a serious gap in his theory. Without more information on how the life space can change, we are hard put to make long-term predictions and even more hard put to make recommendations about teaching, psychotherapy, or other problems in learning.

PIAGET'S COGNITIVE VIEW OF CHILDREN'S LEARNING

The cognitive theorists we have considered so far were interested in describing perception, motivation, and problem solving as they operate in individuals at a given time. As we have noted, they were not much interested in how these activities change for a given individual over time. However, the European cognitive tradition has not neglected such changes. Children reason and solve problems in ways that are often different from the ways of adults, and the process by which juvenile thinking develops into adult thinking has been of interest to a number of psychologists, European and otherwise. Of all the psychologists who have been concerned with this process of cognitive development, the most famous is Jean Piaget (1896–1980). He was a French-speaking Swiss (so his name is pronounced somewhat like "John Peeah*jay*") who spent about the last half century of his life in Geneva studying processes of thinking in children. His early scientific interest was in biology, and at the age of 15 he had already achieved renown for his publications about mollusks. However, his interest in logic and the sources of knowledge led him into cognitive psychology. He first became widely known among psychologists through his book, *The Language and Thought of the Child,* which was published in French in 1923 and translated into English in 1926. This has been followed by so many other books, articles, and lectures, continuing up to the present time, that even a sampling of the titles would be excessively long. Since his writings are not only voluminous but also theoretically rather complex, one can get a better overview of his system from such secondary sources as Flavell (1963) and Phillips (1969). The increasing interest in cognitive theories in recent years has raised Piaget's status in the English-speaking world from that of a somewhat strange outsider who could not be completely ignored to that of a major theorist.

Basic Concepts of Piaget's System

One way of identifying a theorist is by the key intervening variable(s) that he postulates. Piaget used as his favorite intervening variable the *schema* (plural, *schemata*). Schemata are a little more general than most of the cognitions we have considered so far. They are ways of perceiving, understanding, and thinking about the world. One might speak of them as frameworks or organizing structures for mental activity. They are broad types of expectancies, dealing with general ways in which events occur. The formation and change of schemata is the essence of cognitive development.

A child, of course, has schemata relevant to a great many topics, and the number becomes even greater as one approaches adulthood. Piaget was particularly interested in those that might broadly be called scientific. In what ways does a given child understand relationships of size and weight and causality? How does the child reason about physical changes, about constants and variables, about the sources of actions and the nature of living and nonliving things? Though the exploration of these schemata was Piaget's greatest contribution, he has not been unaware of children's social worlds as well. How does a child understand social relationships? How does the child reason about moral issues? What justification can be provided for the rules of games or the rules of decent behavior? Piaget has studied these schemata, too, as well as influencing the research of others interested in those aspects of development.

Schemata can change, and such change is important in cognitive development. The process by which they change is known as *accommodation*. When a child (or any person, for that matter) has an experience which is inconsistent with a schema, there will be some tendency for the schema to change so as to accommodate this new input. For example, it is common for children around the age of 6 to operate on the schema that objects which are light to lift will float and those which are heavy to lift will sink. When asked to make predictions, they indicate that a large (and therefore heavy) block of wood will sink, while a small piece of metal will float. However, as they repeatedly see disconfirmations of these predictions, the schema becomes increasingly difficult to maintain. Gradually they fumble their way toward a new, more adequate schema. For a while they may manage with a group of more specific schemata such as that wood floats, while metal and stone sink. Eventually they achieve a new schema that is as simple and general as the old, but more accurate: that objects of low density float, while those of high density sink.

The process of accommodation by which the child improves his schemata is similar to that by which scientists improve their more technical ones. Indeed, the question of how to differentiate consistently between objects that float and those that sink was once as much of a problem for scholars as it is now for children. All of us sometimes find our views of the world disconfirmed, try to explain why, and (perhaps) learn from the experience. Accommodation applies equally well to an infant discovering that an object which has gone out of sight has not ceased to exist and to Einstein replacing Newton's description of the world with the theory of relativity.

An emphasis on the process of accommodation might suggest that schemata are unstable, constantly being changed by new inputs. Actually, however, schemata tend to be rather stable. A child is no more likely to give up an old schema in response to one or two disconfirming inputs than is a scientist to give up a pet theory because only one or two experiments failed to work out as he expected. Even more common than accommodation is the opposite process, by which schemata influence the interpretation of experiences. This process is known as *assimilation.*

Everything we experience, from the simplest physical stimulus to the most complex new scientific or philosophical idea, is interpreted in the light of what we already know and believe. Lewin emphasized this most strongly, in his claim that it is not the physical environment but the life space that matters to our behavior. Most theorists have not been willing to put the matter quite that strongly, but all have agreed that our reaction to stimulation depends on something other than the physical characteristics of the stimulus. One way of expressing this relationship is to say that the stimulus (however simple or complex) is assimilated into the existing schemata. The meaning of the stimulus is determined by the schemata which the person uses to recognize and interpret it. This "modification" of the stimulus into a part of the individual's total cognitive world is what Piaget means by assimilation.

When a schema is stable and can easily assimilate whatever relevant new experiences come along, a state of equilibrium exists. As new experiences come along that cannot easily be assimilated, disequilibrium results. If accommodation occurs, so that the new schema can assimilate these troublesome experiences, a new equilibrium results. This process of striving toward equilibrium of schemata and experiences—by assimilation where practical, more gradually by accommodation where necessary—sounds rather like the notions of the gestalt psychologists about the characteristics of a good gestalt. Piaget's schemata are more durable than their gestalts, but both involve an organization within the nervous system, resulting from the interaction of experience with existing structures, and always striving toward its best possible form. Though Piaget's background is not that of a gestalt psychologist, his thinking is congenial to theirs.

Piaget is not, however, open to the same criticism as Lewin—that he ignores the external world and talks only about the life space, thus providing no basis for a true theory of learning. Piaget is very much aware of the external world. While the concept of assimilation emphasizes that our behavior is determined by the world as interpreted, the companion concept of accommodation emphasizes that the external world is constantly in a position to modify the way we view it—to "keep our schemata honest," so to speak. Piaget is thus in the position of combining a complex and flexible cognitive theory with an insistence that the influence of the "real world" cannot be ignored.

Stages in Cognitive Development

If we look only at the process of accommodation, we can imagine a person's schemata constantly changing throughout life. Though in a sense this is true, it would not give a very accurate picture of Piaget's writings. Much of what he has written deals not with changes in schemata but with their characteristics at any given period in life. Since schemata change slowly, it is possible to describe the way a person interprets the world at any given time during one's life without worrying about the changes that are slowly going on in those interpretations. One of the most conspicuous features of Piaget's theory is his list of developmental stages. At each stage, children's schemata have certain characteristic features that are different from those of earlier or later stages. Knowing at what stage a given child is now, we can predict with a fair degree of accuracy how he will answer various questions about the way things happen and why.

Many psychologists have described development as a series of stages, and several comments are appropriate to all of them, including Piaget's. For one thing, the number of stages and the boundaries between them are somewhat arbitrary. What one scholar would call two stages, another might call two parts of a single stage. Moreover, a given person at a given time might be judged by one observer to be in an earlier stage, but starting to make the transition to the next stage, and by another observer to be in the later stage, but still showing many remnants of the earlier.

Further, some children will enter a given stage earlier than will other children, and some children will pass through the stage more rapidly than others. The order of stages is assumed to be the same for all children, but the timing is somewhat variable and the ages specified for any given stage are therefore only approximate. In addition there is typically some ambiguity as to why everyone passes through the same order of stages and whether there is any way the order could be changed. Psychologists who describe systems of stages nearly always assume that the order, at least, is fixed, regardless of the environment. It may be possible to speed up progress through the stages, or slow it down, or even stop it completely, but it is not possible to reach a "higher" stage before passing through the lower ones. Though this assumption of stage theories often is challenged, Piaget could defend it in his case by pointing to the way in which schemata build on one another. Since one cannot solve a problem without first having mastered the necessary components, Piaget would claim that one cannot enter a later stage until one's schemata have reached the necessary level of complexity and abstraction, represented by the previous stage.

With these general warnings, let us look at Piaget's system of stages. The matter of distinguishing between main headings and subheadings, mentioned above, is a bit of a problem. Probably the clearest version of his classification is in four stages: sensory-motor, preoperational, concrete operations, and formal operations. Each stage represents an increase over the previous one in the child's ability to think abstractly, predict the world correctly, explain reasons for things accurately, and generally deal intellectually with the world.

The first stage is known as the *sensory-motor.* It extends roughly from birth to age 2. As the name implies, the schemata that develop during this stage are those involving the child's perception of the world and the coordinations by which he deals with the world. It is during this period that the child forms his most basic conceptions about the nature of the material world. He learns that an object that has disappeared can reappear. He learns that it is the same object even though it looks very different when seen from different angles or in different illuminations. He relates the appearance, sound, and touch of the object to one another. He discovers ways in which his own actions affect objects, and acquires a primitive sense of causality. Thus his world becomes increasingly an orderly arrangement of more-or-less permanent objects, related causally to each other and to his own behavior.

The second stage is the *preoperational,* extending from about ages 2 to 7. In this stage the child begins to show the effects of having learned language. He is able to represent objects and events symbolically: not just to act toward them, but to think about them. However, Piaget does not regard this change as due entirely to language. The child has internal representations of objects before he has words to express them. These internal representations give the child greater flexibility for dealing adaptively with the world, and attaching words to them gives him much greater power of communication. However, his intellectual abilities are still very limited compared to those of an adult. His thinking is still decidedly concrete by adult standards. He tends to focus on one aspect of a situation to the exclusion of others, a process that Piaget calls *centering.* His reasoning can be a logician's nightmare, and he finds it difficult to understand how anyone else can see things from a different point of view than his own. He is thus, as the name implies, only in the early stages of acquiring a logical, adult intellectual structure.

The third stage is that of *concrete operations,* extending from about ages 7 to 11. Again, this stage represents an increase in flexibility, in this case over the preoperational. The sorts of operations to which the name of the stage refers include classifying, combining, and comparing. The child in the stage of concrete operations can deal with the relationships among hierarchies of terms, such as robin, bird, and creature. He is aware, as the preoperational child is not, of the reversibility of operations: what is added can be subtracted, and a substance that has been changed in shape can be restored to its original shape. A girl in this stage will not fall into the fallacy that a preoperational girl may, of saying: "I have a sister, but she doesn't have any sister!" Just as the advances of the preoperational stage can be related to the beginning of language, so the advances of the stage of concrete operations can be seen as related to the beginning of school. Again, however, Piaget points out that this is not the whole story. One child may have learned arithmetic operations by rote but fail to apply them when appropriate, while another child may deal effectively with problems without ever having been exposed to arithmetic. Learning of symbolic manipulations may be helpful to the child in going from the preoperational to the concrete-operations stage, but experience with a wide variety of concrete situations is more important.

The fourth and final stage is that of *formal operations,* starting around age 11 and involving improvements in abstract thinking continuing to about age 16. In this stage the capacity for symbolic manipulation reaches its peak. Though children in the previous stage have been able to perform a number of logical operations, they have done so within the context of a concrete situation. Now the person (intellectually no longer a child) can view the issues abstractly. He can judge the validity of syllogisms in terms of their formal structure, independent of content. He can explore different ways of formulating a problem and see what their logical consequences are. He is at least ready to think in terms of a realm of abstract propositions that fit in varying degrees the real world that he observes. (In short, we might suggest, he is ready to study Hull's theory!) He may not demonstrate all of these tendencies in every possible situation—how many of us ever do?—but he has reached the stage at which he is capable of doing so. The intellectual apparatus of formal reasoning that provides the basis for so much human achievement is at least potentially at his disposal.

As the child passes from one stage to another, as well as through substages we have not considered, his schemata are changing through accommodation to new experiences. At each stage he tries to assimilate new experiences to his existing schemata, but often finds discrepancies. (The same observations at a younger age would not have been discrepant, since his schemata were not well enough developed for him even to recognize an inconsistency.) Though a single such discrepancy is merely puzzling, a series of them will gradually produce accommodation and change the relevant schema toward the next stage. Formal schooling helps the process along, but confrontation with discrepant information is critical, and even that produces its effect only slowly.

Of the many schemata that change during development, there is one group that Piaget has studied in particular detail. They are the most studied changes that take place as the child moves from the preoperational stage into and through the stage of concrete operations. They are grouped together under the heading of *conservation,* to which we now turn.

Conservation

Most people, on hearing the word "conservation," probably think of virgin redwood forests or some other natural resource in danger of depletion. Piaget's use of the word, however, is more like that in the physical expression "conservation of matter." It refers to the fact that some quantitative property of matter remains the same in spite of changes in other properties. For example, a lump of clay keeps the same weight no matter how its shape is changed, and a given number of buttons is still the same number whether the buttons are bunched close together or spread out widely over a table top. These constant properties may seem ridiculously obvious to us, but they are not at all obvious to most children in the preoperational stage. Just as an infant must learn that an object remains the same object as it moves, so a somewhat older child must learn that a substance conserves its weight through changes of shape and a group of objects conserves its number through changes of spacing. The mastery of these various forms of conservation takes place typically at somewhat different ages, extending from the beginning to the end of the stage of concrete operations.

A favorite demonstration among Piagetians is to show a preoperational child two pitchers of different-colored liquids, the same size and shape, and equally full. When the child has agreed that there is the same amount in both pitchers, the experimenter pours the contents of one of them into a tall, narrow beaker and asks the child which liquid there is now more of. Some children will say there is now more of the one that was poured ("since it's higher"), others will say there is more of the one that is still in the pitcher ("because it's fatter"), but they generally agree that there are no longer equal amounts of the two liquids. The child has failed to show conservation of volume. This failure may be attributed to two characteristics of the preoperational child. One is his centering tendency: he focuses on either height or fatness and fails to note that the other is also changing in a compensating way, so that volume remains the same. The other tendency is his unawareness of the reversibility of operations. It is obvious to most adults that the liquid could be poured back into the pitcher and would then take up the same space as before; its volume never changed. To the preoperational child, however, the change was more fundamental; he is not aware of its reversibility. These two characteristics of his thinking combine to prevent him from achieving conservation.

Failure to conserve number or weight follows from the same characteristics of the preoperational child. A child lines up eight buttons next to eight pennies and agrees that there are the same number of pennies as buttons. Then the pennies are spread out to make a longer line, and in reply to the experimenter's questioning he now indicates that there are more pennies. This failure of conservation of number represents a centering on the length of the lines at the expense of their spacing, and a nonrecognition that the change in spacing is reversible. Similarly, when a child has seen two balls of clay balance on a scale and has then watched the experimenter mold one of them into a different shape, he is likely to decide that now the changed piece is either heavier or lighter. Again, he is centering on one dimension of the clay at the expense of another, and does not realize that the clay can be restored to its original shape.

Failure to show conservation seems so strange to most adults that one is tempted to think that the problem is merely a trivial misunderstanding about words. Maybe the child really knows that the number, or volume, or weight remains the same, but just gets the words for them mixed up with words for length or height, and so appears not to be showing conservation. This is a tempting interpretation, and there is evidence to suggest that confusion about words does play some part in children's failure to show conservation. However, most people who have worked with children on these problems, asking children the same question in different ways, have concluded that there is much more to it than that. If the child is confused about the words, it is largely *because* he is confused (from an adult point of view) about the whole matter of quantities—what they are and how they behave. However strongly he may defend his "wrong" interpretations, he is still, as Piaget claims, in the process of developing and refining the schemata by which he interprets the world.

THE GESTALT TRADITION AND LEARNING

Gestalt psychology was not primarily a theory of learning, and our examination of Lewin's theory shows why its attempts to incorporate the subject of learning were not always successful. As for Piaget's theories, developmental changes that result from learning are mostly slow changes and it is often difficult to tell just what independent variables are responsible for which changes. As a result, these theories are short on answers to questions that many learning theorists consider of central importance. This does not mean, however, that these theories have no relevance to the issues considered by psychologists of learning. As Lewin notes, his theory (and related theories) can be of considerable value in predicting and understanding individual behavior.

Let us consider a psychologist working with individuals whom she wants to help—perhaps a school counselor working with mildly disturbed children. Since she knows little of the children's life histories, she may well find that the most effective way of understanding them is to reconstruct their life spaces, to "see the world as they see it." She will then have a good basis for guessing what they will do under various circumstances. She may be able to predict more accurately in this way than in any other what events will make a given child less anxious or less hostile or happier. This does not tell her how to help the child change, but it does provide a basis for trying to change the environment in a way that will help. Moreover, once she has identified the chief features in a child's life space, she at least knows where to focus her attempts at changing the way he relates to the world. Many counselors feel that this approach is more useful than any other in understanding and helping individual children and adults.

However, this is not the only approach that claims practical usefulness in dealing with individuals. Skinner, like Lewin, feels that to be useful an approach needs to apply to individuals, not just to the statistical trend of groups of people. To control the behavior of people and animals, he needs independent variables that will work for most individuals regardless of their unique characteristics. The counseling psychologist should be able to use these independent variables to modify a child's behavior in ways that will help both the child and the other people around him.

Here we have two contrasting approaches. Both are relevant to the problems of individuals, both are potentially useful to a counseling psychologist (and to many other people), but their assumptions are widely different. The first is cognitive, growing out of the gestalt tradition and focusing on the individual's life space; the second is connectionist, based on behaviorism and focusing on learning. Each has its devoted followers, and the followers of each have tended to regard the other as either ineffective or perhaps even harmful. Nevertheless, since our counseling psychologist wants to help children by whatever means will work, she might well wish to combine the best of both approaches, to have both a way of understanding the child's life space and a way of changing it.

If so, she would certainly not be alone in that desire. A number of theorists have felt that the cognitive approach, with its emphasis on people's perceptions and beliefs, has more to offer than does the connectionist's emphasis on habits. At the same time, they have not wanted to give up the behavioristic interest in how behavior relates to independent variables in the external world and in how learning can change this relationship. It is these cognitive theorists, influenced as much by behaviorism as by gestalt psychology, that we consider in the next chapter.

chapter 6

Cognitive Theories in the Behaviorist Tradition

During most of the history of American learning theory, connectionist theories have been dominant and what cognitive theories there were have been in the very different gestalt tradition. Only fairly recently has it become popular to combine the basic attitudes and goals of behaviorism with intervening variables of a cognitive sort. Looking back, it seems surprising that it took so long. There were, however, a few pioneers in this approach whose work goes back as far as many of the connectionist psychologists we have considered. Of these pioneers, the most conspicuous was E. C. Tolman.

TOLMAN'S PURPOSIVE BEHAVIORISM

Edward Chace Tolman (1886–1959) spent most of his professional life on the faculty of the University of California at Berkeley. His major work, *Purposive Behavior in Animals and Men,* was published in 1932. Though his system later underwent a number of modifications, its essential spirit remained the same. Writing in the heyday of behaviorism, Tolman was impressed with behaviorism's objectivity, its concern with the precise measurement of behavior, and its faith in the improvability of man. At the same time he felt that behaviorism showed too little appreciation of the cognitive aspects of behavior. We do not simply respond to stimuli, he argued; we act on beliefs, express attitudes, and strive toward goals. What we need, therefore, is a theory that recognizes these aspects of behavior without sacrificing objectivity. To fill this need, Tolman undertook to create what has been called a *purposive behaviorism.*

What is a purposive behaviorism like? Much of its meaning can be inferred from the name. First, since it is a form of behaviorism, it is concerned with objective behavior, not with conscious experience. Moreover, it is concerned with the effect of external stimuli on behavior, not merely with a "life space" inferred from behavior. Second, it is concerned with learning, with the way that behavior changes with changing experience of the external world. It is thus a genuine learning theory in a sense that Lewin's, for example, is not. Third, it is concerned with the purposes that impel and guide behavior. Whereas Watson, Thorndike, and to a lesser extent the other connectionist theorists treat behavior as a matter of responses to immediately present stimuli, Tolman emphasized the relation of behavior to goals. Most of our behavior is not so much a response to stimuli as a striving toward some goal. Stimuli of course guide us toward the goal and determine at every step what means we will use to reach it, but the search for the goal is what gives unity and meaning to our behavior. We may shift from one approach to another as circumstances require, while still continuing to direct our efforts toward the same goal. As a result it would be necessary for anyone who wanted to predict our behavior to know the goal we were seeking as well as the particular stimuli we were encountering along the way. Tolman's system is called a purposive behaviorism because it studies behavior as it is organized around purposes.

The behavior that Tolman wanted to study is *molar* behavior. This term refers, not to the kind of behavior, but to the way in which it is analyzed. Molar behavior is analyzed in fairly large, common-sense units, such as driving to work or cooking a meal. In practice, this is the way all theories of learning analyze behavior. However, some theories include an interest in *molecular* behavior, which is behavior analyzed in terms of single movements of particular muscles. Walking a city block, for example, is a molar act made up of an enormous number of molecular movements—expansions and contractions of the various muscles of the legs and other parts of the body. Guthrie is an example of a theorist who puts a good deal of emphasis on molecular analysis. Tolman, however, states explicitly that he is concerned only with molar behavior. The ways in which molecular movements work together to produce molar acts are of no concern to his system.

Cognitions as Intervening Variables

A given goal may be approached by a great variety of different acts, not only as sequences of responses but also as alternative possible ways of gaining the objective. Tolman's problem was to develop a theory for dealing with this complex variability of molar behavior as it operates in search of goals. To do this, he considered it necessary to take account of the individual's cognitions—one's perceptions of and beliefs about the world. These correspond to Lewin's life space. How could Tolman take them into account without sacrificing the objectivity of behaviorism? His answer was to make use of *intervening variables*. To appreciate the importance of this answer we must see it in historical context. The existing behaviorist theory regarded anything intervening between the stimulus and the response as itself a response, just as physical and potentially just as measurable as any other response. If the word "cognition" had any meaning at all for such behaviorists, it was as a shorthand name for tiny movements of the speech muscles; any other meaning they rejected as a figment of some sloppy mentalistic theorist's imagination. Tolman, however, considered it possible to use the term "cognition" objectively without treating it as a physical, directly measurable movement. He therefore designated cognitions as intervening variables. In doing so he both made the concept of cognition more respectable in behaviorist circles and introduced the concept of intervening variables into psychology.

As an intervening variable, a cognition is not a thing. It is an abstraction defined by the theorist. While it is possible that physiologists may some day find some particular activity in the brain that corresponds to a cognition, this possibility is no concern of Tolman's. The meaning of the word "cognition" is determined by the definition that the theorist gives it. For Tolman, this definition is in terms both of stimuli and of responses, since it intervenes between them. Experience with certain stimuli results in the formation of certain cognitions.

In addition, certain needs produce *demands* for certain goal objects. (Deprivation of food, for example, produces a demand for food.) These demands are also intervening variables. Cognitions and demands work together to produce responses.

The difference between this system and the other cognitive theories we have discussed so far is mainly one of emphasis. For Lewin, the relation of the life space to external stimuli is to some extent a side issue. For Tolman, it is of central importance. He is a theorist of learning, and learning involves changes in cognitions resulting from experience with external stimuli. In this sense Tolman could be considered a stimulus-response theorist even though he is not a connectionist. However, the notion of life space fits easily into Tolman's system. He has, in fact, adopted large parts of Lewin's system into his own. Basically, Tolman's system is a cognitive theory, but with more emphasis on external stimuli than Lewin's and more emphasis on learning and on motivation than gestalt psychology.

Predictions from Tolman's Theory

How is Tolman's theory different from a connectionist one? Both attempt to predict behavior from stimuli and other antecedent conditions. Does the fact that Tolman uses cognitions as intervening variables make any real difference? Consider an individual who makes a certain response to certain stimuli and obtains a reward. What learning does this experience tend to produce? For Guthrie, Miller, Hull, or Skinner, it produces a tendency for those stimuli to be followed by that response, provided other conditions (such as drive, in Miller's case) are appropriate. For Tolman, it produces a cognition that making the response will lead to the reward. If one now has a demand for the reward, one will make the response. How are these two interpretations really different?

The answer to this question is that not all cognitions take the form, "If I do this, I will get that." We form many other kinds of cognitions about the way the environment is structured, about things that go together, about what paths lead to what places. These various sorts of cognitions can then be used when needed to help the individual achieve life goals. Cognitions from several different learning experiences may be put together so that the individual can respond adaptively to new situations. Attention to such combination makes it possible for Tolman's theory to deal with more original and flexible behavior than is covered by the connectionist interpretations of learning that we have discussed so far.

One example of this greater flexibility is in cognitions about what leads to what. Once an individual has learned how to get from one place to another, this knowledge can be used to obtain rewards quite different from the one obtained while learning. A rat that has learned its way around a maze while satisfying its demand for exploration can use this knowledge later to obtain food. This change-over is illustrated in an experiment by Buxton (1940). Rats were given several experiences of spending a night in a large maze. There was never any food in the maze, and the rats were taken out of the maze at different places on different occasions. This variation was designed to ensure that no part of the maze or path through the maze would be rewarded more than any other. After this experience, the rats were fed in the goal box of the maze while they were 48 hours hungry and were then put in the start box of the maze. About half of the rats ran to the goal box without a single error on this first trial, a record far above that of a control group without the previous experience in the maze. Since the rats had never been reinforced with food (or, presumably, with anything else) for following this particular path, it is difficult for stimulus-response theories to deal with this experiment. For Tolman, however, it is simple enough; the rats had formed a cognition (or perhaps a group of cognitions) about how the maze was arranged. They did not make use of this knowledge until they were given a reason to do so. In other words, the learning about the layout of the maze remained latent until food was experienced in the goal box. Hence this study is said to demonstrate *latent learning.* Several different kinds of latent learning have been studied; this experiment illustrates one of them. Whenever learning goes on without its being evident in performance at the time, latent learning is taking place.

Another way in which Tolman's theory achieved greater flexibility than connectionist theories was through its emphasis on learning the location of reward. Once an individual has learned where a given kind of reward is located, that location can often be reached by means other than those originally used. If a shopper finds an intriguing store while exploring the city on foot, the person can return later by car or bus. Similarly, a rat that has learned the location of food may, if the experimental arrangements permit, take a detour to get there faster. This is illustrated by another experiment (Tolman, Ritchie, & Kalish 1946). Rats ran across a table top, through an enclosed alley, and then along a series of elevated pathways by a roundabout route to food (Figure 6.1, part A). After they had learned to use this route, the alley was blocked, but 18 new pathways were made available, leading in various directions from the table top (Figure 6.1, part B). The rats did not, as one might expect from the principle of generalization, choose the doors closest to the one they had previously used. Instead, they tended to choose the one that pointed approximately toward the location of the goal. Many, to be sure, chose other paths, but the goal-pointing path was the only one chosen by a large proportion of the rats. In other words, the rats tended to choose the path that appeared to be a shortcut to the goal rather than those close to the original path. They had not merely learned a route to food; they had also learned the location of the food in space.

The two above experiments are typical of many that were done by Tolman and his students or were done by others but quoted by Tolman in support of his position. Because of their importance for the controversy between cognitive and connectionist interpretations of learning, these studies often were criticized for various details of their procedures and often were repeated by both friends and foes of Tolman's ideas. In some cases it turned out that animals show the insightful behavior predicted by Tolman only under quite special conditions. However, whether or not rats behave according to Tolman's theory in any given situation, there is no doubt that this kind of flexible, insightful behavior does occur in some species (particularly humans) under some conditions. The very fact that Tolman considered these experiments necessary shows how strong a hold connectionist interpretations of learning had on American psychology.

Tolman used a number of terms to refer to the cognitions that are learned in various situations. One popular term is *cognitive map*. It is easy to see how the two experiments discussed above can be interpreted by saying that the rats had cognitive maps of the areas they had explored. Those in the maze had a cognitive map of the various alleys, indicating which were blind and which led on to other choice points. Those in the roundabout path had a map that included not only the path but also the surrounding space with its possible shortcuts. If someone asks how it is possible to have maps in the brain when the brain is made up of nerve fibres that conduct impulses from one place to another, Tolman is not concerned. Cognitive maps are intervening variables, and if they explain learning Tolman does not care what connection they have with physiology.

Another of Tolman's terms is the impressive expression *sign-gestalt-*

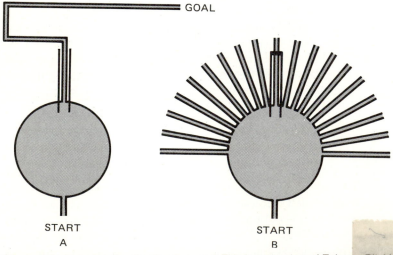

Figure 6.1 *Learning the direction to a goal.* This is a top view of Tolman, Ritchie & Kalish's (1946) apparatus. In part A, rats followed the roundabout route from the round table top to the goal, where they found food. In part B, the original route was blocked and 18 new paths were made available. The rats tended to choose the path pointing toward the goal.

expectation. This is the individual's expectation that the world is organized in certain ways, that certain things lead to others. The inclusion of the word "sign" indicates that these expectations are mainly about stimuli which are signs of certain things, rather than about responses. The word "gestalt" emphasizes that the signs must be considered in context, that the whole pattern of stimulation is important. This term has become one of Tolman's trademarks; in fact his theory sometimes is called sign-gestalt theory.

These two terms, cognitive map and sign-gestalt-expectation, point up the closeness of Tolman's formulation to those of the cognitive theorists we have already discussed. In many respects he was particularly close to Lewin, and he borrowed heavily from Lewin in later formulations of his theory. Tolman's later theoretical publications are full of diagrams of vectors and valences. He also added to Lewin's system of diagrams by making a distinction between *pragmatic performance vectors* and *identification performance vectors.* Pragmatic performance vectors refer to the tendencies actually to go to various places or to make other responses of acting on the environment. Identification performance vectors refer to the tendencies merely to observe things. They are concerned with exploring the situation, with observation of the environment. Thus Tolman distinguishes tendencies to observe the environment, either out of curiosity or in order to decide what to do about it, from tendencies to take action toward some part of the environment.

At various points in his theorizing Tolman borrowed ideas not only from Lewin and the gestalt psychologists but also from Freud, from the reinforcement theorists, and even from Guthrie. His breadth is also reflected in the variety of variables that he took into account in explaining behavior. In addition to all the aspects of the situation, he listed four main kinds of individual-difference variables. Only one of these, we may note, involves learning. The four are heredity; age; training; and endocrine, drug, or vitamin conditions. Using the initial letters of these four, Tolman labeled them the HATE variables. (One wonders how Tolman, a devout Quaker, came to arrive at this particular set of initials.) The HATE variables help to illustrate the breadth of Tolman's concern with different aspects of behavior. Discussions of such diverse factors as age and vitamin conditions are rare in learning theory. They are valuable as a reminder that learning, for all its great importance, is far from being the only determinant of behavior.

Of Rats and Humans

Tolman was atypical among cognitive theorists in having given more attention to the behavior of animals than of humans. (This was also Köhler's emphasis at one stage of his career, but he also did extensive work in human perception.) To some extent the preference reflects the same factors that have influenced behaviorists in general toward animal work: the greater simplicity of animals and the greater opportunity to control their environments. It probably also reflects Tolman's special concern to show that a cognitive system could still be objective, that it need not depend at all on anything the individual says. Tolman himself, in the tongue-in-cheek manner so characteristic of his writing, presented a third possible explanation. He suggested that psychologists typically begin with an interest in solving the great problems of human life, then become frightened by the awesome implications of such a task and flee to safer aspects of the study of behavior, such as learning in the rat. Certainly Tolman was right in saying that many psychologists are aware of a conflict between their desire to attack the great questions of life directly and their desire to concentrate on other questions that are less exciting but that they have more chance of being able to solve. Tolman's own career reflects this conflict clearly.

On the one hand, Tolman was a man of strong social conscience. (He was one of the faculty members who left the University of California rather than sign the controversial loyalty oath in 1950). In 1942 he published a small book called *Drives toward War,* in which he analyzed the psychological causes of war and presented some suggestions for removing them. His analysis of the biological drives, social techniques, and psychological dynamisms leading to behavior—warlike or otherwise—combined experimental, clinical, and historical sources. On the basis of this analysis he suggested several fairly radical changes in our political, economic, and educational systems, changes which he thought would reduce the impetus toward war. Among these was a plan for a world state, along with some psychological suggestions for making this admittedly visionary idea a bit more practical.

On the other hand, Tolman had as his principal ambition the development of a schematic rat world, a system from which he could predict completely the behavior of rats in a laboratory environment. This is reflected in his whimsical dedication of *Purposive Behavior* to *Mus norvegicus albinus* (actually the white mouse, but he meant the white rat). He wanted to include enough different variables and to have flexible enough constructs to achieve this goal completely. When we consider the tremendously complex human social situations that people usually want psychologists to deal with, this seems like a very modest ambition. Tolman did not, however, achieve his goal.

Evaluation of Tolman

If we consider how Tolman combined the best of both connectionist and cognitive theory, what a broad range of variables he took into account, and how early he anticipated future developments in the logic of theory building (e.g., the use of intervening variables), we could easily conclude that Tolman is the greatest learning theorist we have considered. In its conception, his theory may very well be the best there is. The conception, however, was never really carried into execution. Tolman discussed the kinds of laws psychology needs, but he did not develop these laws. He did experiments intended to show that cognitive formulations are better than connectionist ones, but he did not do experiments to make these cognitive formulations precise enough to be really useful for prediction. He pointed the way toward an extension of cognitive theory to include the best aspects of connectionist theory, but he did not carry the program through. He is therefore open to the same criticism as the other cognitive theorists, that he does not give us a basis for predicting from objective stimuli to objective behavior. He gave us a cognitive framework (or perhaps we should say a gestalt!) for interpreting learning, but he did not provide us either with detailed laws of learning like Skinner's or with a general principle of learning like Guthrie's. Thus his system is more a road sign or a pious hope than it is an accomplished fact.

This shortcoming is not really a failure on Tolman's part, however, for his attitude toward his own theorizing was always tentative and whimsical. He regarded theory-construction not as a serious business of building great intellectual edifices for the future but as a half playful trying out of different approaches. As a result he was constantly revising his theory, making suggestions and then abandoning them before he had time to explore their implications. His writings are a mixture of earnestness and whimsy, of high-flown theorizing constantly being pulled up short by a chuckle. His desire to construct a schematic rat world was thus partly an aspiration but also partly a joke. He wanted not so much to build a truly adequate theory as to explore the whole activity of theory building, both playing with it himself and puncturing the excessive claims of others. As a result, he has been widely respected and widely loved, but not widely followed. In fact, of all the major learning theorists in the last 40 years, he may well have been regarded most affectionately by his students but at the same time have had the fewest students follow in his footsteps. This apparent contradiction was analyzed 15 years after his death in a symposium (see Campbell & Krantz 1974), which concluded that to be a "tribal leader," that is, to found a school of loyal followers, one must have a strong and somewhat intolerant conviction of the rightness and importance of one's ideas. Tolman lacked that conviction. Possibly his intellectual style was influenced by his being the younger brother of a distinguished scientist in a better-developed science: physics. In any case, compared to other major theorists, he had little faith in the lasting rightness of his theories, but much interest both in exploring ideas and in encouraging students to develop in their own directions.

Tolman himself put it best. His final theoretical statement appeared in the same book as Guthrie's (and he and Guthrie died in the same year). He ended his chapter with this concluding statement, which thus became in a sense the concluding statement of his professional life.

> The system may well not stand up to any final canons of scientific procedure. But I do not much care. I have liked to think about psychology in ways that have proved congenial to me. Since all the sciences, and especially psychology, are immersed in such tremendous realms of the uncertain and the unknown, the best that any individual scientist, especially any psychologist, can do seems to be to follow his own gleam and his own bent, however inadequate they may be. In fact, I suppose that actually this is what we all do. In the end, the only sure criterion is to have fun. And I have had fun [Tolman 1959, p. 152].

MORE RECENT BEHAVIORISTIC COGNITIVE THEORIES

The same casual approach to theorizing that prevented Tolman from founding a school also made it easier for him to present many tentative suggestions about the interpretation of learning. We have noted his openness to other people's ideas, to aspects of learning that many other theorists neglected, and to different formulations of different kinds of learning. As a result, it has been hard for later cognitive theorists to come up with anything that Tolman had not already suggested. Much of the work of later cognitive theorists, therefore, has been to make ideas quite similar to Tolman's somewhat tighter and more formal than he did. From among the various recent formulations of cognitive theory (see also, e.g., Boneau 1974, Seligman & Johnston 1973), we will look at two whose similarities and differences make an especially revealing counterpoint.

Bolles's Cognitive Interpretation

One attempt to formulate a neo-Tolmanian theory was by Robert C. Bolles (b. 1928) of the University of Washington. Since the University of Washington was Guthrie's stronghold for many years, and Arthur Lumsdaine continues to represent Guthrie's viewpoint there, Bolles (1972) may have been particularly sensitive to a gibe that Guthrie once directed at Tolman. Tolman's theory, said Guthrie, dealt with how a rat's cognitions were formed, but then left the rat buried in thought. If the rat ever got to the food at the end of a maze, he would have to do it by himself, with no help from the theory. Whether or not Bolles found that remark amusing, he certainly did not consider it fair. Why, he asks, should we say that a habit produces behavior while an expectancy produces nothing but the thought? Both habits and expectancies are intervening variables, which produce behavior if and only if we postulate that they do. (It is clear where Bolles stands on the question of whether intervening variables are real entities that we discover or explanatory fictions that we invent.) Hull, for example, says that the right combination of habit, drive, and incentive will produce a given response. Tolman, in contrast, says that a response results from an expectancy that a given response will produce a given outcome, plus a demand for that outcome. Is one formulation any more logical than the other? asks Bolles. Either set of intervening variables, if correctly formulated, permits us to predict what response will occur under what conditions, but neither produces the response any more directly than the other.

How does Bolles formulate a cognitive theory to predict behavior? He begins with three kinds of events about which an organism can learn. The first two sound familiar enough: a stimulus that serves as a cue (S), and a response (R). The third, which refers to a biologically important stimulus, is S*. The kinds of stimulus events to which S* refers are the same kinds that other theorists have called positive and negative reinforcers. A cue event S permits us to predict the occurrence of a significant consequent event S*.

Two kinds of expectancies can be formed about the relationships among these three kinds of events. An S-S* expectancy is a cognition that when S occurs, S* will follow. If we have learned that the sight of an approaching waiter (cue) means we will soon get food (significant positive consequence), we have formed an S-S* expectancy connecting the approach of the waiter with the arrival of food. If a child has had the misfortune to learn that some barking dogs do bite, he has formed an S-S* expectancy connecting the sight and sound of a barking dog with the significant negative consequence of being bitten. The reader will note the relationship of S-S* expectancies to classical conditioning, with S as the conditioned stimulus and S* as the unconditioned stimulus. The S also resembles Skinner's conditioned positive or negative reinforcer, since it predicts a primary positive or negative reinforcer. Where S* is aversive, S also resembles what Miller would call a stimulus for the secondary drive of fear.

The other kind of expectancy is R-S*. Here it is the individual's own act that predicts the biologically significant consequent. If one expects that opening the refrigerator door (R) will reveal food (S*), or that touching a lighted stove (R) will produce pain (S*), one has formed R-S* expectancies. Since Bolles is more concerned with why behavior occurs than with why it does not occur, most of the R-S* expectancies with which he deals are ones in which the S* is positive. However, it may be positive in the sense that it relieves a negative condition, as in the expectancy that if you take this aspirin (R), your headache will go away (S*). An R-S* expectancy thus relates a response to what Skinner would call either positive or negative reinforcement.

There are two questions we can ask about these expectancies. First, how are they learned? The answer to this question is easy enough: by experience. Whenever an S is followed by an S*, an S-S* expectancy is formed or strengthened, and whenever an R is followed by an S*, an R-S* expectancy is formed or strengthened. There is no need to refer to reinforcement, even though S* is the kind of event that others have referred to as positive or negative reinforcers. The acquiring of expectancies is thus a forming of cognitions by a process of learning by contiguity.

Second, how do these expectancies lead to behavior? In other words, what specific assumption does Bolles make to avoid leaving the person or the rat buried in thought? He assumes that when an event S occurs, it will give rise to behavior R if the individual has both an S-S* and an R-S* expectancy connecting that S and that R. For example, a sign "Restaurant" on a building will lead to the behavior of entering the building only if the person has both the S-S* expectancy that the sign really indicates that there is food to be obtained and the R-S* expectancy that going into the building is the way to get to it. The strength of the tendency to make the response will depend on three things: the strength of the S-S* expectancy, the strength of the R-S* expectancy, and the value of S* to the individual. In the example, how sure is the person that the sign indicates food, how sure is he that going into the building is the way to get the food, and how hungry is he? Bolles suggests that in some rough sense an S-S* expectancy corresponds to Hull's K, an R-S* expectancy to $_sH_R$, and the value of S* to D.

In the above example, the S* in the S-S* expectancy is positive and the R in the R-S* is the means of getting to it, so the S* in S-S* and the S* in R-S* are the same. However, this relationship does not always hold. A mistreated child might learn the S-S* expectancy that an angry shout means he is about to be struck. That S* is negative, and an appropriate R-S* would refer to how to avoid it. He might have the expectancy that running away would save him from the blow. In that case, the S* of the R-S* expectancy would refer to safety, while the S* of the S-S* expectancy refers to danger. Thus, for the two kinds of expectancy to work jointly to produce action, they may refer to the same positive S*, or one may refer to a negative S* and the other to its absence. These predictions fit well with common sense, and Bolles does not feel it necessary to make any special distinction between these two kinds of situations.

Although a theory of learning naturally focuses on learned expectancies, they are not the only kind. Both kinds of expectancies can also be innate— resulting from the organism's heredity rather than from previous experience. The fear of a sudden loud noise that infants often show might be considered an innate S-S* cognition that such a noise (S) indicates danger (S*). However, Bolles is more interested in innate R-S* expectancies. The existence of such innate expectancies is indicated by various stereotyped responses which different species of animals make in the presence of food, danger, or other biologically important situations. Most species have fairly stereotyped ways of taking and eating food, and also stereotyped reactions to danger. Among the food responses, we may note not only the various ways of grasping, tearing, chewing, etc., but also such special patterns as the raccoon's food-rubbing ritual (sometimes called "washing"). For danger, fleeing and freezing are the two most common patterns. While a connectionist psychologist would interpret these *species-specific behaviors* as evidence of stimulus-response connections, Bolles prefers to look at them as reflecting innate R-S* expectancies. For example, "freezing in fear" results from a combination of an S-S* expectancy that this noise means danger and an innate R-S* expectancy that freezing means safety. A combination of the two kinds of expectancies can thus predict behavior equally well whether the expectancies are innate, learned, or one of each.

Even with the extra complications discussed in the last two paragraphs, Bolles's system may seem rather spare as contrasted with Tolman's spread of cognitive maps and vectors. Part of this difference is due to the fact that Tolman focused more on the arrangement of events in space, whereas Bolles focuses on the sequence of events in time. Tolman did research on rats finding their way around in mazes, whereas Bolles has worked most on what happens when a rat receives a signal that indicates a shock is soon to follow. Since mazes involve two-dimensional space (or occasionally three-dimensional, if the rat climbs out the top), while time extends in only one dimension, it is perhaps understandable that Bolles feels he can get along with simpler assumptions than Tolman did. However, theories commonly grow from more specific to more general, so Bolles may presently add more complicated assumptions to his now rather simple cognitive system.

Bindra's More Cognitive Interpretation

Bolles is only one of a number of theorists of the late 1960s and the 1970s who have worked on cognitive interpretations of behavior. We will consider one other, who is of interest because of the way his theory both complements and contrasts with that of Bolles. This is Dalbir Bindra (1922–1980) of McGill University. Starting from interests and biases fairly similar to Bolles's, Bindra (1974) comes to conclusions that are even more distinctively cognitive than are those of Bolles.

Bindra's key concept is the *central motive state*. This is an intervening variable that predisposes the individual to act in certain ways with regard to certain positive or negative incentives. There is a central motive state for food, one for danger, and the like. In some ways it resembles Hull's $_sE_R$, since it includes arousal by an incentive, drive for that incentive, and the activation of response tendencies. However, it differs from $_sE_R$ in that it involves a tendency, not just to one response, but to all the responses relevant to the incentive. In the case of positive incentives, such as food, it involves three main categories of behavior: instrumental responses (such as approaching the food), consummatory responses (such as eating the food), and regulatory responses (such as salivating). When a central motive state is active, all three of these kinds of responses are likely to occur. Thus both the behaviors that Skinner would call respondent and those that he would call operant are under the control of central motive states.

What determines whether a given central motive state will be active at any given time? Bindra's answer is in terms so similar to Bolles's S-S* expectancy that we can take the liberty of using that term here, even though Bindra's terminology is slightly different. An S-S* expectancy may be of two sorts, either an expectancy that when S occurs, S* is more likely to occur, or an expectancy that when S occurs, S* is *less* likely to occur than in the absence of S. Thus, if S* is an injury, S could be either a danger signal (S* is more likely to occur) or a safety signal (S* is less likely than usual to occur). Once an S-S* expectancy is learned, presentation of S arouses a central motive state appropriate either to S* or to its absence.

Once the combination of the S and the S-S* expectancy has aroused the central motive state, how do we get from there to actual behavior? Whereas Bolles introduced an additional expectancy, the R-S*, to complete the picture, Bindra rejects this device and admits only the one kind of expectancy, S-S*. How, then, does he avoid leaving the individual buried in thought? To answer this, we must remember that one of the characteristics of a central motive state is that it gives rise to approach or avoidance behavior. When one is presented with food, the central motive state will lead to approaching it. When presented with a signal for food (the S of S-S*), one is likely also to approach it and as a result get closer to the food itself. The S-S* expectancy, by arousing a central motive state, thus automatically produces behavior that moves the individual toward the S*.

To return to the previous example, what happens to the person who sees a sign, "Restaurant," and who has an S-S* expectancy that such a sign indicates the presence of food in the vicinity? He approaches the sign, and thus exposes himself to the sights, sounds, and smells of food from within the restaurant, cues for which he has stronger S-S* expectancies than he has for the sign. (Otherwise he might eat the sign!) He therefore approaches these new cues, and thus finds himself inside the restaurant and exposed to cues even more strongly associated with food. Since the food is surrounded by cues for which the person has S-S* expectancies, and since the strength of the expectancies is stronger for cues closer to the food than for cues farther away, the person is "drawn" toward the food without needing any R-S* expectancies to get him there.

How can we decide which of these two similar cognitive formulations is preferable? If we can think of approach as a simple, automatic form of behavior, then Bindra can predict behavior just as well with one kind of expectancy in his theory as Bolles can with two. However, Bindra's theory is not well adapted to those cases where a person (or animal) must learn particular techniques to get to particular goals. If our hungry traveler, in order to get to the food, must turn away from the sign that says Restaurant and go through an unmarked door, this presumably must reflect an R-S* expectancy that one gets into restaurants by opening doors rather than by getting as close as possible to signs. Similarly, a rat in a Skinner box might be drawn to the lever entirely by an S-S* expectancy that food is to be found near it, but pressing the lever rather than hugging or licking it would seem to depend on an R-S* expectancy. So, although Bindra's system can explain many items of behavior, Bolles's approach seems to be the more general and hence probably the more useful.

Bolles has suggested that this difference between his interpretation and Bindra's may result from the kinds of subjects they had in mind when they developed their theories. Bindra's theory, he thinks, may work quite well for birds, whose response patterns are fairly fixed but who are good at attaching those responses to new stimuli. Pigeons, for example, are quite good at learning when to peck, but the pecking itself is a stereotyped response that not much can be done to change. However, continues Bolles, mammals are better at learning not only when to make approach responses but what particular responses to make under particular conditions. To explain their behavior, we need R-S* as well as S-S* expectancies. In what proportions we need them is, however, largely an unanswered question. Bolles and collaborators have recently begun a research program to try to determine how much of a rat's learning is of the S-S* sort and how much of the R-S* sort. Specifically, when a rat has learned to make two different responses to the same object, and then is punished for one of them, to what extent does he learn a fear of making that response (R-S*) and to what extent a fear of that object (S-S*)? The answers so far are not simple (Bolles, et al. 1980), nor would we expect them to be, but this research represents a promising beginning at using these concepts to clarify just what is learned from a given experience.

COGNITION AND THE COMPUTER

As we have noted, connectionist models were dominant during most of the history of American learning theory, and only recently have cognitive models become preferred by a large proportion of psychologists. Since most people attribute much of their own behavior and at least some of other people's behavior to knowledge, beliefs, and ideas, why did psychologists for so long avoid that type of analysis? Many factors may have contributed to this, but probably the most significant was the desire to treat human as well as animal behavior as part of the natural world of science. Connectionist intervening variables seemed appropriate to that purpose, since they were consistent with a nervous system in which physical input led fairly directly to measurable responses. Cognitive intervening variables, on the other hand, impressed many psychologists as mentalistic, as belonging to a realm of mind or spirit rather than to the physical and biological realm of natural science. Much as Tolman tried to convince the world that this was not the case, that cognitive intervening variables could be as well integrated into the physical world as could connectionist ones, most psychologists of learning were unconvinced, and connectionist theories remained dominant.

What happened to change this situation? Why were psychologists more willing to listen to Bolles in the 1970s than to Tolman in the 1930s or '40s? Part of the reason was biological. As biologists and psychologists became increasingly aware of the complexities of the nervous system, it became less and less clear that the central nervous system operates according to connectionist principles. As a result, cognitive principles came to seem increasingly acceptable. Even more important, however, was another development, one which made cognitive activity not only part of the scientific world but of technology as well. This development was the rise to prominence of computers in science, in business, and eventually throughout society.

The phenomenal rise in the use of computers in the past third of a century has had several effects on psychology. Computers are used to analyze data, to generate stimuli for experimental subjects, to present instructional programs, and in various other ways. For theorists, a particularly interesting application has been the attempt to draw an analogy between the operation of computers and the operation of the human intellect. Computers carry on various processes that bear marked resemblances to human learning, remembering, and thinking. Can the way that computers carry on these processes tell us anything about how humans do so? In these days of computerized games it may be appropriate to begin with a relatively simple connectionist "toy," not even using a computer. A small machine can be built, far less complicated than a computer, that will behave like a real organism in that it moves around, seeks certain goals, avoids others, and demonstrates simple forms of learning. Walter (1953) produced such a machine a number of years ago and named it (imitating biological taxonomy) *Machina docilis* (the teachable machine). This little machine would ride around on its wheels, approaching lights of moderate intensity and moving away from very bright lights. It could be conditioned to approach a whistle that was paired with the turning on of a "reinforcing" light, and this conditioning was subject to both extinction and forgetting. It would avoid obstacles, show "fear" of a stimulus that had been paired with a kick, and behave ambivalently toward other members of its "species." In the days before computers became widespread, when the behavior of machines was widely regarded as something completely different from the behavior of living organisms, such a machine constituted quite a striking demonstration. Even after looking at its wiring diagram, one tended to feel that there was something magical about a "mere machine" behaving in a fashion so lifelike. Now, when computers have taken over many business operations and computerized robots are a stock-in-trade of movies and television, some of the magic has gone out of such a demonstration, but it has still not completely lost its power to beguile us.

For the most part, computer analogs have been of more complex, cognitive processes. They typically involve problem solving, game playing, language comprehension, and the like—not so much models of learning per se as of those behaviors that in humans are the results of learning. A number of them are discussed in Feigenbaum and Feldman (1963) and in Schank and Colby (1973). One impressive model is the "Logic Theorist" of Newell, Shaw, and Simon. This is a computer program whose function is, given the postulates of geometry, to prove certain theorems. The manner in which it goes about doing so is quite comparable to what a good high school geometry student does. It works forward from theorems already proved to try to find ways of turning one of them into the theorem to be proved. It works backward from the to-be-proved theorem to other statements which, if true, would permit the proof, and then treats these statements as subgoals to be proved. Clearly, it deals with cognitive structures rather than with stimulus-response connections or even with the sorts of signals that Bowles considers. Though Logic Theorist's concern with postulates and theorems would appeal to Hull, Tolman would feel more at home with its mode of operation than most of the other theorists we have discussed, and Wertheimer would be proud of its creative problem solving!

Soon after Newell, Shaw, and Simon developed Logic Theorist, it was expanded to deal with a wider variety of problems. The result was known, appropriately, as General Problem Solver, or GPS (Ernest & Newell 1969). A problem may be regarded as any discrepancy between an actual state of affairs and a corresponding desired state of affairs, and the job of a problem solver is to reduce that discrepancy. In real life, problems vary from: "I am in Chicago and want to be in New York, but a snowstorm has closed O'Hare Airport; how can I get to New York?" to "I need an A in biochemistry to get into medical school, but at this rate I'll be lucky to get even a B; how can I raise my grade?" Though a computer program to solve such problems for us would indeed be useful, illustrations of how GPS works are generally more artificial problems. They are, however, still challenging enough to keep most people occupied (and sometimes frustrated) for at least a few minutes. Two examples of such problems that GPS can solve are shown in Figure 6.2.

A computer program that can solve problems as different from one another as logic proofs and the puzzles in Figure 6.2 is clearly quite an accomplishment, and GPS is one of several that can. Nevertheless, some people feel that problems of this sort are rather trivial. Humans have been able to analyze completely the various possible approaches to these problems and to say which will work efficiently, inefficiently, or not at all, so perhaps it is not such a wonderful thing that computers can be programmed to find a solution. However, computers have also been programmed to work on problems that no one has been able to analyze so exhaustively. Chess playing is probably the most famous example. Though no chess-playing program has yet achieved very high ranking in the chess world, some are quite good, and it is not rare for a program to beat its author.

Even though a computer can search the implications of many possible moves very quickly, it cannot win by that power alone. Fast as it is, it still cannot come anywhere near to following every possible sequence of moves through to eventual victory or defeat; there are just too many possible combinations of moves in the course of a game. The program must therefore recognize, as a human player does, what situations are promising and which are threatening and then try to create or avoid those situations. In other words, it "understands" that it is

---

PROBLEM 1

Present state: There are three missionaries and three cannibals on one side of a river.
Desired state: To have all six of them on the other side.
Difficulties: The only way across is a boat that can carry only two people at a time
and must always have at least one person to row it (i.e., it cannot cross
the river empty). If more cannibals than missionaries are ever left
together on one side, the cannibals will eat the missionaries. (Getting
missionaries across in cannibals' stomachs is not considered a solution!)
Question: What sequence of crossings with the boat will accomplish the transfer?

PROBLEM 2

Present state: DONALD
                  + GERALD
                   ROBERT
Desired state: An example of correct addition in which one particular numeral
corresponds to each of the letters above.
Difficulty: The codebook to tell what numeral each of the above letters represents
is lost, and we know only that D = 5.
Question: What code will convert the letters into numerals to give a correct example
of addition?

Figure 6.2 *Two problems that both humans and computers can solve, though not necessarily in the same way.*

typically desirable to trade a knight for a rook or to threaten the opponent's king, but undesirable to lose one's queen or to have one's own king put in check. Each sequence of possible moves is then analyzed according to whether it leads to desirable or undesirable consequences within the next few moves.

Though human players and computer programs are alike in that they examine and evaluate various possible moves, it does not follow that they do so in just the same way. Computers, because of their great speed, can examine more total moves. They are much less efficient, however, in deciding which possible moves to explore most deeply. As a result, they tend to play rather uninspired chess (as do most human players), with little ability to formulate long-range strategy. The best human players can beat the best chess programs partly because of such long-range strategy and partly because of having gradually learned the significance of a great many specific chess positions—which are favorable, which are risky, which call for a particular move or series of moves. Programs might obtain such detailed knowledge about chess positions either by having it included in the original program or by being programmed to learn by experience. So far, neither approach has been very successful, so it will probably be a number of years before the world's chess champion is a computer program. These similarities and differences between human players and computer programs, and their implications for understanding both people and computers, are explored in Frey (1983).

Though these examples suggest (correctly) that computers are more effective thinkers than one would have imagined 40 years ago that any machine could be, they are a long way from being able to do all that humans can do. One of their conspicuous failures is translating from one language into another. Fairly early in the development of computers, it looked as though they should be ideally suited for translation. To translate Russian into English, for example, you should need only to provide the computer with a Russian-English dictionary and to program it with appropriate grammatical rules. These hopes have not, however, been realized. The main reason for the failure is that the meaning of a sentence cannot be determined by vocabulary and grammar alone. Does "We don't have enough different woods" refer to a shortage of forest preserves, cabinet-making materials, or golf clubs? It depends on the context. Does "That kills me!" mean that the speaker is dying? Fortunately not in most cases. Because of such ambiguities, a passage translated into a foreign language and then translated back again by another person may be unrecognizable, as when "He shot off his mouth without thinking" comes back as "He absent-mindedly fired a bullet into his jaw!" Given such difficulties, it is understandable that computerized translation has not yet achieved great success.

What do computer programs tell us about the actual processes of learning and thinking in living organisms? Nothing directly; as just noted, the fact that a computer can be programmed to learn or think by certain processes does not demonstrate that either humans or rats learn or think by the same processes. What these programs can show are the implications of certain assumptions about how organisms learn. A theorist can write a computer program to follow the laws of learning that he thinks organisms follow, then run the program to see what happens. If what happens is similar to the outcome of human or animal learning, this finding makes it more plausible that humans or animals do in fact follow those hypothesized processes when they learn. If what happens is quite different from the outcome of "real" learning, the theorist's assumptions are probably false. Thus the computers provide a more precise way of doing what Hull wanted to do; if he had made use of computers he might have avoided some of the contradictions in his system. The role of the computer program is much like that of mathematical analysis—not to change the logic of theory construction, but to carry out that logic more precisely and more thoroughly.

Though most psychologists working with computers have not been concerned primarily with the arguments between connectionist and cognitive theorists, their work is quite relevant to that controversy. As a piece of engineering, a computer is a connectionist "organism"; its transistors, which do or do not pass currents, are comparable to neurons in the nervous system that do or do not fire. At a molecular level, therefore, a connectionist analysis of a computer would be accurate. At the molar level, however, what we mainly note is the computer's ability to store and retrieve information, reason logically, break problems into subproblems, and otherwise behave in very cognitive ways. A computer is thus a basically connectionist "organism" that gets programmed to operate in cognitive ways. If a "mere machine," built by humans from basically connectionist parts, can operate so effectively in such cognitive ways, cognitions can scarcely be as unscientifically mentalistic as earlier psychologists feared. Perhaps, indeed, there may be a resolution of the connectionist-cognitive argument in the definition of a human being as "the only movable, general-purpose computer that can be produced by unskilled labor!"

In the case of computers, the programming is done by humans. How do humans themselves get programmed? Their programming takes place through a lifetime of experience, some of it arranged deliberately by parents and teachers, some of it happening without anyone having planned it. At first our programs are simple, but they soon get combined into more complex ones. A computer program often includes a command to call some simpler program to do a particular job needed by the larger program. Similarly, a person working on a large task can draw on previously learned ability to do smaller tasks that contribute to the larger one. For example, a carpenter's "program" for building a bookcase will be full of specifications to saw a board or pound a nail. The details of these actions do not need to be spelled out, since the carpenter is already thoroughly familiar with how to do them and can take the details for granted. When the appropriate point in his "program" for the bookcase arrives, he simply has to note that the board should be sawed, and his previously learned "subprogram" of skills will take care of it, after which the main program continues on its way.

The analysis in terms of programs and subprograms could be extended to more than two levels, with programs made up of subprograms and in turn combined into larger programs. The result would be a hierarchy of skills at different levels. This way of analyzing human knowledge and skills has indeed achieved some popularity, and not only in the context of computers, as we will see in the next section.

THE HIERARCHICAL STRUCTURE OF LEARNING

The use of programmed instruction began as an attempt to apply such Skinnerian principles as immediate reinforcement and the gradual shaping of the responses to complex verbal situations in education. However, as more programs were written and the more and less successful ones compared, it became evident that there is a lot more to programming than eliciting and reinforcing responses. Programs need to be constructed in ways that clarify the logical structure of the material. What needs to be learned are not merely particular responses, but a structure of principles from which particular responses can be derived. Programs are successful to the extent that they are organized so as to clarify this structure for the learner.

The importance of the structure of material applies not only to the writing of teaching-machine programs but also to such related topics as industrial and military training. One psychologist who has been particularly impressed by this aspect of practical training is Robert M. Gagné (b. 1916), currently of Florida State University. How, Gagné (1962b) asks, can we most usefully apply psychological principles to training people on such tasks as radar operation, aerial gunnery, or troubleshooting in complex electronic systems? The sorts of suggestions that a typical learning theorist might come up with, such as providing immediate reinforcement or making the crucial stimuli more distinctive from one another, turn out not to be as useful as an optimistic psychologist might hope.

Some are simply not applicable to a given learning task, and those that are, all too often make relatively little difference in rate of learning. What does help is an analysis of the task into its component parts. The psychologist needs to ask the following kinds of questions: "What items of knowledge and skill must a person have in order to do this job?" "How do these items of knowledge and skill depend on one another in such a way that certain ones should be learned before others?" "Into what more basic components can these items be analyzed, and how are they in turn organized?" The answers to these questions tell the psychologist what needs to be taught, in what order, and to some extent how.

When one analyzes a complex task into its components in this way, one finds a hierarchical structure. The final task can be broken down into various component items of knowledge or skill, each of which can then be broken down into subcomponents, and so forth. Gagné (1962a) provides a further analysis of this hierarchical structure in an educational setting, where the focus is on knowledge rather than on manual skills or mechanical operations. Suppose we ask what knowledge a person must already have in order to perform a certain task, given only instructions. The answer will be mastery of some other tasks that are simpler and more general. For example, one can tell an algebra student that the way to solve two simultaneous linear equations is to use one equation to get a value for one of the unknowns and then substitute that value in the other equation. To act on this instruction, the student must know both how to solve a single linear equation and how to substitute one value for another in an equation. If the learner does not have these two items of knowledge at his disposal, he will not achieve the final performance of solving the simultaneous equations, even if the instructions are clear and he attends carefully. If he does have both items of knowledge available, he will quite possibly be able to act on the instructions and carry out the task, but he may not; the instructions could be inadequate to bridge the gap between the components and the final task. Each of the two components, in turn, depends on others. Solving a single equation, for example, depends on knowing that a term can be moved from one side of the equation to another with a change of sign, and that both sides can be multiplied by the same factor, and so forth. These component items of knowledge are necessary, but not always sufficient, to solve a single linear equation. Thus the final performance is at the apex of a pyramid of component items of knowledge.

Given such a hierarchical arrangement of knowledge, in which a performance can only be achieved by those who have already mastered its components, it is clear why Gagné considers task analysis the key to effective teaching. To teach any task, one must at a minimum ensure that all the necessary components are learned, which may in turn require teaching *their* components. When the components are mastered, simple instructions may be enough to obtain the final performance. Often, however, simple instructions are not enough; some more complex presentation may be needed to bridge the gap, to get the components put together in the proper way. Such a presentation should make clear what performance is required, focus attention on the necessary components, identify crucial stimuli, and otherwise point the learner in the right direction. These are what a good teaching program does, in addition to simply providing information, as it moves the learner up the hierarchy to higher and higher levels of knowledge.

Gagné's views have implications beyond either schooling or applied training: they indicate the way in which our whole structure of knowledge and skills is gradually built up throughout life. Early in life, simple items are acquired, such as the skill to grasp an object in the hand, and the knowledge that objects still exist even when they are out of sight. Such items form the components for the next higher level, such as knowledge about the ways in which various objects can or cannot be changed, or skills in performing such manipulations of objects. The learning of spoken language, and afterward of written language, mathematics, and other symbolic systems, makes possible many additional levels, so that the hierarchies of knowledge for an educated adult are extremely complex.

This analysis of cognitive development begins to sound quite a bit like Piaget's. Indeed, the idea that knowledge, skills, and understanding are arranged in hierarchies that gradually develop through life has come to be quite widely held. It is interesting that Piaget's research on children's cognitions, Gagné's work on education and training, and the application of ideas about computers, along with other current approaches, have all converged on this idea about cognitive organization. The idea of hierarchies is not inherently a cognitive idea, for connectionists likewise assume that simple habits get organized into complex skills, but the idea is currently more associated with cognitive thinking. Whether connectionist, cognitive, or a mixture of both, the idea of hierarchical organization is important in the study of learning, thinking, and human development.

chapter 7

Connectionist Moves in Cognitive Directions

Because cognitive interpretations of learning have become much more popular in the past couple of decades, it is easy to imagine that connectionist views have simply been replaced by cognitive ones. Though this interpretation of history would be partially correct, it is by no means the whole story. Even before cognitive interpretations became very popular, their criticisms of connectionist theory were beginning to take effect. Connectionist theorists have always made an effort to explain complex behaviors in their own terms, and they were increasingly moved to do so by the challenging data that cognitive psychologists were presenting. Thus, some of the most significant developments within connectionist theory have been attempts to expand so they could deal more effectively with phenomena that other theorists considered evidence of cognitive processes. Such an attempt is consistent with the influence of computers, as discussed in the previous chapter, since it tried to show that cognitive types of behavior could be derived from basically connectionist principles. The impetus for this theorizing, however, came well before computers had made such an impact on life as they now have.

CONTRIBUTIONS BY HULL, SPENCE, AND AMSEL

One of Hull's many interests was the elaboration of his theory so that it could predict some of the laws of behavior that had been demonstrated by cognitive theorists. Of major assistance to him in this enterprise was his younger colleague, Kenneth W. Spence (1907–1967). After obtaining his Ph.D. at Yale, Spence went to the University of Iowa and spent most of his professional career there, though the last few years of his life were spent at the University of Texas. For two decades before Hull's death, Spence was a major contributor to his thinking and a great producer of research relevant to the theory. Derivation of cognitive findings from the postulates of the theory is something on which Hull and Spence both worked so much, and on which they constantly influenced one another, that it is sometimes hard to decide who contributed what. After Hull's death, Spence became the chief exemplar of his tradition and continued to incorporate cognitive features into the theory.

Fractional Anticipatory Goal Responses

For dealing with cognitive issues, Hull's system included one important corollary that we did not consider in the discussion in Chapter 3. He called it by slightly different names at different times in his career, but the name by which it is best known is *fractional anticipatory goal response.* We can best understand this imposing expression by analyzing it in parts, starting at the end. A goal response is the response of consuming a reward, which by definition is at the goal of a sequence of responses. Thus, when a rat eats food in the goal box at the end of a maze, the rat is making a goal response. An anticipatory goal response is one that occurs before the individual gets to the goal. Strictly speaking, "anticipatory" means only that it anticipates the goal in the sense of coming before it, but clearly something more was implied: the response indicated that the rat anticipated the goal in the sense of expecting it. The anticipatory goal response cannot be a complete goal response, since there is no food to be consumed until the goal actually is reached. The rat in the maze can anticipate the food by licking its chops and salivating, but cannot make the complete eating response until food is available. The parts of the total goal response that can occur before the goal is reached are therefore called fractional anticipatory goal responses.

The abbreviation for fractional anticipatory goal response is r_G. This is usually read as "little r G" which is a sort of pun on the word "little," indicating both that the written letter "r" is lower case and that the goal response referred to is fractional and hence small.

How is the r_G acquired? Like any other responses, says Hull—by reinforced practice. When a rat eats food in the goal box of a maze, it is making a goal response that is reinforced by the drive reduction from the food. This goal response occurs in the presence of stimuli from the goal box, such as its color, smell, and floor texture, and thus is learned as a response to these stimuli. As a result there will be a tendency for the goal response to occur to these stimuli even in the absence of food. However, the stimuli in the rest of the maze are much like those of the goal box. Since in the absence of food such an anticipatory goal response can only be fractional, it is the r_G.

Although Hull limited his formal consideration of r_G to such obvious examples as fractional eating responses, the concept can be applied to any goal response. In the case of humans, there might be fractional anticipatory reading responses, baseball-playing responses, or money-pocketing responses. These could be conditioned, respectively, to the stimuli of the library, the sandlot, and the pay envelope.

The important aspect of the r_G is that it produces stimuli that have a major role in guiding the individual's behavior. A stimulus produced by an r_G is called an s_G. The function of s_G in Hull's system is much like that of Guthrie's movement-produced stimuli. The chief difference is that the s_G in Hull's system has reinforcing properties, which would of course not be included in Guthrie's system. The reinforcing properties of s_G arise from the fact that these stimuli were closely paired with drive reduction during the original goal reaction (e.g., eating). This pairing resulted in their becoming conditioned reinforcers. As a result, any stimulus that produces r_G, and hence also s_G, will have a reinforcing effect.

Hull found r_G very useful in demonstrating that the kinds of behavior studied by cognitive psychologists could be shown to follow from his theory. It proved to be a powerful tool in deriving theorems dealing with movement in free space and with insightful problem solving. When Tolman says an individual has a cognition that food is to be found in a certain place, or when Lewin says that a certain region in the life space has positive valence because it contains food, Hull can say that the stimuli of this place elicit r_G for food. Fractional anticipatory goal responses can thus be seen as cognitions about the location of goal objects. In making such interpretations, Hull was following the tradition of Watson and Guthrie, reducing ideas and expectations to small movements of parts of the body. However, he went into more detail than Watson or Guthrie, and in doing so reduced the gap between connectionist and cognitive interpretations of learning.

By using r_G, Hull could predict that an individual might approach a goal object by a route that he had never before used. Once the individual saw the goal object, or any stimuli commonly associated with it, r_G would be aroused by these stimuli. As a result, the individual would tend to approach the goal object, regardless of whether the route by which he had approached it was one he had ever before used for approaching that goal. His behavior would thus conform to Lewin's prediction, that he should tend to approach a region of positive valence from whatever direction and by whatever means the situation required. It would also fit Tolman's interpretation of behavior as a seeking of goals rather than a running off of habits. Attaining old goals by new techniques is thus one phenomenon, emphasized by cognitive psychologists, with which Hull is able to deal.

Closely related to new approaches is the matter of detours. Much of the emphasis in gestalt interpretations of learning is on finding new ways to reach goals when the old familiar ways are blocked. The new ways involve finding detours around barriers, either in physical space or in Lewin's topological life space. Gestaltists interpret such detour solutions as involving a restructuring of the life space, a realization that it is possible to get around the barrier. Hull concerns himself only with physical space and concentrates on the trial-and-error process by which the detour is discovered. The inexperienced individual, when confronted by a barrier, is likely to spend some time in futile attempts to penetrate the barrier and continue directly on the way to the goal. As reactive inhibition builds up and partially inhibits this direct response, says Hull, the oscillations of this and other responses occasionally make some other response momentarily stronger. Eventually this process results in the individual accidentally finding a route around the barrier. The response of taking this indirect route is reinforced and thus becomes more likely to occur if the individual again encounters that barrier on the way to that goal. Hull derived a number of theorems about the factors that would make such detour learning easier or more difficult. This kind of learning involves problem solving, but without insight.

For an individual experienced in free space, however, the situation is different. In the course of ordinary life, individuals often reach the same goal by different routes. Different habits leading to the same goal come to form a habit family. All members of the habit family have r_G for a certain goal in common. When one of these habits is blocked, another member of the habit family can readily take its place, so that progress toward the goal can continue. Those habits in the family that obtain the goal most quickly and easily are preferred, both because they involve less delay of reinforcement and because they result in less reactive and conditioned inhibition. The habits in the family are thus arranged in a hierarchy of preference, ranging from the most to the least preferred. A less preferred habit will ordinarily be used only if all the more preferred ones are blocked. This arrangement of habits is known as the *habit-family hierarchy*. We might think of the habit-family hierarchy as Hull's equivalent of a cognitive map. In making use of it to explain detour behavior, Hull is in effect saying that the ability to show cognitive behavior, to act as if one has a cognitive map, is the result of prior learning. He is reinterpreting cognitive behavior as a product of prior connectionist learning.

The addition of incentive motivation to Hull's system provided him with another convenient tool for reinterpreting insightful learning in his own terms. One of the points that Tolman emphasized was the distinction between learning how to get to a given place and learning whether to expect a reward there. In making K separate from $_sH_R$, Hull conceded this point. Learning how to get somewhere or do something is a matter of habit strength, which builds up slowly. Learning where a reward is located is a matter of incentive motivation, which both increases and decreases rapidly. It is thus possible for $_sH_R$ to reach a high level while K remains very low. In such a situation, the introduction of a large reward would raise K and thus result in a sudden improvement in performance. This response would constitute a form of latent learning, one of Tolman's favorite phenomena, but it would also be consistent with the later version of Hull's theory.

These applications of Hull's theory to complex, insightful phenomena of learning do not by any means close the gap between connectionist and cognitive interpretations. For one thing, some learning phenomena emphasized by cognitive psychologists are still largely beyond the reach of Hullian explanations. Buxton's latent learning experiment, described in our discussion of Tolman, is very difficult to explain in Hullian terms, even with the aid of habit-family hierarchies and fractional anticipatory goal responses. For another thing, these derivations of Hull's are less precise than many of his others, and there is room for some dispute as to how rigorously the theorems really follow from the postulates. Nevertheless, Hull went far enough in closing the gap between the two kinds of theory to point the way toward a possible eventual amalgamation, in which cognitive principles would be accepted as valid but would be interpreted as the result of prior learning of a connectionist sort.

Spence's Revision of Hull's System

Almost by definition, a system such as Hull's is never completely finished. As new laws are established by new experiments, the postulates are almost certain now and then to require some modification. At his death Hull's system was in a particularly unfinished state, however, since changes that Hull made in the last few years of his life had not yet been carried through to their logial conclusions. The system thus suffered, as we have already seen, from internal inconsistencies. The job of straightening out the inconsistencies and reaching the logical conclusions was undertaken by Spence.

In spite of their close connection, Hull and Spence differed somewhat in their approach to theory. Though Spence was a great exponent of theory construction, he was more cautious about it than Hull. His theory, though it can readily be seen as a revision of Hull's, is less elaborate, less formally stated, and more obviously tentative than Hull's. Even though Hull expected to keep modifying his theory in the light of new evidence, he stated it in the form of a formal, finished structure. Spence stated his more casually, leaving more of the details to be settled by experiment. In particular, Spence regarded Hull's inclusion of specific numerical equations in his postulates as highly premature. With our present information, or lack of it, he believed that such specific equations can only represent misleading pseudoprecision. Spence was more concerned than was Hull about the *boundary conditions* of a theory. These are the limits within which a theory is expected to operate. For example, a theory of education that worked well for explaining and predicting what happens in middle-class American schoolrooms might fail completely if applied to education among African Bushmen, or even to education in American urban ghettos, because education in these other situations is a topic outside the boundary conditions of the theory. Similarly, a theory intended to deal with learning by animals or human babies, where language does not enter in, might not be appropriate for learning by school children or adults. Therefore a theory should specify the conditions to which it is and is not intended to apply. Thus in various respects Spence did not set his aspirations for theory quite as high as Hull, but he is nonetheless a major advocate of theory construction as vital to the development of science.

The chief innovations in Spence's system as compared with Hull's are those concerned with K, the incentive motivation factor. At Hull's death this had still not been fully assimilated into his system. Spence undertook to clarify the status of K, and in doing so made radical changes in the whole basis of the theory.

Hull intended to define all of his intervening variables in terms of the independent variables that produced them and the dependent variables that they influenced. Nevertheless, he was quite willing to speculate about what physiological changes inside the organism might be involved. Habit strength might be related to some change in the neural connections between the sense organ that receives a stimulus and the muscle or gland that makes a response. Drive might be related to a bodily need (as Hull himself suggested) or to a strong stimulus (as Hull suggested and Miller emphasized). But what of incentive motivation? Is there any bodily process to which this construct can be related? Yes, says Spence, there is the fractional anticipatory goal response. Hull never clarified the relationship between K and r_G, but it seemed to Spence that such a relationship existed and should be made explicit. The r_G is assumed to be a response, but one differing from other responses in that the sensations it produces are reinforcing. If an individual has eaten a large quantity of food several times in a certain place, the r_G of eating will be strongly conditioned to the stimuli of that place. Whenever these stimuli are observed, r_G will occur and produce s_G. If the person had eaten only a little food on previous occasions in that place, the r_G and s_G would be only weakly evoked. If food had never been eaten there, they would not be evoked at all. Note, however, that the same condition (amount of food) which determines the strength of r_G also determines the magnitude of K. Let us say, then, suggested Spence, that K is nothing more than the total strength of r_G and the associated s_G. By combining these two concepts, K and r_G, into one, we can both simplify the theory and eliminate some of the uncertainty as to just where K fits.

This change, however, has implications beyond a mere simplification. For although K and r_G in Hull's system have so much in common, they differ in one important respect. For Hull, K is related to a stimulus-response connection: the greater the food reward for making a given response to a given stimulus, the greater the K for that stimulus-response connection. However, r_G is related only to a stimulus: the more the eating that has occurred in the presence of a stimulus, the greater the tendency to make r_G in response to that stimulus. By treating K as nothing more than r_G, Spence has related K purely to the stimulus. Thus the incentive component in the equation for excitatory potential is not the incentive for making a response but the incentive for getting to certain stimuli. If we should refer to these stimuli that evoke r_G as "signs that food is near," the similarity of this theory to Tolman's would be emphasized.

A closely related innovation in Spence's system is concerned with the building up of habit strength. Hull, in the final version of his theory, made habit strength a function of the total number of times that the response had occurred in the presence of the stimulus and had been reinforced. The size of the reinforcement, however, made no difference. Is it reasonable, we may ask, to assume that there is no difference in this respect between a huge reward and a tiny one, but a very important difference between a tiny one and none at all? Spence solved this problem by assuming that H (he omitted the subscripts) does not depend on reinforcement. Whenever a response is made in the presence of certain stimuli, said Spence, H increases. Thus H depends only on practice, not on reinforcement. Reward operates only through K (that is, r_G), not through H.

With these changes from Hull, what does Spence's system look like? As with Hull's, Spence's H, D, and K combine to produce E. However, D and K are added together, not multiplied, so that the equation becomes $E = H(D + K)$. This change has the effect that either D or K alone can activate a response, whereas for Hull, if either $D = 0$ or $K = 0$, then $_sE_R = 0$. As with Hull, various other components enter into the full equation, but this abbreviated form will be adequate for our purposes. In this formula, H depends only on the total number of times that the response has been made in the presence of the stimuli, while K depends on the extent to which goal responses have occurred previously in the presence of the stimuli. Thus drive reduction does not enter into the equation at all, and reinforcement enters only indirectly through r_G.

As a final complication, it must be pointed out that the above applies only to the learning of responses that lead to rewards which can be consumed. Where a response is rewarded by escape from a noxious stimulus (or is negatively reinforced, in Skinner's terms) different laws apply. As in Hull's theory, these have not been worked out as fully as those for positive reinforcement, but one point stands out: drive reduction *is* more important in the learning of these responses. The experiments by which Spence supports this interpretation are ingenious, but it is not necessary to report them here.

Astute readers of this book may already have noticed the many resemblances between Spence's theory and those of a variety of other theorists we have discussed. Like Skinner's, Spence's system is in a practical sense a stimulus-response reinforcement theory. However, Spence attempted to analyze the nature of reinforcement, which Skinner does not, and in the process sounded much like Guthrie. Both H and K depend only on practice: in one case practice in making the instrumental response, in the other case practice in making r_G. In that sense, Spence's theory is as much a pure contiguity theory as Guthrie's. Moreover, r_G is an example of movement-produced stimuli contributing to the maintenance of goal direction, a thoroughly Guthrian notion. Finally, and most interestingly, Spence's theory has a marked resemblance to the cognitive theories, particularly that of Tolman. Though in his earlier years Spence was an outspoken critic of cognitive interpretations, his own work led him over the years to a theory that lends itself well to cognitive purposes.

Spence's theory deals with phenomena of interest to cognitive psychologists in much the same way that Hull's does, but his theory is even better adapted to doing so than is Hull's, because Spence has eliminated reinforcement as a fundamental concept (at least so far as positive rewards are concerned). In place of reinforcement, he has the r_G mechanism, which can easily be regarded as the anticipation of reward. This reasoning completes the separation, begun by Hull, between learning about what paths lead where and learning about where reward is located. In accepting this distinction, which is central to Lewin and Tolman but absent in Skinner and only hinted at in Guthrie, Spence made a large stride toward a more cognitive interpretation of learning. Though often a critic of others' formulations, Spence included elements of other systems in his own system to a greater degree than has any other theorist of learning except perhaps Tolman.

Frustration Theory

In recent years, one important advance in the study of motivation has been the elaboration of the Hull-Spence tradition to include the analysis of frustration. This line of theorizing has received its greatest impetus from the work of Abram

Amsel (b. 1922). In some ways Amsel's relation to Spence has resembled Spence's to Hull, in that Amsel was Spence's student and Spence incorporated many of Amsel's ideas into his own thinking. Since Spence's death there has been no one person who can clearly be considered the chief exemplar of the Hullian tradition, but Amsel probably comes the closest. Several elaborations of the theory have appeared (Amsel 1958, 1962, 1967).

What does frustration theory say? It begins with the concept of r_G, which we have already noted can easily be translated into cognitive terms as an expectancy of reward. When an organism expects reward in a certain place (i.e., makes r_G to the stimuli of that place) and then does not find reward, frustration results. Frustration is conceived to be a drive, produced by the nonfulfillment of an expectancy of reward just as other drives are produced by food deprivation or by injury to the body. Though the detailed reasoning is not always easy to follow, all the effects that frustration is assumed to have in various situations are aspects of its status as a drive.

What are some of the properties of a drive? For one thing, it is a state of high arousal, multiplying habit strength to increase excitatory potential. If frustration is a drive, it should be possible to show that subjects will respond more vigorously immediately after being denied an expected reward than at other times. That subjects will respond thus has been shown by having a rat run down two alleys in succession. He is always rewarded at the end of the second alley, but only part of the time at the end of the first. Once he learns to expect (or at least hope for) reward at the end of the first alley, he should be frustrated on those trials when he does not in fact find reward there. This frustration drive should increase his total drive level, thereby producing a higher excitatory potential for running down the second alley than he would have if he were not frustrated. Thus rats should run down the second alley faster on trials when they are nonrewarded in the first alley than on trials when they are rewarded, a prediction which has repeatedly been confirmed.

Another characteristic of a drive, as Miller emphasized, is that it can be conditioned to new stimuli, to which a subject will then learn a new escape response. In learning of a discrimination, the negative stimulus (S−) is a signal for frustration and so should become a secondary drive stimulus. It should then be possible to place the subject in a new situation where he had never experienced either reward or frustration, turn on the signal, and teach him a new response to turn the signal off. Wagner (1963) and Daly (1969) have shown that rats will indeed learn to jump across a hurdle from one side of a box to the other in order to turn off a stimulus which has previously been a signal for frustration.

Finally, just as subjects can learn to expect reward, they should also be able to learn to expect frustration. Just as r_G (or r_R, R for reward, in Amsel's terms) comes to occur as a subject approaches a place where he has previously been rewarded, so r_F (F for frustration) should also occur as he approaches a place where he has been frustrated. This anticipation of (possible) frustration is assumed to produce competing responses, which interfere with continuation of the goal-directed behavior. It therefore takes longer to complete the response. Spence (1956) included a reference to this effect as a minor part of his system. He suggested that $E = H(D + K)$ is a complete formula only in cases of continuous reinforcement. Where nonreinforcement occurs, it is necessary to expand it to $E = H(D + K) - I$, with I referring to the interference from competing responses produced by frustration. The I would be present in extinction, in discrimination learning (for the nonreinforced alternative), and in partial reinforcement. Using I, Spence was able to derive various phenomena that could not have been explained using only H, D, and K.

It should be noted that I, although it bears some resemblance to Hull's I_R and $_SI_R$, is a quite different concept. Whereas Hull's terms refer to inhibitions against responding, Spence's I refers to the active interference of one set of responses (those elicited by frustration) with another set (those getting the subject to the goal). It applies only in cases of nonreward, while I_R and $_SI_R$ were assumed to be involved to some degree in all responding.

It may seem strange to the reader that frustration should tend to make animals run faster in the two-stage runway, but yet that anticipatory frustration should make them run slower. It is true that theorists attribute so many different properties to frustration that there is a constant problem of maintaining consistency, one with which we can sympathize after studying Hull's system. Nevertheless, it is not difficult to see intuitively how both these opposite effects might occur. The individual who is afraid he is going to be frustrated if he completes some course of action may hesitate and dawdle, easily distracted from a goal toward which he is ambivalent. However, if he reaches the goal and is indeed frustrated, this frustration may well energize him to do something else, something from which he definitely expects reward, with extra vigor. Perhaps the unsuccessful (hence often frustrated) student who dawdles on his way to school but emerges from school onto the playground with a burst of energy bears some resemblance to the rat in the two-stage runway!

The assumed occurrence of r_F has also been used by Amsel to explain a phenomenon that has often troubled theorists, the *partial-reinforcement effect*. We mentioned in connection with schedules of reinforcement in Chapter 4 that it takes longer to extinguish a response following intermittent reinforcement than following continuous reinforcement. This generalization is true not only of the free-operant situation that we were considering there but also of the case where animals receive separate trails in a runway. In such situations it is customary, for some obscure historical reason, to speak of partial reinforcement rather than intermittent reinforcement. In partial reinforcement in a runway, for example, there is a reward at the end of the runway on some trials but not on others. Greater resistance to extinction following partial reinforcement than following continuous reinforcement is known as the partial-reinforcement effect, and it is this effect that Amsel attempts to explain by using the concept of r_F.

When a rat receives partial reinforcement in a runway, he presently begins making r_F. At first, as we have noted, this fractional anticipatory frustration tends to disrupt his running. Nevertheless, on each trial he eventually gets to the goal and is reinforced for his running. Running in the presence of r_F (or, strictly speaking, in the presence of s_F, the stimuli produced by r_F) is reinforced. Eventually, therefore, the s_F become no longer stimuli for competing responses, but rather stimuli for running.

What happens when extinction begins? Rats that have received continuous reinforcement in the runway now begin for the first time to make r_F, which give rise to competing responses (Spence's I). Since extinction involves for them both a decrease in K and an increase in I, the rats extinguish the running response rapidly. For the partially reinforced animals, however, r_F are nothing new and now tend to produce running rather than competing responses. For these animals there is thus only one factor tending to produce extinction—the decrease in K —while the additional factor of I is not involved. The extinction for these animals therefore proceeds more slowly, giving the partial-reinforcement effect.

As with the Hullian theory from which it comes, frustration theory is complex and constantly struggling to avoid getting so enmeshed in its various assumptions that it becomes self-contradictory. Nevertheless, its success in applying the rigor of Hullian theory to as clinically useful a concept as frustration has made it an important feature on the current theoretical scene.

MOWRER'S INTERPRETATIONS OF LEARNING

For all his similarities to cognitive theory, Spence sticks firmly to his connectionist terms and to his insistence that cognitive behavior is basically a matter of responses and stimuli. Another well-known theorist, who also began his work somewhat in the Hullian tradition, has moved toward cognitive interpretations in his terms as well as in his ideas. This is O. Hobart Mowrer (1907–1982), long a professor at the University of Illinois. Originally noted, like Miller, for his applications of learning theory to personality, Mowrer has recently been best known for his concerns with group psychotherapy, drug addiction, and the place of sin in psychopathology. In addition, however, Mowrer attained note as a theorist of learning and of thinking. Beginning with attempts to resolve certain problems within connectionist theory, he became more and more a cognitive theorist as he proceeded.

Mowrer's Older Two-Factor Theory

The problem that Mowrer originally tried to solve was concerned with the nature of reinforcement. Is it, or is it not, a matter of drive reduction? Mowrer agreed with Hull and Miller that the answer is usually that it is. The events that are reinforcing are the ones which relieve hunger or pain or fear or some other noxious state. However, Mowrer was particularly concerned with the learning of emotional reactions, and here the situation seemed to be different. When Miller's rats learned to be afraid of the white compartment, or when a burnt child learns to fear the fire, what is the reinforcement for this learning? A common-sense answer would be that the pain, of electric shock or of a burn, is the reinforcer. Hull and Miller did not accept this common-sense interpretation, but maintained instead that it was a reduction in pain immediately afterward that served as the reinforcer. We can readily see that Hull and Miller tried, by this interpretation, to maintain a consistent drive-reduction explanation of reinforcement. To Mowrer, however, the common-sense explanation seemed preferable. It seemed unreasonable to him that the emotional responses a rat or a person makes when hurt are reinforced by the termination of the pain. If that were true, brief punishment would reinforce any response, while lengthy punishment would have no effect on it. Everyday experience contradicts this idea, and Mowrer did a number of experiments that further contradicted it. These results led Mowrer to formulate a *two-factor* theory of reinforcement.

Mowrer's two-factor theory was much like Skinner's distinction between the conditioning of reflexes and the learning of operant behavior. Several people prior to Mowrer had, in fact, suggested that classical and instrumental conditioning are basically different kinds of learning. It remained for Mowrer, however, to sharpen the distinction and to emphasize its importance for the understanding of all learning situations.

Mowrer referred to his two forms of learning as *sign learning* and *solution learning.* The two are sharply demarcated in various ways. Sign learning involves classical conditioning of involuntary responses of the smooth muscles in the internal organs and of the glands. These are what we call emotional responses, and the most important example is fear. An unconditioned stimulus, such as pain, elicits these involuntary fear responses. Any stimulus that is paired with the unconditioned stimulus can then become a conditioned stimulus for the fear responses. Thus the unconditioned stimulus that elicits the emotional response is also the reinforcer in the conditioning of fear to new stimuli. This form of learning is called sign learning because the conditioned stimulus becomes a sign of danger and thus elicits an emotional response.

Solution learning is the instrumental conditioning of responses that reduce drives. It involves voluntary responses of the striped, skeletal muscles. The reinforcement for this form of learning is the reduction of the drive. It is called solution learning because the response solves the problem posed for the individual by the drive.

So far Mowrer seems to be adding very little to what Skinner had already said. He has substituted the terms *sign learning* for the conditioning of respondent behavior and *solution learning* for the learning of operant behavior. Also, he has restricted sign learning to the emotional responses of smooth muscles and glands. The importance of his contribution is in suggesting the relationship between these two kinds of learning. In a great many cases the drive that is reduced in solution learning is a secondary drive that was previously acquired by sign learning. The learning process thus has two stages. In the first, fear (or possibly some other emotional response) is conditioned to some stimulus by a process of sign learning. This fear response produces stimuli that act as a drive. In the second stage, an instrumental response that reduces the fear drive is learned by the process of solution learning. The instrumental response reduces the fear by getting the individual away from the conditioned stimulus that arouses the fear.

Consider as an example a child who is bitten by a dog. Since the unconditioned stimulus of pain from the bite produces emotional responses characteristic of fear, the sight of the dog becomes a conditioned stimulus for fear. This event is sign learning. On a later occasion, the sight of the dog (or perhaps, through generalization, the sight of any dog) produces fear, a secondary drive. If the child now runs away, thus escaping from the fear-producing sight of the dog, this running response will be reinforced by fear reduction. This event is solution learning. Both stages of the learning process must be considered in order to understand the child's reaction to the dog.

In principle, either stage of the process can occur without the other. In practice, however, it is doubtful if they ever occur independently. When a drive is conditioned (stage 1), there is usually some response available that will reduce it at least slightly (stage 2). Moreover, primary drives for which one learns an instrumental response (stage 2) are likely to have some component of secondary drive resulting from previous learning (stage 1). For example, when a person in the dentist's chair feels a slight pain, the resulting drive is due only partly to the pain itself, and partly to fear. The fear in turn results from the fact that in the past slight pain has sometimes been followed by greater pain and thus become a conditioned stimulus for fear appropriate to the greater pain. Thus pain combines with fear of pain to produce the total drive. A reassurance, such as the dentist's saying, "I'm almost done," can reduce the fear and hence reduce the total drive, even though it cannot reduce the actual pain.

This two-stage analysis of learning by Mowrer sounds very much like that presented by Dollard and Miller. However, by treating the acquisition of fear as sign learning, Mowrer avoids a problem that Miller faced, that of finding a drive-reducing reinforcer for the acquisition of the fear response. For Mowrer, it is the onset of the drive, serving as an unconditioned stimulus, that reinforces the fear response in stage 1, whereas Miller would have to say that the end of the drive reinforces the fear response. Mowrer's view is more consistent both with common sense and with experimental evidence. However, such a sharp distinction between two kinds of learning seems artificial to many people, especially in view of the fact that such principles as extinction, generalization, and discrimination apply to both. As the reader can see by comparing the discussion of Dollard and Miller with the discussion of Mowrer, in most situations it makes little difference which assumption one makes. Although our understanding of the learning process will be very incomplete until this issue (along with many others) is resolved, many practical applications are possible without the answer to this theoretical question.

The Newer Sign-Learning Theory

Since Mowrer (1947) originally presented his two-factor theory, he has modified it by pointing out that solution learning has many of the characteristics of sign learning. Suppose an individual learns not to do something for which he has been punished. According to two-factor theory, in stage 1 of this learning the sensations produced by his own behavior became a conditioned stimulus for fear. In stage 2, the response of changing his behavior away from that which was punished was reinforced by reduction of the fear, and learned. In stage 1, sensations from his own behavior became danger signs. Why, asks the new Mowrer, should we not say the same thing about stage 2: that sensations from the individual's own behavior became signs of hope? When the fearful person felt himself making the new, never punished response, he felt safer, because the sensations from this response had previously been followed by a reduction in fear. This new interpretation of Mowrer's replaces his older two-factor theory with a new, cognitive-sounding one-factor theory. All learning, in this new version, is sign learning.

Through learning, according to this theory, stimuli become signs of fear or hope or disappointment or relief. Even the acquisition of bodily skills can be interpreted as sign learning. When we learn certain movements in riding a bicycle, for example, we are learning that some sensations from our bodies mean we are doing it right, while other sensations indicate that we are about to tip over and must act quickly to keep our balance. The important thing about these stimuli is not that they elicit certain responses but that they have certain meanings, that they are signs of success or of impending failure in our attempt to ride. The history of Mowrer's thinking, in coming to this position, is covered in his book, *Learning Theory and Behavior* (1960).

This new interpretation of learning makes Mowrer more cognitive than any of the other theorists we have discussed who developed their systems within the connectionist tradition. It is therefore interesting to compare him with the two recent cognitive theorists whom we considered in the previous chapter. His earlier system bore considerable resemblance to Bolles's, with sign learning corresponding to the formation of S-S* expectancies and solution learning to the acquisition of R-S* expectancies. Mowrer's newer system, however, is closer to Bindra's, since both agree that all learning is sign learning. They are not, however, saying the same thing. Mowrer still is concerned with the learning of responses, but says that we learn them because the sensations that the responses produce are signs of hope or relief. Bindra, however, is not concerned with the learning of responses at all. Given S-S* learning and central motive states, he regards the responses of approaching and avoiding as natural outcomes, requiring no special additional learning. Mowrer's new system can thus handle situations involving new learning that pose problems for Bindra's theory. Mowrer, however, like both Bolles and Bindra, lacks the full cognitive complexity of Tolman's system. Like them, Mowrer talks about sign learning but not about sign-gestalt learning or cognitive maps. Though his theory is as cognitive as some that emerged from the cognitive tradition, he still shows traces of his connectionist background.

MEDIATING RESPONSES

So far in this chapter we have seen two examples of connectionist theory being broadened to incorporate aspects of the cognitive approach, each primarily the work of one theorist. We turn next to a general approach that has taken many forms and been advanced by many people, without any one person emerging as its main exponent. A number of the major theorists we have discussed in this book have made use of this approach, as have many other theorists we have not mentioned. This approach is the use of what are known as *mediating responses*.

We have seen that Hull and Spence made great use in their theories of fractional anticipatory goal responses and the stimuli they produced. Guthrie made somewhat similar use of movement-produced stimuli, while Miller's interpretation of secondary drive involved strong stimuli produced by the individual's own emotional responses. In all of these cases, the primary effect of a response was to produce the stimuli for further responses, thereby producing a mediating link between the original external stimulus and the final observable response. Such responses are therefore known as mediating responses.

Mediating responses and the stimuli they produce serve a variety of functions in theories of learning and motivation. First, there are drive functions. For example, conditioned emotional responses produce drive stimuli and thus serve as the basis of secondary drive. This function is emphasized by Dollard and Miller and by Mowrer. Second, there are incentive functions. For example, fractional antedating goal reactions produce stimuli that have secondary reinforcing properties. These serve as the basis of the incentive component in Spence's system. The anticipatory muscle readinesses that Guthrie discusses are similar. Third, there are cue functions. Here the stimuli produced by the mediating response serve as the guiding stimuli for further behavior. A striking example is Watson's view that thinking is merely subvocal speech—a series of fractional speech movements that serve the function of talking to oneself. It is this cue function of mediating responses with which we will be mainly concerned here.

In some cases it is fairly clear that mediating responses serve this cue function by changing the orientation of our sense receptors and hence of the stimuli we receive. A person staring at something and a dog pricking up its ears are obvious examples. In such cases we can speak of the mediating responses as *observing responses* (Wyckoff 1952). In other cases we cannot identify any specific observing response, but it is still plausible to say that the mediating response changes the effective sensory input in subtler ways, through a change in attention. Often it is difficult to say whether we are dealing with changes in receptor orientation or in attention at the level of the central nervous system. If it is true, as someone has said, that a man notices a woman's legs, another woman notices her hat, and a thief notices her purse, is the difference in what they look at (observing responses) or in the part of what they look at that they notice (attention)? Perhaps it depends on something as trivial as how far away the woman is, and hence whether it is possible to focus one's eyes on all of her at once. So, although a full understanding of mediation would require knowing just what form the mediating responses take, for our present purposes we can group together all those cases where mediating responses of whatever form serve primarily a cue function.

Cue-Producing Responses

One phenomenon that can be explained by cue-producing mediating responses is what D. H. Lawrence (no relation to the novelist) has called the *acquired distinctiveness of cues.* This term refers to learning about which cues in a situation are important. When a first-grader discovers that it is the shape of letters rather than their size that is important in reading, the cue of form has acquired distinctiveness for him. This acquisition will then affect his subsequent learning of letters and words. The response of paying attention to form is separate from any particular response that he makes to any particular form. This separateness has been demonstrated in several ingenious experiments with rats (Lawrence 1949, 1950) and in an impressively thorough experiment with humans (Goss & Greenfeld 1958).

Acquired distinctiveness of cues is not an unmixed blessing. Once we learn what aspects of a situation to pay attention to and what ones to ignore, we may miss opportunities for useful learning about those we have come to ignore. Such a situation has been labeled *blocking* (Kamin 1968). For example (Haggbloom 1981), rats were trained to run down an alley and were rewarded on every other trial. As a result, they learned to run fast on trials following nonreward (since the next trial after a nonrewarded one was always rewarded) and not on trials following a reward. In other words, they learned to discriminate between the internal cues of just having eaten and of just having not eaten. Once this discrimination was learned, a new cue was introduced: on rewarded trials the alley was always black, while on nonrewarded trials it was always white. They were given as many trials on this new regime as other rats needed to learn to run when the alley was black and not when it was white. However, these rats did not need to learn this discrimination, since they could always respond appropriately on the basis of the internal cues they had already learned to pay attention to: run after a nonreward but not after a reward. What happened when they were tested with the rewarded and nonrewarded trials in random order, so that the only cue was color? In fact, they showed little evidence of discrimination on the basis of color, indicating that the earlier learning about the internal cues had blocked later learning about color. Because of the blocking, they were baffled by the new discrimination problem. How often do people have similar experiences—learning enough so they think they "know it all" and therefore not learning any more?

Another closely related example of a situation where observing responses are important is in the formation of *learning sets*. These were first demonstrated by Harry F. Harlow (1905–1981) of the University of Wisconsin (Harlow 1959). To demonstrate a learning set, an individual is given a long series of discrimination problems. On each problem he is presented with two objects. One of these has a reward behind it on every trial, the other does not. The same one is correct on each trial. He has to find out by trial and error which one is correct, but once he has learned this he can be right on every subsequent trial of that problem. Since the next problem has two new objects, he cannot directly transfer what he has learned on one problem to the next. He can, however, transfer the principle that reward is behind only one object and it is always the same object throughout a given problem. If he understands this principle, he can be correct on all but the first trial of every problem. All he has to do is to choose either stimulus at random on the first trial. If it is correct, he chooses the same one on all the other trials. If it is wrong, he chooses the other one on all the remaining trials. For the completely inexperienced learner, this solution is not as easy as it sounds. For one thing, the right-left position of the stimuli is changed from trial to trial, and some learners tend to respond to the position rather than to the object. There is also a widespread tendency to choose the other one on trial 2 regardless of whether the first one was rewarded on trial 1. These and other systematic wrong ways of responding to the situation are known as *error factors*. Because of the various possible error factors, inexperienced learners are likely to do poorly on the task. How are they to know that the same object, regardless of position, will be rewarded on every trial? Gradually, however, they do learn this principle, so that learning gets better and better from problem to problem. After having experience with enough different problems, all of which can be solved in the same way, learners commonly reach the point where their scores on new problems are nearly perfect. They are then said to have formed a learning set.

A learning set is an example of learning how to learn. It involves being set to approach the problem in a certain way. Since the approach to the problem requires paying attention to certain cues rather than others (form rather than position, for example), acquired distinctiveness of cues is one aspect of the formation of learning sets. Most of the studies of learning sets have been with animals, particularly monkeys. There are large species differences and age differences in the rate at which learning sets are formed, more so than in the learning of a single discrimination. The rate at which learning sets are formed has come to be regarded as one of the best measures of differences in intelligence among animals.

Much of education may be regarded as the formation of learning sets. We hope that in teaching students we are not merely providing them with specific stimulus-response connections, but are giving them the necessary background for continued learning after they leave school. We want them to be able not merely to parrot answers to questions but to solve problems by making use of what they have learned. Studies of learning sets show individuals going through such a process of learning how to solve problems. The solution to one problem cannot be transferred directly to another problem, but the general method of solution can. Just as the "intelligent" behavior of the experienced monkey solving a discrimination problem reflects its prior experience in forming a learning set, so the "intelligent" behavior of an adult human reflects prior experience in learning how to solve problems.

The cue function of mediating responses is particularly valuable for a rapprochement between connectionist and cognitive theory. If our own responses can provide us with cues and if these can include complex verbal cues, we are well on the way to a connectionist cognitive theory. If one can make the responses of drawing a map on paper, can one not also make responses of imagining such a map? If one can give oneself instructions in words, why not in images, in muscular sets, or in any other sort of stimulus-producing response? And if such nonverbal mediating responses are available to humans, why not to animals also? This line of reasoning can be carried to the point where nearly all of the cognitive theorists' statements about life space, sign-gestalt expectations, and cognitive maps are accepted, but all are reinterpreted as stimuli produced by the individual's own responses.

Clearly, not all of the suggestions about mediating responses that have been made by various connectionist psychologists have gone this far. Though Hull, Spence, Mowrer, and Guthrie all make use of mediating responses, none of them regards the response-produced stimuli involved as having the extensive gestalt properties that cognitive theorists favor. Moreover, Wertheimer would probably have considered learning sets more like blind applications of a principle than like true insights, leading to B rather than A solutions. Nevertheless, these various elaborations of connectionist theory help to bridge the gap that separates them from cognitive theory. If they are still far from Wertheimer and only moderately close to Tolman, they are perhaps not so far from Bolles.

Cognitive Aspects of Pavlovian Conditioning

Psychologists in the Soviet Union have shown a related interest in their discussions of the *second signal system.* The kinds of conditioned stimuli that Pavlov studied, which signal the arrival of an unconditioned stimulus because they have been paired with that unconditioned stimulus in the past, are referred to collectively as the first signal system. Words and other arbitrary symbols also serve as signals, but the learning by which they became signals is more complex; they are said to make up the second signal system.

The complexities introduced by the second signal system are illustrated in an experiment quoted by Razran (1961). A boy was conditioned to salivate to the Russian word for "good" or "well" as the conditioned stimulus (S+), while the word for "bad" or "badly" was nonreinforced (an S−). He was then tested with a variety of sentences that did not contain either word but that had definite positive or negative connotations, and was found to salivate much more to the positive than to the negative ones. He produced the most drops of saliva to "The Soviet Army was victorious" and the fewest to "The pupil was fresh to the teacher." In addition to what this experiment tells us about conditioning, it gives us an interesting look at the value system of the Soviet Union!

Interest in such cognitive aspects of classical conditioning has not been limited to the Soviet Union, or even to the portions of eastern Europe influenced by Pavlovian psychophysiology. Researchers in the United States have also discovered that a conditioned stimulus can be something considerably more complex and meaningful than a light or a buzzer. For example, the conditioned stimulus in an eyelid conditioning experiment can be a simple arithmetic problem with the answer correct or incorrect, such as $3 + 2 = 5$ or $4 - 3 = 2$ (Fleming, et al. 1968). If every correct arithmetic problem is followed by an air puff on the eye, but incorrect problems are never followed by the puff, people learn the discrimination and blink only when presented with correct problems. This learning occurs even though the same problem is never repeated; the CS + is any correct problem and the CS− any incorrect problem. However, the discrimination is formed more quickly if it is done the other way around, with all the incorrect problems followed by an air puff, but none of the correct ones. Apparently it seems more natural to these learners for a mildly punishing stimulus, the air puff, to follow something wrong than something right. Oddly enough, however, if the air puff instead follows both correct and incorrect problems, the subjects blink more often to the correct than to the incorrect problem. Clearly there are aspects of classical conditioning that would not be predicted by a simple connectionist theory!

One might suspect that with a problem this complex, what is being learned is not so much a conditioned response as a deliberate, voluntary response. However, specialists in eyelid conditioning have developed techniques for distinguishing voluntary responses from "true" conditioned responses, based on the speed and form of the eyelid closure. The above results are found even when only responses of the true conditioned response form are counted. Apparently it is not just that "simple conditioned responses" are replaced by "higher mental processes," but that conditioned responses are not so simple.

THE SEMANTIC DIFFERENTIAL

This consideration of the evaluative significance of verbal stimuli can serve as an introduction to another aspect of mediation, the meaning of meaning. An important development in this area is the work of Charles E. Osgood and his associates at the University of Illinois on the concept of meaning (Osgood, Suci, & Tannenbaum 1957). They suggest that for every concept a person has, there is a mediating response which provides the meaning of that concept for that individual. (Actually they use the more general term "mediating process," but for consistency we will continue to speak of mediating responses.) These mediating responses are fractional parts of our response to the thing the word names. Thus our response to "sour" might be a slight tendency to pucker the lips and salivate, and our response to "mountain" might be a slight tendency to look upward. The mediating responses may also be part of the emotional response to the thing. We might, for example, smile slightly in response to the word "happy" or become tense in response to the word "danger."

Just what the particular mediating responses are is something we usually do not know. As Osgood and his associates are careful to point out, they may not be responses in the usual sense, like those in our examples, but may be unobservable processes in the central nervous system. We can, however, provide indirect evidence to support the view that the mediating response to a word is similar to the response to the thing that the word names. This view states that both the word and the thing are stimuli for a mediating response that produces further stimuli. These in turn may be the stimuli for some overt, measurable response. The mediating response and the stimuli it produces are similar whether they occur in response to the word or to the thing. This, indeed, is what we mean when we say that the word means the thing. Consequently the final overt response to the word should be similar to the response to the thing. That it is so has been demonstrated by experiments in which a bell or a blue light is used as the conditioned stimulus for some response and then the word "bell" or "blue" is presented. A large amount of generalization is found from the stimulus to its name.

It seemed unlikely to Osgood and his associates that there are as many unique mediating responses for meanings as there are words in the English language. Considering the many ways in which the meanings of different words are related, they thought that a fairly small number of different mediating responses should be enough to explain most of the meaning of words. Since they could not study the mediating responses directly, they undertook instead to study the different mediating responses in terms of the *dimensions of meaning.* In order to make this study, they developed a technique known as the *semantic differential.*

In the semantic-differential method, one begins with several pairs of opposite words. These might be such pairs as good-bad, strong-weak, hard-soft, and wet-dry. Each of these pairs defines a dimension of meaning running from one extreme to the other, as from good to bad or from strong to weak. Any other word can then be rated according to where it falls on each of these dimensions. A given person might rate the word "friend" close to the good end of the first dimension, halfway between strong and weak on the second, and a little closer to soft than to hard on the third. This pattern of points on the various dimensions then defines the meaning of the word "friend" for this person according to this method. With two words, or with two people rating the same word, the difference between the patterns indicates how different the meanings are.

Some of the dimensions that are used with this method turn out to be closely related, so that any word that is rated high on one is likely to be rated high on the other, and vice versa. Good-bad, for example, would be highly related to right-wrong. We can then conclude that these are really the same dimension. Over a long series of studies it is possible to determine how many really separate dimensions are needed to describe the meanings of words. It would then be plausible to suppose that each of these separate dimensions represented a separate mediating response. These several different mediating responses, occurring at the same time with different intensities in response to a stimulus word, would determine the meaning of that word. Osgood and his associates have found that a considerable part of the meaning of words can be accounted for with just one such dimension: the *evaluative dimension.* This includes such pairs as good-bad, beautiful-ugly, and kind-cruel, all of which are concerned with the desirability or value of the word being rated. Much of the remaining meaning is carried by two other major dimensions: strong-weak and active-passive. We can tell a great deal about the meaning of a word by seeing where it is rated on these three main dimensions.

There are, of course, limits to the meaning that can be given merely by placing a word the proper distance between good and bad, between strong and weak, and between active and passive. Some concrete descriptive words, such as "yellow" or "wet," have a good deal of meaning not accounted for by the three primary dimensions. Nevertheless, it is striking how much meaning is carried by the three, and especially by the evaluative dimension. How much real difference in meaning is there, for example, between "good," "nice," "fair," and "decent"? To the average person, probably very little, since they all are concerned primarily with evaluation. Whatever its limitations, the semantic differential has served both as a useful tool in practical studies and as a valuable approach to the quantitative understanding of meaning. Though a number of stimulus-response theorists have suggested that thinking involves the operation of mediating responses, Osgood's work on meaning is the most ambitious attempt to study the implications of this view in quantitative terms.

SOCIAL LEARNING AND MODELING

As far back as people have speculated about one another's behavior, one thing they have noted is the tendency people have to imitate one another. Nevertheless, modern learning theory paid little attention to the topic of imitation until Miller and Dollard wrote their book, *Social Learning and Imitation* (1941), which was discussed in Chapter 3. Even then, although the book was widely quoted, there was not much further theorizing or research on the topic for some years thereafter. More recently, however, imitation has finally come into its own as a major topic in learning theory.

An Analysis of Modeling

Of the various people who have contributed to this resurgence of interest in imitation, probably the most influential has been Albert Bandura (b. 1925) of Stanford University. He and Richard Walters collaborated on a book in which they presented their views, not only on imitation, but on a range of related topics (1963). Their one small book, in fact, covered much of the same range of topics, including social learning processes, personality development, and psychotherapy, that Miller and Dollard covered in the two books on which they collaborated.

As regards imitation, Bandura and Walters start at about the point where Miller and Dollard stopped. The form of imitation that Miller and Dollard analyzed in detail was like a simple version of follow-the-leader. They showed that rats could learn to follow (or not follow) other rats in a T-maze, and that children could learn to make (or not make) the same response that an adult or another child made. The responses the rats or the children made were ones that they would have made in that situation anyway; all the leader did was to provide a cue as to which response would be reinforced. Certainly humans, probably monkeys, and perhaps various other species can learn by imitation in considerably more complicated ways than that. A person can learn how to perform some fairly elaborate sequence of operations by observing someone else doing it and then modeling his own behavior after what he has observed. Whether or not a person can acquire completely new responses by imitation is largely a matter of definition, but he can surely learn to arrange simple responses in a complex sequence purely by observing and imitating someone else.

Consider how hard it would be to learn to drive a car if every step in the process had to be shaped by Skinnerian procedures. Reinforcing the learner for each successive approximation to the final correct use of each of the controls would not only be maddeningly slow, it would also give little assurance that the learner would survive the training course, considering how a person would be likely to drive who had achieved only a first approximation to mastery of the steering wheel and the brake. The fact that a learner can observe and imitate an experienced driver greatly increases both the speed of learning and the chance of living to the end of the course!

The reader may feel that this example ignores the importance of language. A person can learn a lot about how to drive a car by observation, but he can also learn a lot by being told how to work the controls and what sorts of precautions to take. One would guess that certain aspects of driving could be better acquired by watching and others by listening, while a combination of both might be better still. Bandura and Walters do not worry much about this distinction. They are really concerned with a concept even more general than imitation: *modeling.* When one models one's behavior after someone else's, that someone else may be called the model, and the whole process referred to as modeling. Modeling thus includes not only simple imitation of one person by another, but also those more pervasive processes (often called identification) by which a person tries to be the same kind of person as another. Given this broader concept, the model need not be a particular real person whom one observes. He or she may instead be a character in history or fiction or a generalized ideal person whom one has only heard described. When we think in terms of modeling one's behavior after that of some real, imaginary, or hypothetical person, the distinction between learning by observing and learning by being told becomes less important. One may still ask which will work better in a given case, but both are examples of modeling and hence, in a sense, of imitation.

The example of learning to drive a car refers to the acquisition of at least relatively new responses. Considering all the skills and social behaviors that people acquire from one another, such acquisition of new responses is certainly a very important kind of imitation. However, it is only one of three processes of imitation that Bandura and Walters consider. The second involves the inhibition or disinhibition of already learned responses. In other words, the person has already learned to make a response, but he learns by observing other people whether or not to make a given response under a given set of conditions. In the case of *inhibition,* he learns from observing someone else not to make the response that he otherwise very likely would have made. Teachers hope that such inhibition by observation will take place when they reprimand a student for being noisy in class—that other students will learn thereby not to be noisy either. As with every other hope in education, it often does not work that way, but it works often enough to illustrate that observational learning of inhibition is a real process. *Disinhibition* refers to the case where a person has already both learned how to make a response and learned not to make it in a given situation, but now observes someone else making the response and proceeds to do so also. The inhibited response has been disinhibited through a process of imitation. Just as the inhibitory effects of imitation were illustrated by what teachers hope will happen, the disinhibitory effects may be illustrated by what they fear may happen after they have trained a class to be quiet. One student making a commotion may have a disinhibitory effect, inducing the rest of the class to abandon their inhibitions and join in rowdy noise-making.

The third way in which imitation can operate is by eliciting an already learned response. Such elicitation is particularly noteworthy in children, though common enough in adults; as soon as one person starts to do something, several other people want to do the same thing, although they had given the possibility no thought until that moment. This tendency can be a nuisance if the resources for that one activity are limited (only one set of crayons for a dozen children who suddenly want to color), but a benefit if the activity is one that requires a number of people for best results. It is not always easy to tell whether a given case of imitation is elicitation or disinhibition, since both involve an increased tendency to perform an already learned response when one observes someone else doing it. In principle, however, the two processes are distinctly different, since in elicitation the sight of the model creates a positive desire to perform the activity, while in disinhibition the desire is already active and all that is needed is some indication that the desire can safely be indulged.

Both the second process of imitation (inhibition and disinhibition) and the third (elicitation) depend at least in part on the consequences of the activity to the model. If the model is punished for whatever was done, the result is likely to be inhibition, and the chance of the model's being imitated goes down. If there is no obvious consequence, good or bad, the model may be imitated either through disinhibition or through elicitation, but the chance of imitation is greater if the model is conspicuously rewarded for his behavior. In effect, reward or punishment of the model acts much like reward or punishment of the observer, in that we tend to imitate those we see rewarded and refrain from imitating those we see punished. This process by which consequences to the model influence the behavior of the observer often is called *vicarious reinforcement*.

Although vicarious reinforcement is important for the second and third kinds of imitation, it seems not to be very important for the acquisition of new responses. That is, an observer learns what it was that the model did, and becomes able to imitate it irrespective of reinforcement to the model. What reinforcement to the model does is to influence whether the observer will show what he has learned about the model's behavior. Studies have shown that even when children do not spontaneously imitate a model, they can still imitate the model with a good deal of accuracy if specifically asked to do so. Studies have also shown that whether or not the children spontaneously imitate the model depends considerably (though by no means entirely) on the reinforcement or punishment that the model received.

Much of the research that Bandura and Walters did dealt with the imitation of aggressive behavior. Both were concerned with the problems posed by aggression, and Bandura in particular worried about the extent to which aggressive models on television might contribute to aggressive behavior by the children who watched television. Research by Bandura and others has amply demonstrated that children learn the aggressive responses they observe and that in many cases their subsequent play is influenced into more aggressive forms by what they have observed. This change in behavior involves the learning of new responses, the disinhibition of old ones, and probably the elicitation of old ones without disinhibition. It is less clear to what extent observing aggression on television induces viewers to engage later in real-life aggression. As with so many practical applications of psychology, speculation goes well beyond data, and there is plenty of room to argue both sides of the case. At a minimum, however, we can say that televised aggressive models could well influence the behavior of some viewers.

Bandura's Social Learning Theory

Whereas Walters died not long after their book was published, Bandura has continued to work and write on modeling and its implications and applications. In doing so, he has dealt increasingly with the "how" and "why" of modeling (Bandura 1971). As regards the "how," his interpretations are quite cognitive. The main thing that goes on in modeling is learning by observation. The observer sees what the model does, notes what the consequences to the model are, remembers what he has learned, makes various inferences from it, and either then or later takes account of it in his own behavior. What is learned is not responses in the connectionist sense, but knowledge about responses and their consequences. On this matter, therefore, Bandura is clearly with Tolman and Bolles rather than with Guthrie, Hull, or Skinner.

If we ask for a more detailed treatment of the topic, we are likely to be disappointed. How does an observer convert knowledge about what a model has done into responses that he himself might make? Anyone who has either given or received coaching in a skill knows that observing someone else's behavior does not automatically convey the ability to imitate it accurately. What prior learning is needed before one can imitate effectively? Also, is there any difference between the observational learning involved in modeling and that involved in learning about the layout of the physical world, as in Tolman's cognitive maps, or about sequences of impersonal events, as in Bolles's S-S* cognitions? Bandura is certainly not unaware of these issues; he has been concerned with such matters as how observational learning is coded in memory. Nevertheless, his main interest is in social learning and its practical implications, and he has not attempted (nor have most other theorists) to give a really detailed explanation of the internal processes that make it possible.

As for the "why" of modeling, Bandura is more specific. Imitative behavior, like other behavior, depends on reinforcement. If we are reinforced for imitating, we do it; if punished for it, we don't. If we are reinforced for imitating some models and not others, we form a discrimination and imitate only the one set. This is not to say that reinforcement for imitation is the only factor influencing imitation, since in any particular situation we may infer in various ways whether imitation is or is not likely to be reinforced. (Vicarious reinforcement is an example of such inference.) Nevertheless, in the long run imitative behavior depends primarily on its consequences to the imitator. On this issue, therefore, Bandura at first sounds like as straightforward a reinforcement theorist as Skinner.

This appearance is, however, somewhat deceptive. Bandura and Skinner agree that reinforcement is a major determinant of behavior. Skinner stops there, since behavior is all he is interested in studying. Bandura, on the other hand, is also interested in what goes on inside the "empty organism"—not physiologically, but in terms of the cognitions that are learned. He therefore points out that reinforcement is not necessary for observational *learning,* but only for imitative *behavior.* We acquire the information that makes imitation possible simply by observation, whether or not we are reinforced for using that information, imitatively or otherwise. However, this observational learning may still be indirectly influenced by reinforcement, in that we pay more attention to events connected with reinforcement than to other events. Since attention is necessary for observational learning, this makes reinforcement important for the learning as well as for the performance, but only in a complex, indirect way.

Though Bandura differs from Skinner in being interested in cognitive intervening variables, he resembles Skinner in his interest in practical implications. His early concern with the problems of aggression has already been mentioned, and he has since written a book on the topic (Bandura, 1973). Again like Skinner, he has taken a good deal of interest in behavior modification and has demonstrated the importance both of modeling the desired behavior and of modifying the person's cognitions. In treating phobias, his interest is less in reducing fear and more in increasing the sense of *self-efficacy,* that is, the feeling of being able to deal with a situation in spite of fear (Bandura, Adams, & Beyer 1977). His approach to these and other topics, an approach both behavioristic and cognitive, with a heavy emphasis on modeling, has been labeled *social learning theory* (Bandura 1977).

Social learning theory, like the positions of Tolman and Bolles, occupies an intermediate position between connectionist reinforcement theory on the one hand and the more elaborate cognitive-developmental theories on the other. Though it emphasizes cognitions, it interprets them as more easily modified than does, for example, Piaget. Suppose children who do not spontaneously show conservation of volume are shown models demonstrating conservation as liquid is poured from one dish into another. How will their own responses to subsequent tests of conservation be influenced? Sullivan (1967) has shown that a large majority of the children will then not only show conservation of volume of liquid but also generalize conservation to the amount of clay in a lump as its shape is changed. Similar results have been found for children's moral judgments (e.g., Cowan, et al. 1969), thus challenging the views both of Piaget (1932) and of Kohlberg (1964) that such judgments change only gradually through a fixed sequence of stages. A defender of stage theories would argue in reply that the modeling has really only changed the children's verbal behavior in that situation, not their underlying cognitions about the physical or moral world. If Skinner got into the argument, he would probably maintain that conservation and moral judgment are nothing but verbal behavior, thus supporting Bandura's conclusion but not his cognitive assumptions. This is clearly a multisided issue, and far from settled.

chapter *8*

Mathematical Analyses of Learning

As theories of learning become increasingly formal and attempt to make more exact quantitative statements about behavior, they increasingly tend to adopt language and concepts from mathematics and from more precise branches of science and technology. We have seen examples of this tendency in Lewin's topological life space, in Tolman's vectors, and particularly in Hull's and Spence's equations. Some theorists have gone still further in making mathematical analyses or concepts from engineering central to their theories. Such theories have been particularly prominent in recent years, reflecting the increasing use in modern society of computers, servomechanisms, and probabilistic interpretations of events.

Beginning about 1950, there was a burst of interest in a statistical approach to learning. This approach assumes that the processes in learning are not entirely predictable, but vary randomly in certain ways that can be described statistically. Just as actuaries cannot predict who will marry or die this year, but can predict within a small margin of error how many marriages or deaths there will be, so statistical learning theorists do not claim to predict what a given learner will do on a given trial, but do claim to predict the average behavior of one individual over many trials or of many individuals on a single trial. Whereas Hull worked out a system for making exact predictions and then added the factor of oscillation to show the inevitable random component in behavior, the statistical theorists make this randomness the basis of their systems. One might satirize the difference in approach by saying that Hull started with perfect order and eventually had to make a concession to chaos, while the statistical theorists start with chaos and proceed to find order in it!

156

ESTES'S STIMULUS-SAMPLING MODEL

Since the several statistical models that appeared in the early 1950s had a lot in common, we will look only at the one developed by William K. Estes (b. 1919), who began his career as a statistical learning theorist at the University of Indiana, pursued it for some years at Stanford and at Rockefeller University, and is now at Harvard. His original system and a number of elaborations are presented in Estes (1959).

Estes studied with Skinner during the period that Skinner was at the University of Minnesota, and he received his Ph.D. in psychology there in 1943. His work with Skinner on the effects of punishment was an important contribution to Skinner's thinking on that topic. However, his interest in building mathematical models of learning is of course a departure from Skinner's antitheoretical bias. Moreover, the assumptions in Estes's theory seem to show the influence of Guthrie, with whom he did not study, more than of Skinner.

Estes's system may be spoken of as a *model* of learning because, at least at the beginning, it makes no attempt to be a complete, all-encompassing theory. In this respect it is more modest than the systems of Guthrie, Skinner, or Hull, and perhaps reflects some of the same concern about boundary conditions that Spence expresses. Rather, the model is a very simplified statement of assumptions from which a few aspects of learning can be predicted with (one hopes) a good deal of accuracy. It is a model in the same sense as a three-dimensional model of an atom, with wooden balls for electrons, protons, and neutrons. No one claims that such a classroom model is a complete and accurate representation of an atom; we know very well that electrons are different from wooden balls and that their orbits are not much like pieces of wire. Nevertheless, there are certain respects in which the model and the real atom are alike. Given these similarities, the model enables us to predict certain things about the way the atom itself will behave. To the extent that a model enables us to predict some aspect of reality, it is useful. We need not argue whether or not it is true, since at best it is never more than a partial representation. This is much the same logic of theory construction that Hull used, but Estes carried it further, beginning with a simple model and expanding it gradually at the same time that he was testing its usefulness.

One way to look at Estes's model is as an attempt to make certain ideas of Guthrie's more precise, to turn a part of Guthrie's broad, practically oriented theory into a model appropriate for laboratory study. The reader will remember that Guthrie regarded the learning of a skill as the conditioning of a great many particular stimulus-response connections. Estes simplified this suggestion by grouping all possible responses into two categories: those that produce a given outcome and those that do not. Thus, in Guthrie's terms, he is concerned with acts rather than movements, or, in Tolman's terms, with molar behavior. Estes would record, for example, only whether a basketball player successfully shoots a basket or not, without regard to the innumerable muscle contractions that go to make up either outcome. Similarly, a circus dog either jumps through the hoop or does not, regardless of whether the jump is graceful or clumsy and regardless of whether not jumping through involves jumping and missing, sitting quietly, or running away. In this way Guthrie's concern with what the learner does is changed into a concern with what he accomplishes, with the successful and unsuccessful outcomes of his behavior. (Note, however, that success is defined by the observer, not necessarily by any purpose of the learner's.) Since these two classes of responses (or, strictly speaking, of response outcomes) constitute the two possible acts, Estes calls them A1 and A2.

Stimulus Elements

Having simplified the matter of responses, Estes is prepared to face the complexity of stimuli. He regards any stimulus situation as made up of many small stimulus elements. In principle, such an assumption is clearly realistic. At any given moment we are being bombarded by a great number and variety of stimuli. As we read a book, we may be stimulated by the words on the page, the pressure of the book on our hands, the furniture around us, and the sound of a passing car, to give only a very incomplete list. Altogether these make up the stimulus complex that influences our behavior. However, if we try to analyze this complex into specific components, we immediately find ourselves in difficulty. Is the pressure of the book on our hands a single element, or is it ten elements for our ten fingers? If the temperature and the texture of the book's cover enter into the sensation, are these additional elements? It is a good example of Estes's model building that he does not concern himself with this question. If it is reasonable to suppose that there are such stimulus elements, Estes does not care just what the elements are, or how many there are, or how you decide where one element ends and another begins. He wants to know whether learning acts as if it is under the influence of such elements, not whether such elements "really" exist in the sense of being separately identifiable.

Another problem about this analysis of stimulus complexes into elements is that it implies that these elements operate separately, that there are no effects of patterns, or gestalts. Since we do not know what the elements are, it is hard to judge just how unrealistic this assumption is, but it certainly seems likely that there must be patterning effects of some sort. Estes eventually considered this issue, as we will see, but his original model used the assumption that there are no patterning effects, that each element operates independently of each other. Again the question is not whether this assumption is true but whether it is useful. To answer this question we must wait until we see the predictions Estes has been able to make from a model that included this assumption.

So far Estes has divided all the possible responses in a given situation into two classes, and he has divided all the possible aspects of the stimulus situation into an unspecified large number of elements. He now further assumes that each element is conditioned to one or the other of the two response classes. In other words, each stimulus element tends to evoke either A1 or A2. An element cannot be conditioned at the same time to *both* A1 and A2, nor can it ever be conditioned to *neither*. (If it seems unreasonable that all elements must be conditioned to one or the other of these response classes, keep in mind that all possible responses are included in one or the other class.) Accordingly, at any given moment, all elements can be classified as either conditioned to A1 or conditioned to A2.

The use of the word "conditioned" in this connection does not mean that there has necessarily been prior learning. It might be clearer just to say that every element is "attached" to one or the other response class, so that that stimulus element tends to produce that response. However, these connections are subject to change, with stimulus elements which were formerly attached to A1 becoming attached to A2, or vice versa. In fact, for Estes such changes are what is meant by learning. These changes are a process of conditioning, and hence Estes speaks of an element as being conditioned to a response when it tends to elicit that response.

Stimulus Sampling and Conditioning

To understand how the conditioning process operates in Estes's model, we must first look at the process of *stimulus sampling*. Estes assumes that only a small part of the stimulus elements in a given situation actually influence the response on any given trial. Estes refers to all of the stimulus elements in a given situation, taken collectively, as S. At any particular moment, only a small fraction of the elements in S are actually effective in determining the response. Which elements will they be? Estes assumes that the individual samples elements randomly from S. We need not assume that this sampling process is conscious and deliberate, as though the individual were window shopping before an array of stimuli. The sampling may be explained by momentary changes either in the environment or in the individual's attention. Again, however, it is important to note that Estes does not try to explain just how this sampling occurs. He assumes that it does occur, and whether it is a good or a bad assumption depends on whether it leads to valid predictions.

Each element has a certain probability of being sampled on a given trial. It is mathematically simpler to assume that all elements have the same probability of being sampled. Since the whole concept of stimulus elements is hypothetical anyway, there should be no objection to assuming that these probabilities are equal. Moreover, Estes has demonstrated that, at least for certain purposes, it makes very little difference whether one makes this assumption or not. He therefore assigns the Greek letter θ (theta) to represent the probability that any given element will be sampled on any given trial. Put another way, θ represents the proportion of all the elements in S that are sampled on any one trial.

On successive trials, different groups of elements are sampled. This sampling is random, so that each element has the same chance of being sampled on each trial. Whether or not an element was sampled last time has no effect on its chance of being sampled this time. Moreover, whether or not any one element is sampled this time has no effect on any other element's chances this time. Hence the degree of overlap among successive samples is determined solely by chance.

This assumption, like so many others in Estes's model may seem unrealistic if we think of stimulus elements as particular identifiable sources of sensations. The important question, however, is whether Estes can use these simplified assumptions to make correct predictions about learning.

Let us consider two successive trials. For the sake of simplicity, let us say that in this situation θ is equal to .1. This means that one-tenth of the elements in S are sampled on each trial. Since the sampling is random, we can find the proportion of elements sampled on both trials by multiplying .1 times .1 to obtain .01. This means that one-hundredth of the elements in S are sampled on both trials. How many are not sampled on either trial? Since .9 of the elements (1 minus .1) are not sampled on the first trial, and .9 are not sampled on the second, we find the number not sampled on either trial by taking .9 times .9, which gives .81. By subtracting .81 from 1.0, we find that .19 of the elements *were* sampled on at least one of the two trials.

The stimulus elements sampled on a given trial are the ones that determine which response, A1 or A2, will occur on that trial. But if some elements are attached to A1 and others to A2, which of these two responses will occur? The answer to this question shows why this is called a statistical learning theory. Estes does not tell us definitely which response will occur; instead he gives the answer in the form of a probability statement. The probability of A1 is equal to the proportion of the elements in the sample that are attached to A1. Thus if 60% of the elements that are sampled on a given trial are attached to A1 and the other 40% to A2, there are 60 chances in 100 that A1 will occur on that trial and 40 chances that A2 will occur. Since the sample is drawn randomly from S, we could just as well say that the probability of A1 occurring on that trial is equal to the proportion of all the elements in S that are attached to A1.

Since the prediction of which response will occur is in the form of a probability, we can never say for sure which response will occur (unless the probability of A1 is either 1.00 or 0). This uncertainty of prediction may seem like a considerable weakness. However, Estes is really only saying, a bit more bluntly, what the other theorists we have considered also said. Guthrie said that the combination of stimuli would "tend" to be followed by the movement. Skinner discussed the factors controlling rate of emission of an operant, but he never tried to predict exactly what that rate would be. Hull, as we have noted, accomplished the same thing by including the concept of oscillation. Thus predictions from Estes's theory are no less definite than those from other theories. He has, however, put the whole theory in terms of probabilities: the probability that an element will be sampled and the probability that a given response will occur. (These probabilities can in principle be converted into speeds if desired.) Since probabilities are analyzed by statistical techniques, Estes's theory is called a statistical theory.

In his original formulation, Estes assumed that learning is by the principle of contiguity. This relation means, in his formulation, that whenever a response occurs, all the stimulus elements sampled on that trial become conditioned to that response. Nothing is said about reinforcement as such. This formulation is particularly well suited to classical conditioning. Consider a case of eyelid conditioning.

We will call an eye-blink response A1 and the absence of a blink A2, so that on every trial either A1 or A2 but not both will occur. On the training trials the blink always occurs, since the unconditioned stimulus is always presented. As a result, all the stimulus elements sampled on a given trial become conditioned on that trial to A1 (the response of blinking). On successive trials, additional elements are sampled and become conditioned to A1, so that the proportion of the elements in S that are conditioned to A1 keeps increasing. Whenever an element is conditioned to A1 it is of course also unconditioned to (or "disconnected from") A2. Thus conditioning is a process of transferring elements from being conditioned to A2 to being conditioned to A1. As this process goes on, the probability of a *conditioned* eye-blink response (A1) increases. The unconditioned blink occurs on every trial, since it is elicited by the unconditioned stimulus, but the conditioned blink may or may not occur, its probability depending on the proportion of elements conditioned to A1.

Learning Curves

With all this background of assumptions, we are finally ready to look at the predictions that follow from them. First, what of the shape of the learning curve? Suppose we take the situation in which, at the beginning of learning, all the elements in S are conditioned to A2, so that the probability of a conditioned A1 response is zero. This case would be very near that in eyelid conditioning, where the chance that the subject will make a response to the conditioned stimulus before conditioning has begun is quite small. In this state all the elements sampled on the first trial will already be conditioned to A2 (not responding). However, on this trial they will become conditioned to A1. On the next trial another sample will be drawn. Most of the elements in this new sample will be conditioned to A2, but a few will be conditioned to A1 because they will have been sampled, and hence conditioned to A1, on the previous trial. Only those that are attached to A2 can become conditioned to A1, since the rest already are attached to A1. Thus the number of elements transferred from A2 to A1 will be less on the second trial than on the first. (Remember that the total number of elements sampled is the same on all trials.) On the third trial still more of the elements that are sampled will already have been conditioned to A1, so that even fewer will be transferred from A2 to A1. Learning will continue in this fashion, with fewer elements being transferred from A2 to A1 on each successive trial, until all the elements in S are conditioned to A1. At that point, no further learning can take place.

If we know the value of θ, we can make predictions about the proportion of elements in S that will be conditioned to A1 at the end of each trial. Let us return to the previous discussion of sampling in which we assumed for convenience that θ was equal to .1. At the end of the first trial, .1 of the elements in S had been sampled once. As a result, .1 of the elements were then attached to A1. After two trials, .19 of the elements had been sampled at least once, so that .19 of the elements were then conditioned to A1. The increase in the proportion of elements conditioned to A1 was .1 as a result of the first trial and .09 as a result of the second. In both cases, this increase was .1 of the elements still conditioned to A2. In other words, on each trial, 10% of the elements still conditioned to A2 were transferred to A1. This value, .1, is the value of θ. If we continued these calculations further, we would see that this ratio fits a general principle: on each trial the proportion of elements transferred from A2 to A1 is equal to θ times the proportion still conditioned to A2. However, since fewer and fewer are still conditioned to A2 on each trial, the actual number of elements transferred from A2 to A1 is less than on the previous trial.

This formulation has resemblances to both Guthrie's and Hull's discussions of the learning curve. Guthrie assumed that conditioning of a movement to a stimulus occurs on one trial, but that conditioning of an act requires many trials because it is made up of many stimulus-movement connections. Similarly, Estes assumes that an element is conditioned to A1 on one trial, but that the change in probability of A1 is gradual because there are so many elements to be conditioned. Thus in this respect Estes has taken an idea very much like Guthrie's and changed it from a loose verbal interpretation to a precise mathematical one. The mathematical description of the learning curve then turns out to be identical with Hull's. The advantage of Estes's formulation over Hull's is that instead of simply postulating that the curve should have this shape, he has derived this curve as a prediction from the more basic assumptions of sampling. He has, in a sense, out-Hulled Hull.

Other Aspects of Learning

Once a reader has grasped the fundamental assumptions ("postulates," in Hull's terms) of Estes's system, he can exercise his ingenuity by trying to predict how Estes will deal with various phenomena of learning. The phenomenon of generalization poses no problem. If a response has been learned to one set of stimuli, generalization is indicated by the occurrence of that same response when another, similar set of stimuli is presented. For Estes, a "similar set of stimuli" is one which has a number of the same stimulus elements as the original training set. If all of the elements in the first set are conditioned to A1, and if half of the elements in the second set are also in the first set, then at least half of the elements in the second set are conditioned to A1. The probability of an A1 response to the second stimulus set cannot then be less than .50.

Discrimination is more of a problem. If two stimulus sets have a number of elements in common, how can an individual learn consistently to give response A1 to one of these sets and response A2 to the other? For such perfect discrimination to be established, it would be necessary for all the elements in one set to be conditioned to A1 and all those in the other set to be conditioned to A2. Such a situation is impossible, however, since some of the same elements are in both sets. To deal with discrimination, we must assume either that the individual learns not to pay attention to those stimuli that are in both sets or that he responds to patterns of stimuli rather than simply to total numbers of elements. Either of those solutions gives a more cognitive flavor to an otherwise connectionist theory. It is probably not coincidence that Estes himself, since developing this theory, has more recently gone into other, somewhat more cognitive, lines of theorizing.

Drive, however, should be an easy topic to predict within the framework of stimulus-sampling theory. For Estes, as for Guthrie and for Miller, drive is a stimulus (or, more precisely, a set of stimulus elements). Estes's principal contribution in this regard has been to argue that Hull's intervening variable D is unnecessary. Hull used D to refer to the general energizing function of all drives. In an ingenious mathematical example, Estes showed how what appears to be an overall energizing effect of drive could be explained as simply a matter of the number of drive stimulus elements conditioned to different responses. This revision does not necessarily mean that drives do not have an energizing function, since Estes's example is hypothetical, but it throws the burden of the argument on Hull's supporters.

Extinction, for Estes, is simply another example of conditioning. If in acquisition, stimulus elements are conditioned to response class A1, then in extinction they are reconditioned to A2. The laws of learning are exactly the same in acquisition and extinction. This interpretation is essentially the same as Guthrie's. Guthrie says that extinction is learning to do something else, which raises the question, "What else?" Estes can dodge this question because, by definition, any response that is not A1 is A2. In extinction, A1 is being replaced by something else, but Estes considers only the rate at which that replacement goes on, not the details of what the "something else" looks like.

Forgetting and Spontaneous Recovery

Spontaneous recovery is a bit more of a challenge, but again Estes deals with it in a typically Guthrian fashion. To do so, he has to consider a larger category of stimulus elements than before. He assumes that S, the set of stimulus elements from which a learner samples in a given learning situation, is only a subset of all the elements that are sometimes available for sampling in that situation. In other words, if we consider all the stimulus elements that might be available for sampling in a certain learning situation, only some of them will actually be available for sampling on any given occasion. This seems like a quite plausible assumption. There are many characteristics of learners, teachers, and other aspects of a learning situation that vary from one occasion to another. If the learner is more tired or more distracted on one occasion than on another, for example, this difference could be expected to affect what stimulus elements were available for sampling on the two occasions. We can therefore divide all the stimulus elements that might be available during this learning into two categories: S (those available on a given occasion) and S′ (those not available on this particular occasion but potentially available on others). On any two occasions, some elements will be in S on both occasions, some in S the first time and in S′ the second, some in S′ the first time and in S the second, and some in S′ on both. This assumption makes it possible to predict not only spontaneous recovery but also various other phenomena of learning.

Consider a learning situation in which originally all stimulus elements are conditioned to A1 (see Figure 8.1, part A). In the course of conditioning, all of the elements in S are sampled at some time and become conditioned to A1. The next day the individual is tested for retention. By then, 20% of the elements in S have moved into S' (i.e., are no longer available for sampling) and have been replaced by elements that were formerly in S' (Figure 8.1, part B). Since all of these new elements in S are still conditioned to A2, 20% of the elements now in S are conditioned to A2. As a result, the probability of an A1 response drops from 1.00 at the end of the first day's training to .80 at the beginning of the session on the second day. This drop would ordinarily be described as 20% forgetting. The more different the conditions are on the second day than on the first, the more elements will leave S between the two days and the greater will be the amount of forgetting.

In this context, spontaneous recovery may be regarded simply as the forgetting of extinction. Suppose that over a series of days acquisition training is carried out until all the elements in both S and S' (i.e., all the potentially available elements) are conditioned to A1. Unless there was additional training involving some of the same elements, forgetting would thereafter be impossible. (This is an untestable assumption, since we could never be sure that no such training had taken place.) Suppose now that extinction is carried out for one day until all elements in S are conditioned to A2. If 20% of the elements in S move into S' before the next test and are replaced, S will then consist of 80% elements conditioned to A2 and 20% conditioned to A1. This means that 20% of the response strength before extinction will have recovered spontaneously. A whole series of extinctions on successive days would be necessary in order to prevent any further spontaneous recovery.

This formulation of spontaneous recovery and forgetting emphasizes the importance of practice over a series of occasions. It takes not merely a lot of practice, but practice spaced in time to give maximum possible learning. Herein rests one of the difficulties with cramming and with very concentrated courses. Estes's theory, like Guthrie's, thus supports the view held by many educators that

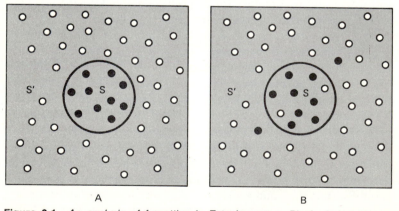

A   B

Figure 8.1 *An analysis of forgetting in Estes's system.* Black circles represent elements conditioned to A1, open circles those conditioned to A2. In part A, all the elements in S have been conditioned to A1. In part B, a day later, 20% of these elements have drifted out of S into S' and have been replaced by elements still conditioned to A2. As a result, only 80% of the elements in S are now conditioned to A1. The probability of an A1 response has therefore dropped from 1.00 to .80 during the elapsed time.

learning is most effective when there is time enough to spread out the process. Reviewing learned material every now and then, or taking a series of courses in which each begins with a review of the previous one, are procedures that fit well with this interpretation of learning.

Reinforcement

What does Estes have to say about reinforcement? Relative to many other theorists, very little. So far as he is concerned, a reinforcer is simply any event that determines to which response class the stimulus elements that are sampled will get conditioned. What other properties a reinforcer may have, such as perhaps being a reduction in drive, do not interest him. He is, then, somewhat like Skinner in the way he interprets reinforcement, but he puts less emphasis on the importance of the topic than does Skinner, thus increasing his resemblance to Guthrie.

Estes's treatment of reinforcement also resembles Skinner's in another respect: both are greatly interested in intermittent reinforcement. What happens, asks Estes, if some of the trials in a series end with reinforcement (thus conditioning all the elements sampled on that trial to A1) and other trials end with nonreinforcement (conditioning all the sampled elements to A2)? A favorite learning situation for answering this question is the *light-guessing experiment.* Here A1 and A2 are defined not as making or not making a given response but as making one of two possible guesses. The learner is seated in front of a board with two light bulbs on it. On each trial he is instructed to guess which of the two lights will be turned on. After he guesses, one and only one of the lights does go on, and which one it is does not depend on his guess. The two possible guesses are response classes A1 and A2, and the two possible *events* (the left and the right light going on) are called E1 and E2. Thus E1 reinforces A1 and E2 reinforces A2. However, Estes assumes that E1 conditions all the sampled elements to A1 and E2 conditions all the sampled elements to A2, regardless of which response occurs on that trial. In other words, the left light going on reinforces the response of guessing "left," even if the guess the learner made was "right." This assumption that a response which does not occur on a given trial can nevertheless be reinforced on that trial is a departure from the usual assumptions of connectionist reinforcement theories.

If E1 always occurs in this situation, the individual gradually learns to make A1 consistently. (He also rapidly becomes bored with the experiment.) What if E1 occurs 75% of the time and E2 occurs 25% of the time, in a random order so that the learner can never be sure which light will go on on any given trial? What usually happens is that he comes to make A1 75% of the time and A2 25% of the time. Any reader who is ambitious enough to work through the mathematics can confirm that this is just what Estes's model predicts. (To do so, the reader will have to decide what percent of the sampled elements will be conditioned to A1 by E1 or to A2 by E2, when the probability of A1 is greater than, equal to, and less than .75. It will take a little thinking, but this opportunity to obtain an insight experience while studying a connectionist theory really should not be missed.)

This finding, so satisfying to Estes, has disconcerted many other theorists because of its apparent irrationality. If the learner wants to guess correctly as often as possible, the best strategy is to guess the more frequent event all the time. A cognitive theorist might expect an individual to follow such a rational strategy, since it would be the best possible insightful solution to the problem. Instead, however, subjects follow the irrational behavior that is predicted by Estes's conditioning model. Why? Many experiments have been done and many words written in attempts to explain this "irrational" behavior to other people's satisfaction. (Some situations have been found in which learners do adopt the "rational" solution, but they are not typical.) Estes, however, can take pride in having correctly predicted an unexpected finding.

How does Estes's approach compare with those of other theorists we have considered? In his approach to theory construction he is most like Spence, building an abstract formal theory but proceeding slowly, with a close eye both on new data and on the boundary conditions. However, Estes has put more emphasis on stimulus factors and less on the nature of reinforcement than has Spence, and the kinds of experiments he has done are rather different from Spence's. His interpretations of most topics are much like Guthrie's, but more detailed mathematically than Guthrie's. His interpretation of reinforcement, however, is most like Skinner's.

ALL-OR-NONE MODELS

Though the postulates in Estes's system differ considerably from those in Hull's, they lead to the same prediction of a gradual, negatively accelerated learning curve. However, not all statistical models have this property. Just as the early 1950s were characterized by a burst of interest in the kind of statistical model just described, the late 1950s and the 1960s were characterized by a somewhat different kind of statistical model. Since this latter kind predicts that learning will be sudden rather than gradual, these interpretations may be grouped together as *all-or-none models*.

We should note that at the level of the individual stimulus element, Estes's sampling model, like Guthrie's theory, is an all-or-none model. It yields a gradual learning curve only because there are assumed to be a large number of stimulus elements. Suppose that there was only one element, with θ being the probability that this one element would be sampled on a given trial. As long as this element remained conditioned to A2, the probability of A1 would be zero, but as soon as the element became conditioned to A1, the probability of A1 would jump to 1.00. When this jump occurred would depend on when the one element was first sampled. On each trial the probability of the element being sampled, and hence conditioned to A1, would be equal to θ. Even if all learners had the same value of θ, some by chance would sample the one stimulus element earlier, others later. With repeated trials, the percentage of A1 responses in a group of subjects would increase gradually, since more and more of the subjects would have sampled the one element and hence would now be making A1 responses. For any one learner, however, the transition would be sudden, from never giving A1 to always giving it. Only for the average of a group would the increase in probability appear gradual.

Psychologists are so used to averaging learning curves from groups of subjects, in order to smooth out the fluctuations that individual curves commonly show, that they often do not even look at the data which might tell them whether individual learning curves more closely approximate the gradual or the sudden form. However, Skinner and his followers had criticized the use of averaged curves, Guthrie had emphasized all-or-none learning at the molecular level, and the gestalt psychologists had studied cases of sudden insight. Then in the late 1950s gradual versus all-or-none learning became a major focus of controversy and research.

Estes, having led in the earlier many-elements models, was also a leader in developing one-element models. He suggested that even though memorizing a list of items is gradual, the learning of any one of these items may well be all-or-none, and presented evidence in support of that view. The evidence has since been challenged, but the view remains important. He also suggested that, in a one-element model, it is more appropriate to speak of a stimulus pattern than of a stimulus element; since the stimulus as a whole is what gets conditioned, it is the total configuration of the stimulus that is or is not sampled and attached to A1 on any given trial. Thus some of the flavor of gestalt theory enters into statistical learning theory. These views are summarized in Estes (1964).

It should be evident from the above that there is not so much a controversy between gradual and all-or-none interpretations of learning as a question of which are appropriate for what kinds of learning. The simpler an item to be learned, the more likely it seems that it would be learned in an all-or-none fashion, while the more complex it is, the more likely it seems that multiple connections would have to be acquired and learning would therefore be gradual. But why limit ourselves to these two extremes: that learning is sudden and complete or that it is gradual and continuous? If we can have either a one-element or a many-element model, why not a two-element model?

In a two-element model, learning would be expected to involve three stages: the initial stage in which neither element has been conditioned to A1, an intermediate state in which one element has and the other has not, and a third in which both have been conditioned to A1. The process of acquisition would therefore involve two sudden increases in the probability of making a correct response. There are numerous situations in which one might plausibly expect learning to be of this form. In conditioning, it may be necessary first to learn what to pay attention to and then what to do about it. In memorizing a foreign language vocabulary, it may be necessary first to learn a response and then to hook it up with the appropriate stimulus item. In each case the learner who has mastered the first part but not the second would be intermediate in performance between the learner who had mastered both and the learner who had mastered neither.

Since one of these two learning tasks would have to be mastered before the other, the specific model of two elements waiting to be sampled seems a bit inappropriate, but the more general idea of randomly determined transitions from one state to another is quite appropriate. Various forms of learning do indeed seem to fit a two-element model, which thus provides yet another alternative mathematical description of learning.

ANOTHER ANALYSIS OF THE LEARNING CURVE

Models of learning in which stimulus elements—whether few or many—are conditioned to responses are by no means the only kinds of mathematical models of learning. One other kind is simply a mathematical description of the typical or basic learning curve. Hull's equation for the growth of habit strength is one example; other people have had other equations that generated other kinds of learning curves. A different approach, one that Estes (1976) himself now favors, is to focus not on responses but on expectancies; what gets conditioned to a stimulus is not a response but an expectancy, regarding, for example, which of two lights will come on. This more cognitive version fits better with much current theory, but it does not always lead to different predictions from the connectionist models we have been looking at so far. It is not surprising that there are numerous mathematical models of learning, since a mathematical model is not a separate theory but rather a way of making any kind of theory more precise and testable.

One description of the learning curve that has become popular fairly recently was developed by Allan R. Wagner (b. 1934) and Robert A. Rescorla (b. 1940), both then at Yale. As a theory, it lies midway between elaborate models such as Estes's original stimulus-sampling model and the simple presentation of an equation for the learning curve. It is less elaborate than Estes's model in that it consists only of mathematical statements about the learning process, without referring to stimulus elements that are sampled or that drift in and out of S. However, it is more complex than other mathematical equations for the learning curve in that it takes account of more than one specific stimulus at a time. What makes it unique is that it deals with *stimulus compounding,* the simultaneous presentation of two stimuli. This feature of the theory makes possible some interesting and sometimes surprising predictions.

It is only for convenience that experimenters present only one stimulus at a time, and indeed in discrimination training they present two or sometimes more. Stimuli in "real life" are commonly combined in all sorts of ways, as Estes's concept of stimulus elements implies. Rescorla and Wagner's focus on stimulus compounding is therefore quite realistic. Though their research has been primarily on Pavlovian conditioning, it may well have broader implications.

Consider a classical conditioning situation in which the conditioned stimulus is sometimes a light, sometimes a musical tone, and sometimes the compound of the light and tone together. Each of these three possible conditioned stimuli can be presented either with the unconditioned stimulus (reinforced) or without it (nonreinforced), which makes six possible kinds of trial. Many sorts of training and test sequences of different kinds of trials are then possible. We could, for example, present reinforced trials with the light and reinforced trials with the tone, then test to see how much of a response there is to the compound of light and tone. Alternatively, we could present reinforced trials with the light alone and nonreinforced trials with the compound, then present the tone alone as a test. The possible sequences are almost unlimited, and it is with such sequences that the Rescorla-Wagner theory deals.

The Rescorla-Wagner Model

How would Rescorla and Wagner go about predicting the growth of conditioned response strength to these three conditioned stimuli: the light, the tone, and the compound? Specifically, how does what is learned to one of the three affect what is learned to another? Rescorla and Wagner's answer to this question may seem a bit strange, but the predictions that follow from it are striking enough to make it worth a little effort to understand Rescorla and Wagner's ideas (Rescorla & Wagner 1972).

The strength of the tendency to give a conditioned response is designated as V. The variable V is thus much like Hull's $_SE_R$ and fairly similar to Estes's p. Each stimulus (e.g., the light and the tone) has a separate value of V, so a subscript must be used to identify which V we are talking about, such as V_L for the tendency to respond to the light and V_T for the tendency to respond to the tone. It is then possible, in dealing with the compound, to add together the separate tendencies to make the conditioned response to the light and to the tone and get a total response tendency, which is designated $\overline{V}$. In this example, then, $V_L + V_T = \overline{V}$. It is this sum, or combined value, that is the most distinctive feature of the model.

Rescorla and Wagner interpret the effects of learning trials in the same way as does Estes. On each trial when the conditioned stimulus is followed by the unconditioned stimulus (i.e., on each reinforced trial), the value of V increases. There is an upper limit to the possible value of V, corresponding to the possible upper limit of 1.0 for the value of p in Estes's model. Such an upper limit is called an *asymptote*. As V increases toward the asymptote, the amount by which it increases on each trial is a constant fraction of the difference between the present value of V and the asymptote. This constant fraction is what Estes labeled θ. (Rescorla and Wagner have a more complex way of expressing it, a way that is necessary for some of their predictions, but since those are not the predictions we will be looking at, we can ignore that part of their model.) When the conditioned stimulus is not followed by the unconditioned stimulus (that is, on extinction trials), the value of V moves down toward zero, and each such trial reduces V by a constant fraction of the difference between its present value and zero.

The distinctive features of the model appear when the light and the tone are compounded. It is now $\overline{V}$ (the sum of V_L and V_T) that approaches the asymptote at a constant fraction of the distance left to go. As $\overline{V}$ increases over trials, both V_L and V_T naturally also increase. However, V_L and V_T can increase as a result of reinforced trials with the compound only as long as $\overline{V}$ is less than the asymptote. Once $\overline{V}$ reaches the asymptote, $\overline{V}$ can no longer increase, so further reinforced trials with the compound cannot increase either V_L or V_T. This implication of the model gives rise to some unexpected predictions, a few of which we will consider here.

Some Nonobvious Predictions

The most obvious prediction is that no matter how much training we give with the compound of light and tone, there will not be as much conditioning to either the light or the tone as if it were not compounded with the other. Either the light or the tone alone could be conditioned until its V reached asymptote. When they are compounded, however, they can only be conditioned until the sum of their two Vs $(\overline{V})$ reaches the asymptote, at which point each V separately will still be less than the asymptote. The presence of each stimulus in the compound thus reduces what is learned about the other stimulus in the compound.

Suppose that instead of training the two stimuli in compound from the start, we first trained with the light alone and only then began presenting the compound, also with reinforcement. By the time we began presenting the compound, V_L would already be fairly close to the asymptote, so $\overline{V}$ would also have to be close to the asymptote. As a result there would not be much room for $\overline{V}$ to increase further, which in turn means that there would not be much room for either V_L or V_T to increase further. This does not matter much for V_L, since it is already fairly high, but it does matter for V_T, which is quite low. If we give a long series of reinforced trials with the compound and then test with the tone alone, there should be little response to the tone in spite of all the training, since little conditioning to the tone took place on all the trials when it was reinforced as part of the compound. However, since conditioning would have taken place if the tone had received the same number of reinforced trials alone, the light in the compound is said to *block* conditioning to the tone. As we saw in Chapter 7, blocking has been demonstrated in both classical and instrumental conditioning, again confirming the predictions of the Rescorla-Wagner theory.

Though we might not have predicted blocking if we were not already familiar with it, it is still not particularly surprising. A third prediction of the theory, however, is so unexpected that it can be presented as a puzzle: If the theory is correct, under what conditions would reinforced training *reduce* the tendency to give the conditioned response? Remember that according to the theory less conditioning to a stimulus takes place when it is presented in a compound and reinforced than when it is reinforced alone. Suppose, then, that a light and a tone were each given a large amount of reinforced training, separately, so that V_L and V_T each came close to the asymptote. If the two stimuli were then presented together in a compound, $\overline{V}$ $(= V_L + V_T)$ would be *greater than* the asymptote. Since the effect of reinforced training is always to move V toward the asymptote, reinforced training with the compound would have to move both V_L and V_T down, also toward the asymptote. Thus reinforced training would produce (partial) extinction of the response to both stimuli in the compound. Strange as this prediction seems, it has been confirmed by experiments. One way of looking at it is to say that the two stimuli together create a stronger expectation of the unconditioned stimulus than the compound does; hence, the phenomenon has been labeled *overexpectation* (Wagner & Rescorla 1972).

Finally, the Rescorla-Wagner theory is useful in explaining *conditioned inhibition* (not to be confused with Hull's intervening variable by the same name), a phenomenon studied by Pavlov. Conditioned inhibition, as we saw in Chapter 2, results when a conditioned stimulus is reinforced when it occurs alone but nonreinforced when it occurs in a compound. The other element in the compound, which has been presented without reinforcement but has never been paired with a reinforcer, then becomes a *conditioned inhibitor*. When we call it an inhibitor we do not mean merely that it will not elicit the conditioned response, as would be the case if it had never been reinforced. Rather, it has active inhibitory properties. This active inhibition, once established, can be demonstrated in at least two ways. One is to present the stimulus alone and reinforce it—the usual procedure for conditioning. It will take longer to condition than if it had not had the previous inhibitory training. Another way is to condition some other stimulus and then compound this new conditioned stimulus with the conditioned inhibitor. The response to the compound will be less than it would be to the conditioned stimulus alone, and also less than if the conditioned stimulus had been compounded with a brand new stimulus that had never received any kind of training. Both of these methods show that the conditioned inhibitor tends to prevent the conditioned response from occurring, which is what is meant by inhibition.

By now the reader should be familiar enough with Rescorla and Wagner's theory to be able to explain the phenomenon of conditioned inhibition in their terms. Consider what happens in the two kinds of trials. When the compound is presented there is no unconditioned stimulus, so the response strength to both stimuli goes down (toward zero). One of the stimuli keeps recovering its response strength by being reinforced on trials when the other stimulus is absent. The other stimulus, however, since it occurs only in the nonreinforced compound, keeps going down in response strength. We might at first imagine that it would simply approach the asymptote of zero, when it would have no effect, excitatory or inhibitory. Remember, however, that it is V of the compound ($\overline{V}$) that approaches zero. Since this must happen while the V of one of the elements in the compound remains greater than zero, it follows that V for the other element must become *less than* zero in order for $\overline{V}$ to approach zero. That element is then a conditioned inhibitor.

Of all the theories considered in this book, Rescorla and Wagner's is perhaps the most difficult to understand. However, it represents what a model is supposed to be: a set of assumptions from which precise, quantitative predictions follow, some of which explain already known phenomena and others of which make unexpected new predictions that can be confirmed or disconfirmed by experiments. This presentation has been designed to show some of these interesting predictions. The entire theory includes a number of other features not discussed here; further complexities have been added by Frey and Sears (1978).

Whether this line of theorizing can eventually incorporate enough features to be the "theory of the future" remains to be seen.

THE CONTRIBUTIONS OF MATHEMATICAL
LEARNING THEORY

What have the mathematical learning theorists accomplished? They have shown how much of learning can be predicted from a formal, mathematical model. They have done new and interesting experiments. On the other hand, part of their success comes from having dealt with a fairly narrow range of learning situations, and many problems have arisen as they have expanded into new areas. Some of their mathematical precision, like Hull's, is more apparent than real, since we can never know the value of θ for any situation in advance, but must always get data in order to compute θ.

Statistical learning theory, being more an approach than a specific set of answers, has adopted a number of forms, of which we have considered three. Estes himself has been constantly finding new ways to look at the issues of learning. In recent years he has interested himself more in verbal learning, thinking, and other topics somewhat removed from the approaches discussed here. However, he has also recently returned to probability learning theory, with a modified set of assumptions and a new set of ingenious experiments for testing them (Estes 1976). (Rescorla and Wagner's model is more recent and still undergoing modification.) It still remains to be seen how much of a contribution mathematical learning theory will ultimately make. At least it has provided psychology with a new set of conceptual tools and has perhaps pointed the way, by slow degrees, toward the kind of precise, general learning theory that Hull envisioned.

chapter 9

Issues in Motivation

Why do we want what we want, seek what we seek? Why are we sometimes relaxed, sometimes working busily but quietly, and occasionally wildly excited? These are the questions of motivation, and to many people they are the most central issues in psychology. Attempts to answer them are part of nearly all the major theories of learning, since these topics are not only important but also closely related to the processes of learning. However, there have also been a number of contributions to the analysis of motivation that were not closely associated with any of the major theories we have considered. In this chapter we will examine some of them.

INTERPRETATIONS OF REINFORCEMENT AND DRIVE

One topic on which there have been important recent developments is the nature of reinforcement. No theorist questions that the effects of our actions influence whether we will repeat these actions (which is the basic principle of reinforcement), but they disagree widely on how this influence should be interpreted. What, if anything, do all reinforcers have in common that makes them reinforcing? Guthrie, though he avoids the term "reinforcement," says in effect that all reinforcement involves is stimulus change. Skinner and Estes for the most part ignore the question, saying simply that whatever reinforces behavior is a reinforcer. Hull, Miller, Mowrer (as regards solution learning, even when it is reinterpreted as another kind of sign learning), Lewin, and Tolman all interpret reinforcement as some kind of drive reduction, even though some of them do not speak either of drive or of reinforcement. Miller's drive, cue, response, and reward can be roughly translated into Lewin's terminology as tension, path, approach vector, and valence, or into Tolman's as demand, sign, expectancy, and goal object. While these may not be the neatest of translations, they illustrate that the drive-reinforcement interpretation, in whatever words, is a widely recognized one.

New Descriptions of Drives

There are currently three trends in the interpretation of reinforcement, two that work within this drive-reduction framework and one that does not. Within the drive-reduction framework, there has been a concentration on what drives are innate. In the past, connectionist psychologists who used the concept of drive have tended to treat as primary, or innate, only a few drives, such as hunger, thirst, sex, and pain, that are clearly physiological. Cognitive psychologists, on the other hand, have been more likely to discuss such motivational tendencies as pride, ambition, or affection, which have no apparent physiological basis. These latter motivational tendencies are regarded by connectionist theorists as the result of complex learning processes, including the acquisition of learned drives. There is not necessarily any disagreement between these two points of view, since cognitive theorists have tended to take little interest in the origins of the tensions or demands they discuss. The chief importance of these interpretations is that the connectionist theorists have had to make assumptions about the learning of motives that are extremely difficult to support by experiments. Although Miller was quite successful in demonstrating a learned drive of fear, other learned drives that are predicted by theory have proved very difficult to demonstrate in the laboratory. As a result, there has been increasing interest in the possibility that there may be far more primary drives than have previously been recognized.

One such drive (or perhaps category of drives) that has received much attention is that which is satisfied by new experience. It is known variously as a drive of curiosity or exploration or manipulation or novelty seeking. Its existence is supported by many lines of evidence. Harlow (whom we have discussed before) showed that monkeys would work to unfasten a clasp device over and over again, even though neither food, escape, nor any other obvious reward was given for doing so. Butler showed that monkeys in a closed cage would press a lever to open a window so they could look out. If the monkeys were kept in the closed cage for several hours before the lever was made available, they would press more (indicating higher drive following deprivation). If the lever no longer opened the window, their rate of pressing would drop (indicating extinction). Such novelty-seeking behavior is found not only in monkeys, which have long been famous for their curiosity, but also in rats. Montgomery and Welker have made extensive studies of rats exploring new places and of the responses they will learn in order to be able to do such exploring. These and other related studies are discussed by Berlyne (1960) and by Welker (1961).

A second kind of drive that has been investigated is satisfied by activity. This is different from the kind of drive we have just discussed in that the activity does not have to produce any novel stimulation. Such activity occurs when a rat runs in an activity wheel, which is a sort of voluntary treadmill. A rat in such a wheel can, if he chooses, get exercise by running, but no exploration is involved, since the wheel just goes around without getting anywhere. Kagan and Berkun (1954) have shown that a chance to run in such a wheel will reinforce lever pressing, and Hill (1956) has shown that rats do more running in the wheel when they have been deprived of activity for a long time.

A third kind of drive has been referred to as contact comfort. It was first analyzed in detail, as were so many interesting phenomena, by Harry Harlow. Contact comfort is a drive which is satisfied by certain kinds of physical contact. Harlow (1958) originally studied it by rearing baby monkeys with *surrogate mothers*, wire models that gave milk like real mothers. He found that monkeys not only preferred a "mother" covered with terry cloth to one made of bare wire, but ran to the terry cloth "mother" when frightened. They did so even if the wire "mother" supplied milk and the cloth "mother" did not. These and other findings in his experiments suggested to Harlow that contact comfort, exemplified by the baby monkeys' attraction to the cloth surrogate mother, is an important factor in personality development. It may well play a major part in personality development, not only in the attachment of infants to their mothers, but also in other aspects of love, in sexual behavior, and in the development of social relationships.

The importance of these various drives is not simply in the recognition that people and animals seek new experience, activity, and pleasant sensations of touch. All of these tendencies have long been known. Rather, their importance is in the recognition, supported by experimental evidence, that they may well be just as much a part of our innate, biological nature as hunger, sex, or pain. This recognition does not by any means answer all our questions about why we seek companionship, achievement, or glory. (Some of the unanswered questions are discussed in Hill 1968.) Nevertheless, it helps to bridge the gap between the drives usually employed in laboratory studies of learning and the motives we all recognize in ourselves and others.

Optimal Arousal

The second trend involves a modification of drive theory—the theory of *optimal arousal*. Different versions of this theory have been presented by several writers; one good collection of ideas about it is Berlyne and Madsen (1973). The optimal-arousal theory holds that reinforcement consists not necessarily of a decrease in drive but rather a change in drive toward some optimal level. The term *arousal* is preferred to *drive* in discussing this interpretation, so as to avoid confusion with more conventional drive theory. If the present level of arousal is higher than the optimal level, a decrease will be reinforcing, as in the ordinary drive interpretation. However, if the present level is below the optimum, an increase rather than a decrease will be reinforcing. When the level of arousal is exactly at the optimum, reinforcement is presumably not possible for the moment. However, both the level and the optimum are constantly changing, so any such limitation is quite temporary.

Optimal arousal theory allows for the often observed fact that people frequently seek more stimulation rather than less. Conventional drive interpretations, such as Miller's, have not been very successful in explaining such behaviors as riding on roller coasters, reading exciting stories, or just complaining of boredom and expressing a wish that something would happen to break the monotony. Since optimal-arousal theory states that increases as well as decreases in arousal can be reinforcing, it has less trouble with such occurrences. However, the recognition that either kind of change in arousal, up or down, can sometimes be reinforcing carries with it a responsibility to indicate when one will be reinforcing and when the other. This responsibility in turn requires knowing a lot about the determinants both of the present level of arousal and of the optimal level.

One additional assumption (or postulate, in Hull's terms) about the relation between stimulation and arousal represents a start toward making the theory more specific. This assumption states that the level of arousal is an increasing function of the intensity, the complexity, and the novelty of the stimulation. More intense stimuli, and more novel ones, are more arousing than those that are weaker or more familiar. This assumption, along with the one we have already mentioned—that moderate levels of arousal are more reinforcing than either high or low levels—forms the basis of optimal-arousal theory.

Several predictions follow from these two assumptions. If novelty and complexity remain constant, moderate stimuli should be reinforcing as compared with either weak or intense stimuli. If intensity and complexity remain constant, stimuli that are somewhat different from those we are used to should be preferred both to thoroughly familiar ones (which would be judged uninteresting) and to highly unfamiliar ones (which would be judged incomprehensible). If intensity and novelty remain constant, stimuli that are moderately complex should prove more reinforcing than those that are either dully simple or overwhelmingly complex. Finally, if more than one aspect of the stimulus varies, then the higher the stimulus is on either intensity, novelty, or complexity, the lower should be the optimal value of the other variables. Thus, a highly novel stimulus should be more reinforcing if it is mild and simple, whereas among very familiar stimuli the more intense and complex ones should tend to be preferred.

This assumption that arousal is an increasing function of intensity, novelty, and complexity fits in well with a concept that has been quite popular among theorists in the Soviet Union—the *orienting reflex*. Although the term implies that individuals tend to orient themselves in varying degrees toward stimuli as they appear, what is actually measured in the orienting reflex is primarily the general arousal produced by a stimulus. The greater the galvanic skin response, the change in heart rate, or the increase in muscle tension produced by a stimulus, the greater the orienting reflex to that stimulus is said to be. Measures of central-nervous-system activity, such as the electroencephalograph (EEG), also give indications of the strength of the orienting reflex. The orienting reflex is greater for more intense stimuli than for milder ones and shows some tendency to be greater for more complex stimuli than for simpler ones. If the same stimulus is presented repeatedly (thus making it more familiar), the orienting reflex progressively decreases. However, it can be restored a good part of the way to its original strength in either of two ways—by changing it in some way or by just waiting for a while—either of which has the effect of making it more novel. Thus the orienting reflex serves as evidence that the level of arousal is affected by various aspects of stimuli in the way that optimal-arousal theory says it should be.

The reader will have noted that optimal-arousal theory attempts to deal with some of the same phenomena that drive theory has tried to deal with by postulating such drives as exploration and activity. To say that there are drives which can be reduced by exploring new things or by becoming more active is to say that sometimes an increase in stimulation produces a decrease in drive. Thus both drive theory and optimal-arousal theory are getting away from the older version of drive theory—particularly closely associated with Miller—that what is reinforcing is a reduction in the level of stimulation. Drive theory makes the shift by looking at each drive separately without worrying about whether it conforms to any general notion about drives as states of high stimulation. Optimal-arousal theory, however, keeps the idea of an overall level of arousal that is closely related to reinforcement, but broadens its interpretation of just what the relationship to reinforcement is.

Responses as Reinforcers

The third trend in the interpretation of reinforcement, outside the drive-reduction framework, relates reinforcement to the learner's own responses to a goal. Reinforcement depends not on what happens to the individual (drive reduction, for example) but on what the person does. This wording sounds like something Guthrie might say, though actually the idea is more like Spence's. The extent to which r_G is conditioned depends, in Spence's system, on the amount of goal activity that takes place. A lot of eating in a given place results in strong conditioning of r_G to that place. How reinforcing it is to get to a given place depends, therefore, on how much eating (or other goal activity) takes place there.

Various people besides Spence have advanced this idea. One, Fred Sheffield (b. 1914), drew his inspiration from Guthrie. Sheffield maintained that the act of consuming a goal object, rather than any form of drive reduction, is the essential factor in reinforcement. Will a response that leads to some goal object be reinforced by the goal object and learned? This depends, says Sheffield, on whether the goal object is consumed. Food, for example, is reinforcing to the extent that we eat it. Our own activity of eating provides the reinforcement for whatever response brings us to the food.

Sheffield did several experiments to support this position. For the most part, however, they were inconclusive. He showed, for example, that drinking a saccharine solution is reinforcing for rats, even though saccharine is completely nonnutritive (Sheffield & Roby 1950). This finding certainly argues against the view that all reinforcers involve reduction in a body need, since saccharine does nothing to reduce the body's need for food. The study does not show, however, that the drinking activity was what produced the reinforcement. One could just as well say that the sweet taste of saccharine is the critical reinforcing factor.

Sheffield's point of view can be elaborated by noting that every species of animal has some stereotyped responses by which it consumes rewards. In the case of food rewards, these include not only such obvious responses as chewing and swallowing, but also such related behaviors as the raccoon's "washing" of its food. Whereas the behaviors by which animals obtain food are fairly variable and subject to learning, the eating responses are much more stereotyped and less subject to learning. Because they involve consuming a reward and also because they consummate the whole process of food getting, they are called consummatory responses. All sorts of motivated behavior sequences end with consummatory responses; not only eating but also drinking, chewing (especially in rodents), copulation, elimination, and in various aggressive species, attacking. It is the opportunity to engage in these species-specific consummatory responses that serves to reinforce the whole chain of instrumental behavior leading to them. This biologically oriented extension of Sheffield's theory has been developed in considerable detail by Glickman and Schiff (1967).

A more general formulation of the idea that responses are reinforcing has been presented by David Premack (b. 1925), currently at the University of Pennsylvania. He simply states that of any two responses, the one that occurs more often when both are available can reinforce the one that occurs less often, but not vice versa. This relationship is illustrated by an experiment with children (Premack 1959). The children were given an opportunity to engage in two activities, eating candy and playing a pinball machine. Some did one of these two more often, some the other. Premack then arranged the apparatus so that for half the children the candy dispenser would work only if the child first operated the pinball machine. To the children who preferred playing, the new arrangement made little difference—they just went on happily playing the machine. For children who preferred eating to playing, however, this change did make a difference—their rate of playing went up, indicating that candy was reinforcing the playing. So far this is a familiar relationship—food reinforcing an instrumental activity. For the other half of the children, the arrangement was reversed, so that the pinball machine would work only if the child first took candy from the dispenser. To the children who preferred candy, this change made no difference. The children who preferred playing, however, ate more candy under this arrangement than before. In this case, playing reinforced eating.

In this experiment, for any one child only one of the two activities could function as a reinforcer. This is not, however, a necessary restriction. For example, Premack (1962) has also studied the reinforcement relationships between running and drinking in rats. If a rat has spent a day without water, but with continuous access to an activity wheel, he will run for the reinforcement of a chance to drink, as we would expect. If, instead, the wheel is locked so that he cannot run unless he first drinks, this relationship will have no effect on how much he drinks—running will not reinforce drinking.

However, the situation can be reversed by having the same rat live for a day with water always available but with no chance to run. Now the tendency to run will be high and to drink will be low. Consequently, running can be used to reinforce drinking—if the rat has to drink in order to unlock the wheel and run, his drinking will increase. On the other hand, requiring the rat to run in order to be able to drink will now have no effect on the amount of running. These somewhat complicated relationships are diagramed in Figure 9.1.

Thus the same animal can be either in a state where drinking reinforces running or a state where running reinforces drinking, and in each case the reverse does not apply. All that is necessary to change him from one state to the other is to do something (in this case, deprive him of drinking or of running) that will change his relative tendency to engage in these two activities.

In a conventional schoolroom, where one of the most difficult demands on pupils is to sit still for long periods of time, we would expect from Premack's analysis that it would often be possible to use access to the playground as a reinforcer for a certain amount of quiet work, but rarely possible to do the reverse. However, in a strenuous program of physical education, it might be possible to reinforce a student's putting forth his last ounce of athletic effort by rewarding him with the chance to sit quietly and read a book. This latter arrangement would of course be expected to work better for the less athletic and more bookish students. Both individual differences and situational differences determine what activities can reinforce what other activities for a given individual at a given time.

In Premack's interpretation, then, there is no special class of consummatory responses that act as reinforcers. Any kind of response can reinforce any other kind of response, says Premack. All that is necessary is for the reinforcing response to be one that the learner makes more frequently than the response being reinforced. Actually, the relationship is more complex than that. We must consider not only whether, e.g., a rat chooses to spend more time running or drinking, but also how much drinking it has to do to earn a given amount of running, or vice versa. Under some such "work requirements," the less frequent activity might actually reinforce the more frequent activity (Timberlake & Allison 1974). Consider, for example, a boy whose free choice would be to spend four times as many hours playing baseball as painting fences. We might (inspired by Tom Sawyer) make fence painting a scarce opportunity that had to be earned: eight hours of baseball playing for every hour of fence painting. Under those conditions, the boy would probably do even more baseball playing than otherwise, reinforced

Characteristics	I Deprived of drinking	II Deprived of running
Tendency to drink	High	Low
Tendency to run	Low	High
If must run to be able to drink	Increases his running	No change in running or drinking
If must drink to be able to run	No change in running or drinking	Increases his drinking
Does drinking reinforce running?	Yes	No
Does running reinforce drinking?	No	Yes

Figure 9.1 *The reversibility of reinforcement.* Columns I and II give the characteristics of two states that a rat can be in with regard to the relative reinforcing effects of drinking and running.

by the less frequent activity, fence painting. A more general statement of Premack's principle would thus be that in order for one kind of response (such as painting) to reinforce another (such as playing), opportunities for the reinforcing one must be scarcer relative to what the person would freely choose. This elaboration of the theory brings it surprisingly close to the demand law in economics, an interesting link between fields that has been explored by Allison (1979).

Premack's interpretation has the same drawback as Sheffield's—that we do not know whether it is the activity itself or the consequences of the activity that acts as the real reinforcer. However, for many purposes this difference is unimportant. If we know how often an individual chooses to do any two things, we can predict (according to Premack's theory and its later elaborations) the reinforcing effects of making one contingent on the other in various ways. To the extent that the relationship holds, it gives us a powerful predictive tool, regardless of how it may finally be explained.

CYBERNETICS

At least since the Industrial Revolution, some theorists have thought of animals and sometimes even people as just glorified machines. Until quite recently, however, it has been evident that the emphasis in that suggestion would have to be on "glorified," since no machine could come close to the performance of humans or even of the higher animals. Now the suggestion is beginning to look more realistic, though it is still a long way from accurate. Two characteristics have seemed to separate humans and at least some animals on the one hand from machines on the other: intelligence and purpose. We have already seen how computers can be programed to behave in seemingly quite intelligent ways. As for purpose, there are various devices, called control mechanisms or servomechanisms, that show at least rudimentary forms of purpose. The study of such mechanisms is called *control theory* or *cybernetics.*

The term "cybernetics" was coined by Norbert Wiener (1948). The word is derived from the Greek for "steersman," since it is concerned with devices that keep some operation, like the sailing of a ship, on its proper course. In order to keep an operation on course, it is necessary to compensate for any deviation in either direction. If a ship drifts off course, either to port or to starboard, the helmsman must move the rudder the proper amount and direction to bring the ship back on course. This illustration presents the general concept of *negative feedback.* Negative feedback involves adjustments in a system to keep it in a steady state by compensating for any deflections from that state.

Negative Feedback

The concepts of cybernetics emerged from the branch of engineering concerned with control mechanisms. Such mechanisms operate by negative feedback. The thermostat is a simple familiar example. The purpose of a thermostat is to regulate a particular variable, temperature. In the terminology of control systems, temperature is the *controlled quantity.* At any given time the thermostat is set to maintain the temperature in a room at a given constant level, the *set point*. When the room temperature drops below the set point, the thermostat turns on the furnace so that the temperature will rise. Then when the temperature rises above the set point, the thermostat turns the furnace off and lets the temperature fall. In such a system, the output (a change in temperature) is fed back to the thermostat as input—hence the term feedback. The effect of the feedback is to produce a change in the opposite direction (warmer if it is too cool, cooler if it is too warm), which is why it is called negative feedback. We will have something to say about the relation of negative feedback to its opposite, positive feedback, in the next chapter.

When a person performs any skilled act, he is constantly guided by sensations from his muscles, usually also from his eyes, and often from other sources. These sensations warn him whenever he is starting to make a mistake and thus enable him to return to the proper procedure. This response often happens so quickly and automatically that he is unaware of it, but it occurs nonetheless. This behavior is an example of negative feedback, with the output being fed back to control the operation and keep it on course.

A similar process operates in the body's physiological regulation. Body temperature, blood sugar level, alkalinity of the blood, and a great variety of other physiological variables must be maintained within some range in order for the body to function properly. They are, then, controlled quantities, and the optimal level for each of them is its set point. Negative feedback operates at the physiological level to correct deviations either up or down from the set point. These automatic regulatory processes are known collectively as *homeostasis*.

To maintain all these physiological controlled quantities close to their set points over long periods of time, it is not enough to have homeostatic mechanisms at the physiological level. To make homeostasis possible, we must eat, drink, breathe, and in most environments also move around, change clothes, and engage in many other activities. When we discuss these more molar activities, we are clearly in the realm of motivation. Just as there is a set point for level of blood sugar at a given time, so is there also a set point for amount of food intake over a period of time. We are aware of deviations from this set point—sometimes being hungry, at other times uncomfortably stuffed—and eat or stop eating to correct them. Over a period of time this negative feedback is often remarkably effective in maintaining the set point. When people are free to eat whatever amount they wish, neither dieting nor under social pressure to eat more than they want, their weight often stays quite stable for months or even years. It may not be the weight they would most like to be at, but it is the level that their free food consumption maintains, and therefore a set point.

As we noted earlier in this chapter, hunger is only one of many drives or motives that have been observed, even in animals. Among humans there is an even greater variety. For a great many of them, the most desirable level is neither the maximum nor the minimum possible, but somewhere in between. We want a certain amount, but not too much, of exercise and rest and companionship and solitude and adventure and security. Each of these motives, then, can be considered a controlled quantity. When we get too little of any of these controlled quantities, we seek more, and when we get too much, we try to cut down. Whereas optimal arousal theory says that this is true of general arousal, a cybernetic theory of motivation says that it is also true of most of the things we desire.

When we proceed to more complex purposive behaviors, the same principle applies. A student going through college may discover that he is getting failing grades. If the discovery leads him to work harder and thus bring up his grades, he affords an example of negative feedback. In the unlikely event that he studies so hard as to affect his health, he can cut down his studying. In both cases he discovers a deviation from his progress through college, one that threatens the success of his education, and he corrects the deviation so as to continue on his progress toward the degree.

The feedback model represents a middle position between connectionist and cognitive theory. Like connectionist theory, it is concerned with fairly mechanistic connections between stimuli and responses. Stimuli serve as the input, responses as the output, and the individual as the system. Negative feedback is the process by which stimuli and responses control each other in continuous interaction with one another, sometimes referred to as a *closed loop.* Feedback theory resembles cognitive theory, however, in its concern with ways in which purposive behavior is maintained by a flexible control system that takes account of the structure of the environment. Moreover, feedback theory is useful not only in dealing with the behavior of individuals but also in analyzing the behavior of groups. The system it describes can as well be a club or a school class as an individual person. A variety of applications of cybernetics to behavior is presented by Smith and Smith (1966).

The Place of Cybernetics in Learning Theory

Cybernetics as the answer to questions discussed in the two previous sections of this chapter is clear. Reinforcement is a change in a controlled quantity, bringing it closer to its set point. All of the theories of reinforcement we have discussed so far can be incorporated within this framework. Drives, for example, involve controlled quantities with low set points. Our set point for pain, for instance, is very low, so it is nearly always a reduction in pain rather than an increase that brings that particular controlled quantity closer to its set point. The theory of optimal arousal reflects the fact that the set point for general arousal is typically neither very high nor very low, so decreases from high to medium arousal and increases from low to medium are both reinforcing. The basis of Premack's theory is the rate at which we make any given response when free to respond as much or as little as we like. That rate is the set point for that response, and we do what we have to in order to control the rate of responding as close as possible to its set point. If the response is restricted to a rate below its set point, any other response that moves it up toward its set point will be reinforced. Cybernetics is thus a very broad theory of motivation and reinforcement.

The great strength of feedback theory in psychology is the range of topics to which it applies. It is a method of analysis that applies to units as small as a flick of the hand or as large as a person's aim in life. It shows that the

coordination of a movement, the pursuit of a goal, the regulation of a physiological function, and the operation of a motive can be viewed as basically the
same thing: maintenance of a set point through the process of negative feedback. Moreover, the various levels at which this process operates are interrelated. For example, a coordinated movement, which has set points for speed
and direction, may be the means of bringing some other controlled quantity
back to its set point (as by getting a glass of water to the mouth and thus
reducing thirst). It is possible to think of all our activities as arranged in a
hierarchy, interrelated in such a way that maintaining the set point of each one
serves to correct a deviation from the set point of the next higher one. This idea
is too complicated and speculative to pursue here, but the interested reader can
find discussions of it in Powers (1973).

The great weakness of feedback theory in psychology, at least for the
purposes of this book, is that it is not a theory of learning. Like Lewin's theory,
it tells us how a system operates but not how its operation changes as a result
of learning. Presumably one learns what techniques are successful in bringing any
given controlled quantity back toward its set point, but cybernetics tells us
nothing about how that learning occurs. Thus, although it is a theory of motivated
behavior within which learning can be studied, cybernetics is still tangential to
the study of learning.

OPPONENT PROCESS THEORY

During the 1950s and 1960s, Richard L. Solomon (b. 1918), currently at the
University of Pennsylvania, was involved in various experiments that involved
giving electric shocks to dogs. His initial interest was in how the dogs learned a
response that permitted them to avoid the shock, but later he became increasingly
interested in the dogs' emotional responses to the shocks, including the response
to shocks that could not be avoided. He and his collaborators observed that when
dogs were first exposed to electric shocks, they appeared terrified by the experience. For a few minutes after the shocks were over, the dogs acted unfriendly and
stealthy, before returning to their more typical active, friendly behavior. After a
number of days of being shocked, their reactions were considerably different. The
reaction to the shocks was much less extreme, more one of anxiety or annoyance
than terror. More striking was the change in behavior just after the shocks ended:
the dogs were even more active and friendly than usual; they seemed to be
expressing their joy that the shock was over.

At about the time Solomon was making these observations, he learned
about a study of skydivers (Epstein 1967) and noticed a marked resemblance
between their reactions and those of the dogs. Before their first few jumps, the
skydivers were highly anxious, and afterward they experienced first a sort of
emotionally drained numbness and then a few minutes of pleasant liveliness. After
a number of jumps, their reactions were quite different. Before the jump their
arousal was in the form of nervous eagerness rather than anxiety, and afterward
they spent a couple of hours in a state of exhilaration. For both dogs and skydivers
one thing remained the same: the period just after the frightening experience was

(not surprisingly) more pleasant than just before the experience. The whole level, however, had changed, from frightened before and fairly unemotional after to less emotional before and pleasantly excited afterward.

Thinking about these changes in the ways dogs and people react to situations that are originally frightening, Solomon wondered whether there might be similar changes in an experience that was originally pleasant. A striking example came to mind: morphine addiction. Early in the addict's experience with morphine (before he becomes an addict), the initial reaction to taking the drug is highly pleasant, while the effect of its wearing off is fairly neutral. After many exposures, the person (whom we can now call an addict) gets less pleasure from the administration of the drug, but finds its wearing off very unpleasant (withdrawal symptoms). Though the directions are reversed, the kinds of changes are the same as with the dogs and the skydivers: the emotional reaction at the beginning lessens, while its ending produces an opposite reaction that gets larger and larger.

The Theory

Eventually Solomon and J.D. Corbit collected a number of such examples and to explain them stated a theory (Solomon & Corbit 1974) known as the *opponent process* theory. First, this is a *hedonic* theory; that is, it refers to pleasure and displeasure. Second, it might be summarized by saying that for every feeling there is an opposite (but not exactly equal) reaction. The original feeling and the opposite reaction are the opponent processes that give the theory its name. Third, the opponent process increases with repeated exposures, producing the changes noted in the examples above. Thus there are opponent processes that counteract both pleasure and displeasure, weakly so at first, but more and more strongly with repeated presentations of the pleasant or unpleasant experience.

Figure 9.2 makes these ideas more explicit. The graphs in Panel A of the figure show what happens when a pleasant stimulus (such as an addictive drug) is first presented. When the stimulus is presented (top), the immediate effect is hedonically positive, as shown in the middle graph. This positive (pleasant) effect (called the *a* process) increases rapidly to a maximum, remains at that high level as long as the stimulus is on, and then drops rapidly back to zero when the stimulus is turned off. (In the case of a drug, the "stimulus on" period is the time that the drug remains active in the body.) This simple sequence of the *a* process is represented by the solid line. Shortly after the stimulus goes on, its opponent *b* process also begins, as represented by the broken line. Compared to the *a* process, the *b* process not only begins later but also increases more slowly and to a lower level. When the stimulus goes off, the *b* process again lags behind the *a* process: it continues for a short time after the stimulus is gone and then drops slowly toward zero. Since the *b* process tends to counteract the *a* process, we can determine the net effect of combining them by adding them algebraically (that is, taking account of sign), as shown in the bottom graph. As long as the stimulus is on, the *a* is much stronger, so the *b* process has only a slight counteracting effect. However, since the *b* process is still going on after the *a* process has returned to zero, the net effect at the end will be negative. Thus the ending of a pleasant experience is not just neutral but slightly unpleasant.

Panel B of the graph shows the situation for the same stimulus after it has been presented many times. The *a* remains the same, but the *b* process has now increased in strength. Thus when we combine the two there is still a pleasant period just after the stimulus goes on and an unpleasant period just after the stimulus goes off. The relative sizes of these two, however, are much different than before. Whereas at first the initial pleasure was strong and the displeasure at the end mild, now it is just the reverse. As for the period in between, while the stimulus remains on, whereas before it was quite pleasant (though not as much as the initial few moments), now it is barely pleasant at all. The *b* process has not completely counteracted the *a* process during that period of time, but it has come very close to doing so.

If we were graphing an unpleasant primary process, as with the shocked dogs or the skydivers, we would get exactly the same graphs except that the up and down directions would be reversed. The *a* process would now be in the negative direction and the *b* process in the positive direction, but the *b* process would still lag behind the *a*. Moreover, the *b* process would still increase with repeated presentations of the stimulus until it almost but not quite counteracted the unpleasant *a* process.

Some Implications

The most interesting examples of opponent processes are not necessarily the most practical on which to do research. One that lends itself well to quantitative research is *imprinting* in ducklings. The attachment of ducklings to their mother

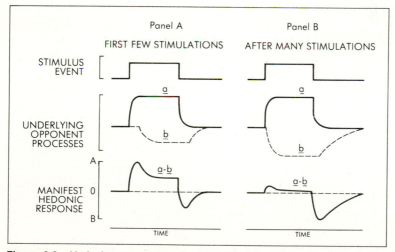

Figure 9.2 *Hedonic opponent processes.* Each panel shows the time that a stimulus is on (top), the *a* process with its opponent *b* process (middle), and the resulting manifest hedonic reaction (bottom). From Solomon (1980). Copyright 1980 by the American Psychological Association. Adapted by permission of the author.

appears to be learned rather than innate, and the process by which it is learned is called imprinting (Lorenz 1952). What most students of imprinting have studied is the duckling's response of following the mother, which can be considered to involve a pleasant *a* process. Solomon and his collaborators chose instead to study the distress calls that the duckling makes when separated from the mother —the opponent *b* process. The number of distress cries in the first minute after separation from the mother makes a good quantitative measure of the strength of the *b* process. In one study (Hoffman, et al. 1974) ducklings received 12 exposures of 30 seconds each to the mother with intervals of separation between. For different groups of ducklings the lengths of the separation periods were different. When these intervals were 1 minute each, the number of distress calls increased from one interval to the next. This change indicates that, as the theory predicts, repeated presentations were strengthening the *b* process. Where the separation intervals were 5 minutes long, however, no such increase occurred. This difference led the researchers to conclude that repetition increases the strength of the *b* process only if the repetitions are close enough together. How close is close enough would vary from one situation to another, but for any particular *b* process there would be a *critical delay duration,* the period within which the stimulus must be presented again in order for the repetition to strengthen the *b* process. With intervals between presentations that are longer than the critical delay duration, the increase in strength of the *b* process would not occur.

It should be noted that the increase with repetition in the *b* process, provided the repetitions come within the critical delay duration, results only from the fact that they occur. This is not a matter of conditioning or even of learning, as that term is often used. Nothing else has to be paired with the *b* process in order to produce the change. It is the repetition of the *b* process itself which strengthens it, as in the repeated use of a muscle. Of all the forms of learning we have considered so far, the only one resembling it in this respect is the habituation of the orienting reflex (Chapter 7). This kind of change resulting simply from exposure, has, however, received increasing attention in recent years (see, e.g., Hill 1978).

Why should there be such opponent processes? We may note that *b* processes, by counteracting *a* processes, tend to move hedonic states back toward zero. Thus neither pleasure nor displeasure is able to become very powerful without being counteracted by negative feedback. This tendency would suggest that affective neutrality is a more adaptive state than either strong pleasure or strong displeasure. Perhaps either kind of strong affective state is too much of a strain on the organism, and homeostasis must be restored to keep us from being emotionally worn out. In any case, opponent process theory resembles traditional drive theory in one respect: both regard a reduction in arousal as the standard tendency of the motivational system.

Although the *b* process can thus be seen as a negative feedback mechanism correcting a deviation from a set point of affective neutrality, it is not a very efficient one. It undercorrects while the stimulus is on and then overcorrects after the stimulus goes off, pushing the controlled quantity in the opposite direction.

As the b process becomes stronger, its undercorrection during the stimulus becomes less, but its overcorrection at the end becomes greater. Using the steersman analogy from cybernetics, it is as though the boat is constantly buffeted by strong and rapidly shifting currents, so that the steersman can never completely compensate for them while they are flowing, but then shoots off in the other direction when the current for which he was correcting suddenly stops. Presumably it would be a wild ride indeed if the steersman were not there to exert at least some degree of control.

At a more philosophical level, the theory suggests that the pursuit of pleasure is bound to be less successful than one might hope, since a pleasant a process not only often carries an unpleasant b process along with it but also keeps strengthening that b process. On the other hand, it also suggests that life's misfortunes are not as bad as they might be, since so many unpleasant a processes have opponent b processes that not only blunt the displeasure but provide a "sweet aftertaste." (Neither Solomon nor anyone else claims to know just how many a processes have opponent b processes strong enough to be important, only that a great many of them do.) As Solomon (1980) comments, it is a puritan's theory. Ralph Waldo Emerson would probably feel that it captures much of the spirit of his essay on compensation.

Chapter *10*

Memory

The theories we have discussed so far in this book for the most part have not had much to say about memory. This silence may well seem strange, since remembering what we have learned is such an important aspect of learning, while forgetting what we have learned is so often a problem. To a considerable extent, however, learning theorists have tended either to take both remembering and forgetting for granted or (like Guthrie) to explain them in general terms without looking at them in much detail.

A CONNECTIONIST APPROACH TO MEMORY

In spite of this relative lack of interest in the topic, learning theorists have not entirely neglected memory. In particular, there has long been a moderate degree of interest among connectionist theorists in verbal learning and memory. Though we remember (or forget) all sorts of things—events, faces, scenes, skills, feelings—the remembering of words and other verbal materials is particularly prominent, at least for those of us who are either students or teachers. Moreover, both words and trigrams are the sorts of simple units that can easily be analyzed as stimuli and responses. It is therefore not surprising that until recently the study of memory focused mainly on memory for verbal material and was done largely by connectionist psychologists (though also, as we have seen, by gestalt psychologists). Hull and collaborators, for example, wrote an impressively elaborate deductive analysis of the process of serial memorization. The greatest interest in the topic was not among the theorists we have mentioned, however, but among other psychologists who, though connectionist in their biases, were less inclined to the building of grand theories. They preferred instead to construct smaller theories dealing with specific topics in verbal learning and memory, which are sometimes called miniature theories. This approach began with the early German psychologist Hermann Ebbinghaus, whose classic experiments on memory (using himself as subject) began the experimental study of the topic (Ebbinghaus 1964). In America, the most prominent examplar of this tradition is Benton J. Underwood (b. 1915) of Northwestern University.

Interference as a Source of Forgetting

Underwood should certainly be classified as a connectionist psychologist, for most of his analyses are in terms of verbal responses and the stimuli, usually also verbal, that elicit them. Many of his experiments are simply concerned with finding the relationships between independent and dependent variables, with little interest in theoretical interpretations. In this respect he resembles Skinner. When he does act as a theorist, however, his interpretations are relatively formal: though he does not put them in the Hullian form of postulates and theorems, he does make them specific enough to be clearly testable with experiments. He uses the term reinforcement, but without much concern as to what the nature of reinforcement is. A cautious, step-by-step approach, with great emphasis on proper research methods, characterizes all of his work.

One of Underwood's many interests in verbal learning has been the question of why we forget. Once something has been memorized, why do we not remember it forever? Of the various explanations that have been offered, by far the most influential has been the *interference* interpretation, that we forget because our retention of any given item is interfered with by all the other items we have learned that resemble it in some way. Though we have mentioned only Guthrie as having such an interpretation, actually a number of the theorists discussed in this book agree that forgetting is caused primarily, if not exclusively, by such interference.

Underwood agrees on the importance of interference in forgetting, but raises a question as to which of two sources of interference is the more important. If we forget any given thing because of interference from something else that we learned afterward, this effect is known as *retroactive interference*. The second thing we learned has in some sense replaced the first in memory, so that it is harder to retrieve the first. Traditionally retroactive interference has been regarded as the major form of interference (again, think of Guthrie's explanation of forgetting). However, it is also possible that the interference with any given material could come from other material that had been learned before. This effect is known as *proactive interference*. These two possible forms of interference are diagramed in Figure 10.1.

At first glance proactive interference seems like a less plausible cause of forgetting than does retroactive interference. Once the new material has been learned, and the old material therefore supposedly unlearned, or at least pushed into the background, why should it interfere with retention of the new? Underwood points out that what happens to the first material when the second is being

Group	Period 1	Period 2	Period 3	Period 4
A	Nothing	Learn Key List	Learn Other List	Test on Key List
B	Learn Other List	Learn Key List	Nothing	Test on Key List
C	Nothing	Learn Key List	Nothing	Test on Key List

Comparisons of key-list scores on the retention test in Period 4:
  C–A = amount of retroactive interference
  C–B = amount of proactive interference
  B–A = extent to which retroactive interference is greater than proactive (if
        negative, proactive is greater)

Figure 10.1 *Retroactive and proactive interference.* By comparing retention of one list (here called the key list) by groups with different experiences of learning another list, we can measure the amounts of proactive and retroactive interference. Note that the retention interval between learning the key list in Period 2 and testing in Period 4 is the same for all three groups, so differences in performance on the test cannot be attributed to any differences in elapsed time.

learned is comparable to extinction. But what happens to an extinguished response with the passage of time? Very often it shows spontaneous recovery. Why should we not expect that the material which was learned first would remain only temporarily extinguished, and then return through spontaneous recovery to interfere with the material learned second? If this process does indeed take place, the passage of time should serve not only to increase the effect of proactive interference but also to decrease the effect of retroactive interference through the recovery of the material to be remembered. Underwood (1948) found that this expectation is indeed what occurs. With the amount and difficulty of the interfering materials held constant, retroactive interference produced much more interference with retention five hours after learning than did proactive, but after a two-day interval there was practically no difference between them.

Which Kind Is More Important?

This experiment of Underwood's demonstrates that proactive interference is just as plausible an explanation of forgetting as is retroactive. It does not, however, give us much basis for deciding how much each of these processes actually contributes to everyday forgetting. Underwood's impression about the relative importance of these two processes came from another line of evidence. He noted that when college students memorized a list of words or trigrams, the amount that they remembered from the list a day later depended greatly on how much prior experience they had had in memorization. We might expect that the more experienced memorizers would show an advantage, and indeed they do if we look at the rate of original learning. However, if both experienced and inexperienced memorizers keep on working until they have mastered the list, and then stop, it is the inexperienced memorizers who retain more after an interval of time (Underwood 1957). This difference does not seem so surprising when we consider that all the previous lists learned by the experienced group were building up proactive interference with retention of the final list. If there are many previous lists to produce proactive interference, this effect can be huge. In one experiment (Keppel, Postman, & Zavortink 1968), subjects learned a series of paired-associate lists at two-day intervals and were tested for retention of each before learning the next. On the average they remembered 70% of the items on the first list and only 5% of the items on the thirty-sixth list, even though the lists were equally difficult and were tested the same length of time after being learned. Clearly, differences in proactive interference alone can make remarkable differences in the amount of forgetting.

Does it follow that proactive interference from things we have learned previously is the major cause of our ordinary forgetting? Not necessarily, since experiments that vary only the proactive interference do not tell us about the effects of the retroactive interference or of other possible causes of forgetting. However, if we are concerned with forgetting over periods of days or weeks, there is likely to be much more other material that can interfere proactively (given the previous years we have had to learn such material) than retroactively (which would have to be learned during the days or weeks of the retention interval). It thus seems highly plausible that proactive interference is the most important cause of forgetting.

Though the above line of argument with its supporting data represents a major contribution to our understanding of forgetting, Underwood was not satisfied to leave it at that. He went on to gather new data, and not all of what he found fits well into his explanation of forgetting. Because Underwood's theory of forgetting is fairly simple and quite close to data, it has the sort of self-correcting character that Hull sought but did not always achieve. Through his application of simple learning principles to more complex forms of learning and through his constant checking of predictions against data, Underwood has provided not only an interpretation of forgetting but also an impressive example of careful, small-scale theory building.

COGNITIVE APPROACHES TO MEMORY

Although the approach to memory that we have considered so far has not been closely associated with any of the major schools of learning theory, it has been very much a connectionist approach. Responses to stimuli are learned; they compete with one another; and they undergo extinction and spontaneous recovery. Increasingly, however, a different approach has become popular. Rather than focusing on the responses, it focuses on the information that makes the responses possible. Though it differs substantially from the cognitive theories we have looked at so far in this book, it is still more a cognitive than a connectionist approach. It has led to substantial changes both in the ways memory is studied and in the ways it is talked about by theorists.

In the connectionist view of memory, what is remembered or forgotten is responses, and the main reason for some responses being forgotten is competition from other responses to similar stimuli. The alternative point of view that was popular through much of the 1960s and '70s regarded the units as items of information and memory as a matter of storing and then retrieving those items. For the connectionist view the appropriate analogies are telephone switchboards or mazes through which to find one's way. For the newer view the appropriate analogy is a library where information is stored. These items of information are cognitive units, even though they may still be measured by the making of a response. If this approach is not as cognitive as Tolman's cognitive maps, it is at least in a class with Bolles's S-S* and R-S* expectancies.

Three Memory Stores

Perhaps the best-known version of this approach was presented by Richard C. Atkinson (b. 1929) and Richard M. Shiffrin (b. 1942), both then of Stanford University (Atkinson & Shiffrin 1968, 1971; Shiffrin & Atkinson 1969). It regarded memory as made up of three *stores,* that is, locations where information can be stored for some period of time. We do not need to take the concept of location literally. If information is received via the senses and can then affect behavior at a later time, it must have been stored in some form during the interval. There seem to be three different forms of storage, in terms of how long it lasts, how it is retrieved, and why it cannot stay stored longer than it does. These differences make it natural to think of three different stores located in three different places, but we do not have to look at it that way. The three stores are intervening variables, and whether we accept them depends on whether we can use them as a basis for predicting the laws of memory, not on knowing where they are located or even whether they have any specific location at all.

The first of the three stores is the *sensory register.* It is first in the sense that all information arising via the senses is registered there first, hence the name. Actually it may be misleading to speak of it in the singular, since in a way there are as many sensory registers as there are senses. All information that we receive, whether by vision, hearing, or in any other way, goes at once into a sensory register. It remains there for less than a second (for vision) or slightly longer (for hearing and perhaps other senses) and is then lost. Moreover, it is stored in just the form that it is received, like a copy of the image from the retina of the eye or of the sound from the inner ear.

We can demonstrate this very short storage of information in its original form by showing someone an array of 12 letters for 1/20 of a second and then, as soon as the display is turned off, giving her a signal to report either the top, middle, or bottom row of letters. People average about three out of four correct, and since they did not know which row they would be asked to report until after the display was gone, we can presume that some image of the array lasted long enough for them to "read" the letters from it (Sperling 1960). (If we had simply asked them to read all 12, they would still have gotten only four or five right, indicating that the image is very short lived.) The sensory register is thus rather like a television picture: it contains a lot of information, but only for a very short time.

The sensory register holds information too briefly to be of much interest to students of learning. The second store holds information considerably longer, and not necessarily in its original form. This is the *short-term store,* also known as *short-term memory* or as *working memory.* The most common example of information in the short-term store is a phone number one has looked up and wants to remember just long enough to dial it. It is not remembered in any permanent sense; in fact it is often forgotten in a matter of seconds. Still, as contrasted with the sensory register, it is held long enough to be used in fairly complex ways. If dialing a number does not seem very complex, consider the information one holds while doing arithmetic in one's head. You may, for example, remember a number long enough to multiply it by another number, but as soon as you have the product, you start to forget it. This example will also help to show why the short-term store is also called working memory.

Only a limited number of items can be kept at any one time in this short-term store or working memory. As soon as additional items are added, some of those already there have to go. This means that items can be kept in short-term memory almost indefinitely as long as one concentrates on those particular items. If for some reason you had to look up a phone number in one place and then spend some time going to the phone without being able to write it down, you could still remember it. However, if getting to the phone required remembering other new information or making calculations, these other uses of working memory might take over the limited space and make you forget the number you intended to dial. This interference between the old and the new material may look a lot like retroactive interference, but the interpretation is rather different. The interference is not between two responses to the same stimulus, one of which will be retained over a long period, but between two items, one of which will be retained in working memory when there is not room enough for both.

The capacity of the short-term store is about seven times. This capacity is about the same regardless of the kinds of items one is remembering, as long as they are familiar enough to function as units. Thus, the letter sequence c-a-t, being a familiar word, would be a unit, and one could expect to hold about seven such units in working memory at a time. However, the same sequence rearranged, t-c-a, might be only a meaningless sequence of three letters and therefore represent three units in working memory. The capacity of the short-term store is not always exactly seven units, but it is rarely less than five or more than nine. This regularity, consistent across both different individuals and different kinds of items, is one manifestation of what George Miller (1956) (not to be confused with Neal Miller) referred to as "The Magical Number Seven, Plus or Minus Two."

Although rehearsal is a good way of keeping an item in working memory, it is not always necessary. Items do not drop out of the short-term store just because they are not rehearsed; they drop out because they are replaced by other items. Suppose you read a short series of letters and are tested a number of seconds later to see how well you remember it. If you spent the intervening seconds doing mental arithmetic, you are likely to have forgotten the letters, since the arithmetic required using working memory for numbers, which crowded out the letters. If, on the other hand, you spent the time listening intensely to try to detect a faint signal, you would remember the letters much better, even though you had not had a chance to rehearse them. There would have been nothing to crowd the letters out of the short-term store, so they would still be remembered.

Finally, the *long-term store* is closer to what we considered in the previous two sections, though still substantially different. Whereas in the previous section we asked how responses are memorized and what determines how they are retained, now we ask how items enter the long-term store and how they are later retrieved from that store. Although there is no way to be sure, the working assumption is that the long-term store has unlimited capacity and that nothing is lost from it. When we forget something that was once in the long-term store, the reason is that we can no longer find it, but it is still there available to be found if we can select the right search strategy for retrieving it.

Although the long-term store corresponds to what Underwood analyzed, the nature of the analysis is rather different. We might think of the long-term store as a filing system of a library, where a great deal of information is stored on a permanent basis for use when needed. Each item of information is filed under a number of headings and may be retrieved whenever there is a call for any of these headings. The headings may be of various sorts: by topic (e.g., everything I know about magnetism), or by occasion (e.g., everything that happened to me during the winter of 1981–82), or by place (e.g., the locations of the major public buildings in Philadelphia), or a number of other possibilities. Some items of information carry many such tags and thus are fairly often retrieved from the long-term store, while others have few such labels and are rarely retrieved. Hence, an item that seems to be completely forgotten may still be retrieved if one hits on the right search label.

When an item is retrieved from the long-term store, it goes into the short-term store, which again justifies the latter's alternative title of "working memory." As with any other item, it stays there for some period of time and then is crowded out by other items. When that happens, however, it is not lost, but returns to (or remains in) the long-term store. Atkinson and Shiffrin suggest the metaphor of a photocopier: when an item is in the long-term store, a copy is put in the short-term store when needed, used there, and then discarded as a new item would be, while the original item remains unchanged in the long-term store.

If nothing is ever lost from the long-term store, why does it typically get harder to retrieve items the longer they have been in the long-term store? The answer is that typically the older items have more items that can be confused with them; and it is harder to find the correct item among all the incorrect ones. Again, this sounds a good deal like proactive and retroactive interference. However, the ways of thinking about the process are still rather different. The interference is not a matter of competing responses that show extinction and spontaneous recovery, but rather of a more-or-less organized clutter in which it gets harder and harder to find what you want when there are more items to be searched through. The age of a memory is not a crucial factor in itself; what matters is whether the way it is labeled matches the search device you are currently using. This approach thus puts less emphasis on what happens to items after they are learned and more emphasis on the ways one goes about looking for them. A good memory therefore depends on the relationship between the way items are labeled as they go into the long-term store and the way they are searched for when the time comes to retrieve them.

How, then, do items get into the long-term store? The basic answer is by rehearsal. The more an item is rehearsed in the short-term store, the greater the probability that it will move into the long-term store. However, what is rehearsed, and perhaps stored, is a particular version of the item, that is, the item *encoded* in a certain way. Encoding is a major determinant of whether an item is stored in a form that can later be retrieved, and so has been studied by a number of psychologists in ways that go beyond Atkinson and Shiffrin's theory.

The Process of Encoding

What does encoding consist of? There are many possibilities, and the applied psychology of memory is largely the study of devices for effective encoding. At the theoretical level, we will consider two approaches that have received a good deal of attention in recent years.

One approach was presented by F. I. M. Craik and R. S. Lockhart (1972). This approach maintains that how well something is remembered depends on how deeply it is processed. What is meant by depth of processing is best indicated by an example. People were given a list of words and asked to make one of three decisions about each word: (1) whether it was in capital or lowercase letters, (2) whether or not it would rhyme with "right," or (3) whether it referred to something commonly found in the home. There were no instructions to remember the words, but afterward the people were in fact asked to try to remember them. Memory was least good for (1), better for (2), and best for (3). Craik and Lockhart explained these differences by saying that question (1), dealing only with the form of the word, required little processing, question (2), dealing with its sound, required more, and question (3), dealing with meaning, required the deepest processing. The deeper the processing, in turn, the better the memory for the words.

Obviously the three questions call for different *kinds* of processing, but what does it mean to say that they require different *depths* of processing? Though deeper processing takes longer, which automatically gives it an advantage in memory, that is not the main answer. Primarily, deeper processing involves those aspects of a word that are most relevant to remembering it. The letters in which it is printed make up a superficial aspect of the word, one unrelated to what is essential about that word. The sound with which the word ends is a slightly more distinctive characteristic of the word but still not as distinctive or basic as the meaning. Processing that involves the meaning is the deepest kind, the kind involving what is essential about the word to be remembered. This, as well as simply the time involved, makes it the most efficient kind of processing.

This emphasis on different depths of processing leading to different lengths of retention can be seen as an alternative to the distinction between short-term and long-term stores. Perhaps, rather than having two different places that items are stored, we have some items that are processed shallowly and are quickly lost and others that are processed more deeply and therefore retained longer. However, we can also use the two sets of ideas together, with the depth of processing determining whether or not an item moves from the short-term into the long-term store. In any case, the idea of different depths of processing offers one answer to the question of why some items are remembered for a long time and others are not.

A different approach to the questions of encoding has been developed by Allan Paivio (1971). He suggests that information is stored in memory in two forms, verbal and imaginal. Verbal representation of information is, of course, in words, whether isolated words, single statements, or complex sequences of related statements. Imaginal representation is in terms of images, which can be of any form (e.g., the sound of a tune or the smell of fresh-ground coffee), but is primarily in the form of visual images, or mental pictures. Some items of information are stored in one form, some in the other, and some in both.

What determines how an item will be represented in memory? In general, it will be stored in any form that it can be. Anything that can readily be expressed in words will be represented verbally in memory and anything that can be coded as a picture will be represented imaginally in memory. Many items, therefore, will be represented in both ways. Pictures that can readily be described, and words or statements referring to something that can readily be pictured, would lend themselves to double representation, both verbal and imaginal. Other items, however, are so much easier to represent one way than the other that they are likely to be stored in only one form. A picture of some complex design for which there is no easy description in words would probably be represented only imaginally in memory, while a word like "truth," which is hard to picture, would probably be represented only verbally. Paivio assumes we are so experienced in applying words to all sorts of things that most stimuli get stored verbally, whereas quite a number of more abstract stimuli do not get stored imaginally. Most items therefore are stored either in both verbal and imaginal form, or only in verbal form.

A key assumption of Paivio's theory is that it is easier to retrieve an item from memory storage if it is represented there in two ways than if it is represented in only one way. There are, so to speak, twice as many ways that one can find the item if it is stored in two forms. It follows from this that concrete words, such as "house" or "dog," that can easily be pictured should be better remembered than abstract words, such as "truth" or "eternity." This prediction has been confirmed.

Psychologists are used to analyzing variables as matters of degree rather than simply present or absent, so Paivio does not stop with saying that an item can easily be coded in one way or in two—he goes on to ask how easily. He gave people a series of words and asked them to form a visual image of each and signal as soon as they had done so. He then used these data to give each word an imagery score: the faster an image could be formed, the higher the score. If the theory is correct, words with high imagery scores should be easier to remember than words with low imagery scores. This prediction has been tested and confirmed in several different forms of memory experiments.

If instead of words a person is given pictures to remember, it should be very easy to represent them imaginally, even more so than for concrete words. At the same time, given our tendency to label the things we see with words, they should also be at least moderately well represented verbally. Memory for pictures should thus be especially good—better than for words. This prediction too has been confirmed.

Paivio's theory helps us to understand why certain tricks for remembering things (*mnemonic devices,* as such tricks are called) work as well as they do. One such mnemonic device, useful when learning pairs of items, is to form a mental image of the two items interacting in some way. Thus, to remember that "hat" and "train" go together, one might imagine a train racing along the tracks with a hat perched on top of the locomotive. (If the image looks silly, so much the better, say some experts.) When a whole series of items is to be remembered, one suggestion (dating back to ancient Greece) is to imagine a building one knows well and picture each item at some particular place in the building. One can then mentally "walk" through the building, retrieving one item from the living room sofa, another from the kitchen sink, and so forth. The reader will readily recognize that both of these methods are useful mainly for concrete items, those with high imagery scores. Given that kind of item, there is evidence to indicate that both of these mnemonic devices are quite helpful in increasing the number of items one can commit to memory in a given amount of time (Bower 1972).

Schemata in Memory

These various approaches to memory, in terms of stores and encoding, dominated the study of memory through much of the 1960s and '70s. Quite recently another, even more cognitive, approach has become increasingly prominent. It is not, however, a new approach; it goes back both to the gestalt psychologists and to the early British psychologist Frederic C. Bartlett (1932). It is also closely related to Piaget's work. This approach treats memory neither as responses to be retained nor as items to be stored but as a pattern of understanding. When we are exposed to new material, we incorporate it into the existing structure of our knowledge and beliefs. In this process, the original material may be distorted to fit better with the existing structure. Perhaps it would be more appropriate to say not that the material is distorted but that what is remembered is a new construction, one which depends both on the presented material and on the existing cognitive structure. When asked to recall the new material, what we come up with is this new construction, which reflects the original material but may differ from it in any of various ways.

As with Piaget, this cognitive approach makes heavy use of the concept of *schema.* As used here, a schema may be thought of as a basic pattern or prototype on which specific experiences represent variations. When we have an experience and afterward try to remember it, we first remember the schema and then work on the details. If some of the details are inconsistent with the schema, we may remember them incorrectly, not as they actually happened but as the schema suggests that they should have happened. On the other hand, a detail that could not have been remembered in isolation can, if consistent with the schema, be given correctly by a mixture of memory and of inference from the schema. Details are not remembered in isolation, therefore, but rather are incorporated into existing schemata. Even an item that is not consistent with the schema is still linked to it, either remembered incorrectly or remembered correctly as a strange (and perhaps, therefore, especially memorable) anomaly.

This gestalt-oriented view of memory helps to make a number of social phenomena easier to understand. Hence it has been popular with social psychologists. They have noted a number of kinds of schemata that affect not only our memory but our perception and understanding of the world around us. For example, there are schemata about people that lead us to organize the things we see other people do under various headings, such as "intelligent" or "athletic" or "generous." Once we have decided that someone shows one of these traits, it serves as a schema leading us to expect certain behaviors from the person but not to expect others and to remember some better than others. Another example is our understanding of stories. We expect a story to start somewhere and go somewhere, with one event leading to another and with the characters motivated in normal ways. Items in the story that fit our story schema are usually easier to remember than ones that don't, which we say "don't make sense." Moreover, we may "remember" details that were not a part of the story at all, but that are consistent with it and fill in gaps in the original presentation (e.g., Mandler 1978, Spiro 1976). This process reduces the distinction between "true memory" on the one hand and inference from schemata on the other. Our social world can be seen as made up of schemata that give the world order and make the world easier both to remember and to deal with effectively, but that also sometimes lead us to inaccurate memories and mistaken conclusions.

One kind of schema that has received considerable attention is a *script* (Schank & Abelson 1977). This is a typical sequence of events that would occur in a given setting. We have schemata about what normally happens at a baseball game, a cocktail party, or an evening at the theater. Each of these schemata constitutes a script that helps us to make sense out of the sequence of events. Thus, if we read in a story that "with three balls and two strikes on the batter, he hit a home run," we know that there were at least six pitches to that batter. If we later try to recall the story as completely as possible, we may give the incident as, "the batter sent the sixth pitch into the stands for a home run." Because we have such scripts for familiar situations, we can reconstruct and elaborate stories from minimal information, whereas people unfamiliar with the situation (i.e., lacking the script) would find the same minimal version of the story quite difficult both to understand and to remember.

Just as classical gestalt theory treated perception and thought as much the same process, so this gestalt-ish approach to memory treats memory and inference as, if not the same thing, at least almost inextricably interwoven. Other people might ask, "Do we actually remember a given item, or do we infer that it must have been there and then act accordingly?" People using the analysis in terms of schemata, however, are likely to conclude that the two cannot be distinguished. Our cognitions about a given event may be formed in any of various ways, but once formed they usually influence our behavior in much the same way regardless of how they were formed. To say that some cognitions represent "real memories" and others do not is pointless.

A striking example of the equivalence of cognitions from different sources is found in studies of eyewitness testimony. For example (Loftus 1975; Loftus, Miller, & Burns 1978), people were shown a sequence of slides of an automobile accident, in which a stop sign figured prominently. Afterward, the people were asked a number of questions about what they saw, among which was the question, "Did another car pass the red Datsun when it was stopped at the yield sign?" Subsequently, when asked about the sign, a substantial proportion of them said without hesitation that it was a yield sign. The proportion who said it was a yield sign was so much greater among those who had been asked the misleading question than among those who had not, that the question clearly had a major effect. How could we differentiate this effect from "really" remembering the kind of sign one had actually seen?

One way to distinguish the two might be to show two otherwise identical pictures side by side, one with a stop sign and the other with a yield sign, and ask which picture they had actually seen, so that the emphasis would be on the visual memory image. As it turned out, however, those that had been asked about the nonexistent yield sign still showed a tendency to choose the yield sign as the one they had actually seen. One might go even further, telling the observers that there might have been a discrepancy between what they saw and the context of the questions they had been asked, and then asking them both what they had seen and how the question had been worded. This method was also tried, but it did not lead those who had chosen the yield sign to recognize their error. The misinformation from the leading question had apparently been incorporated into their memory of the incident and there was no way to separate that part of their memory from the part based on what they had actually seen.

A Parting Thought   Of the various topics we consider in this book, memory is the one that most illustrates the recent upswing in cognitive theorizing. The approach discussed in the second section of this chapter has largely (though by no means entirely) replaced that from the first section as the dominant approach to memory. That is, the view of memory as a system of storing and retrieving information has become more popular than the view of memory as facilitation and inhibition of responses. One might say that a "library" model of memory ("Do we have that item in our library collection and how can we find it there?") has to a considerable degree replaced a "switchboard" model ("Do our wires still have the connections so that each incoming signal will activate the correct mechanism?"). It is a change that Tolman would have applauded.

Moreover, even within cognitive theory, the use of the concept of schema seems to be gaining in popularity. Memory is regarded less as a collection of items in a library and more as a total view of some topic. Information is incorporated into an existing schema and in some cases modifies the schema. Since an item of information cannot be analyzed apart from the whole pattern of which it comes to form a part, this is distinctly a gestalt view of memory. Thus, at least in the area of memory, cognitive theory has come very much into its own.

Chapter *11*

Biologically Based Theories

Learning theorists have always assumed in principle that our behavior depends on the characteristics of our bodies in general and of our nervous systems in particular. In other words, they have seen psychology in some sense as a branch of biology. In practice, however, they have often paid very little attention to biology. They have typically justified this decision by claiming that biologists do not yet know enough about the detailed functioning of the nervous system to be able to make useful predictions about behavior. Given the recent increases in knowledge about neurophysiology, biochemistry, and behavioral pharmacology, it can certainly be argued that this is no longer an appropriate position for psychologists of learning to take. However, in view of the biological expertise needed to explore these various biological bases of behavior, we will not attempt to do so in this book. Instead, we will look at two relatively nontechnical ways in which biology and the psychology of learning have moved closer together.

BIOFEEDBACK

Both Skinner and Mowrer (in his earlier theory) made sharp distinctions between the kind of behavior that could be modified by classical conditioning and the kind that could be modified by instrumental learning. For Skinner, this was the distinction between respondent and operant behavior; for Mowrer it was the distinction between sign learning and solution learning. Though many theorists have accepted this distinction, evidence is increasingly accumulating that the distinction is not a hard and fast one. Of the various lines of evidence, the one that has aroused the most interest in recent years is the instrumental conditioning of the usually involuntary activities of smooth muscles, glands, and brain cells. The technique by which this has been accomplished is known as *biofeedback*.

What Biofeedback Is

A great deal is constantly going on in our bodies of which we are only dimly if at all aware: digestion, circulation of the blood, secretion from many glands, and a host of other functions. In addition to being largely unaware of them, we also have almost no voluntary control over these functions. Perhaps our lack of control is due to our lack of awareness, and if we knew what was happening, we could bring them under voluntary control. Biofeedback is the process of providing information to an individual about his bodily processes in some form which he might be able to use to modify those processes. If a device can provide continuous measurements of our blood pressure, or skin resistance (GSR), or brain waves (EEG), or any other bodily condition, it can also make that information continuously available to us. Information about the individual's biological processes is fed back to him from the recording instrument—hence the term "biofeedback."

This kind of feedback is closely related to, but not identical with, the feedback that is central to cybernetics. Cybernetics is primarily concerned with negative feedback, in which the output is fed back in such a way as to counteract deviations and maintain a steady state. However, cybernetics also includes a concept of *positive feedback,* in which information about deviations is used to increase those deviations. Negative feedback says: "Get back on course!" Positive feedback says: "Now you're shifting in the right direction; let's have more of the same!" Since negative feedback acts to prevent change, it is not closely related to learning, which is a process of change. Positive feedback, however, produces change. Reinforcement of a new response is an example of positive feedback, since the reinforcer tells the individual to continue making that new response rather than to return to previous behavior.

It should be clear that in this context positive does not necessarily mean good or negative mean bad. In fact, in cybernetics they tend to have the opposite implications: negative feedback is considered the "good" kind that keeps a system functioning normally, while positive feedback is the "bad" kind, enhancing deviations from normality so that the system goes out of control. Students of learning tend to see the matter somewhat differently, however. For example, when Skinner gradually shaped an animal to make some response the animal would normally never make, he was using positive feedback deliberately to get the system away from its normal functioning. Rather than saying that positive or negative feedback is either good or bad, we might say that negative feedback is the conservative force and positive feedback the radical force in a system and that depending on circumstances, "radical" can imply either progressive or destructive.

Although biofeedback can be used as either positive or negative, most of the interest has been in positive feedback, which makes the emphasis more like that in any other learning situation than like that in cybernetics. As information is fed back to a person about some change in a body process, he is encouraged to try to increase that change. For example, he may be told to try to increase his GSR or to decrease his blood pressure, and is then given information about his GSR or blood pressure so that he knows exactly when he is succeeding. It is not even necessary that he know what change in his body is being fed back. He may simply be told to try to keep a certain signal light on as much of the time as possible. The experimenter knows, but the subject does not, that the light is on whenever, for example, his blood pressure is lower than its average pressure in the five minutes before the biofeedback began. In that case, the only information the feedback conveys to the subject is his success or failure in the task. In other words, it is a simple reinforcer.

At first, of course, a subject in this situation has no idea how to make the light go on; he can only engage in trial-and-error behavior. If he succeeds in getting the light on a higher and higher percentage of the time, this will provide evidence of learning based on the reinforcement provided by the biofeedback signal light. Success with this procedure in modifying blood pressure or GSR, which are usually unconscious responses of smooth muscles and glands, would provide clear evidence that solution learning (in Mowrer's terms) is not limited to responses of the striped muscles.

A number of studies have indeed achieved success with this method of changing autonomic behavior (Katkin & Murray 1968, Kimmel 1967, Yates 1980). It has worked for blood pressure, heart rate, GSR, volume of blood in a particular part of the body, and the alpha brain-wave rhythm. It has been demonstrated in both humans and animals. In studies of biofeedback, many precautions are needed to ensure that the results are really due to reinforcement by the feedback rather than to changes in activity, nervousness, boredom, stimulation from the signal, or a variety of other possible factors. Although there is still some controversy about the effectiveness of biofeedback independent of all these other factors, enough evidence has accumulated so that many psychologists are prepared to take biofeedback quite seriously. What, then, are its implications?

Implications of Biofeedback

From a theoretical point of view, changes as a result of biofeedback in behavior that is usually involuntary obscure the distinction between respondent and operant behavior. They clearly refute Mowrer's (and others') suggestion that such behavior cannot be modified by the procedures for solution learning (instrumental learning). While it does not eliminate the distinction between respondent and operant behavior, it does suggest that the two blend into each other rather than being clearly separate. Perhaps it would make more sense to say not that a given behavior is either respondent or operant but that it is respondent or operant to some degree. To the extent that any response is elicited reliably by a given unconditioned stimulus, it can probably be modified fairly easily by classical conditioning. However, it cannot be so easily modified by instrumental conditioning because it varies so little from time to time that it is hard to find one form of it to reinforce and another form of it not to reinforce. However, to the extent that a given behavior varies from time to time, rather than being elicited consistently in the same form, it can be modified by instrumental conditioning. If this formulation is correct, then what seems to follow is that our bodily processes are more variable from moment to moment, less respondent and more operant, than most of us had realized. Given this fact, it is only necessary to make people aware of that variability through biofeedback for them to be able to start controlling it.

From a practical point of view, biofeedback has seemed to many people to have important ramifications. Medically, it offers some hope for people with hypertension to lower their blood pressure without drugs, simply through instrumental conditioning (Benson, et al. 1971). Likewise, some sufferers from tension headaches have been taught to relax those muscles through biofeedback from the muscles of the forehead and the neck, thus reducing the tension that produces the headaches (Budzynski, et al. 1973). In physical therapy, paralyzed people have achieved greater control over whatever muscles are at all functional by receiving biofeedback which tells them when they have succeeded in tensing one of these muscles even slightly (Ingles, Campbell, & Donald 1976). Thus the paralytic patients learn how to contract barely functional muscles, while sufferers from tension headaches learn just the opposite—to relax chronically overactive muscles, both of these through biofeedback that tells them what their muscles are doing. Eventually, some enthusiasts hope, we might all achieve the degree of control over our bodily processes that has been claimed for the yogis of India, with all the benefits this might convey in health and effective functioning.

Psychologically, particular attention has been focused on control of brain waves. The alpha rhythm, a brain-wave pattern of around 10 Hz, occurs primarily when the person is awake and alert but with his eyes closed and feeling comfortably relaxed. If biofeedback can be used to increase the proportion of time that alpha waves occur, might the person not become more relaxed? If so, might he not also become better adjusted and be in generally better mental condition? Such extravagant claims of this sort have been made that what real benefits there may be have been cast somewhat into disrepute. In fact, it is not even clear that very large increases in alpha can be produced through biofeedback apart from other factors, let alone that any large psychological benefits result (Paskewitz & Orne 1973; Strayer, Scott, & Bakan 1973). Like many new techniques, biofeedback may suffer more at the hands of its overly enthusiastic supporters than at those of its detractors. However, it remains a promising technique for giving people greater control over the processes of their own bodies, with consequences that may in some cases be beneficial.

BIOLOGICAL CONSTRAINTS ON LEARNING

"Development" refers not only to the changes within an individual from conception to death, but also to the changes in a lineage over generations—in other words, evolution. Biologists and physical anthropologists have taken a strong interest in these evolutionary changes, but psychologists have for the most part been little interested in them. Though learning theorists have done research on a variety of species, they have seldom focused on the differences among species, differences which are products of evolution. Rather, they have been mainly interested in the similarities among species, with the differences commonly being dismissed as inconvenient irrelevancies.

Skinner's attitude may be taken as representative. He recognizes that species differ in their responsiveness to different stimuli (e.g., dogs are color blind, while pigeons have excellent color vision); in the responses they can easily make (e.g., grasping by monkeys but not by dolphins); and in the reinforcers that affect their behavior (e.g., raw worms as positive reinforcers for robins but not for humans). To study learning in different species effectively, therefore, it is necessary to find the right stimuli, responses, and reinforcers for each species. When that is done, however, different species will react to the same independent variable in the same way. A thirsty rat pressing a lever for drops of water, a hungry pigeon pecking a key for access to a hopper of grain, and a human pulling a vending-machine-type plunger for cigarettes will show the same reactions to their schedules of reinforcement. Put all three on a fixed-ratio 5, for example, and their response patterns will be indistinguishable.

This view that the basic laws of learning are the same for different species has been a fundamental tenet of most learning theories. It serves to justify the fact that out of all the species in the world, learning theorists have made greatest use of rats; moderate use of pigeons, monkeys, dogs, and humans; and only slight use of all the rest. It also serves to justify applications of learning theory based largely on rats or pigeons to complex human clinical and social issues, as in the publications of Skinner and of Dollard and Miller. Without this assumption, learning theory would be a substantially different enterprise.

Along with this assumption has gone another: that stimuli, responses, and reinforcers can be paired up in any way, and all ways are equally effective. In other words, how much one learns from a given series of experiences depends on the distinctiveness of the stimuli, the ease of making the required responses, and the effectiveness of the reinforcers, but it does not depend on which stimuli are used with which reinforcers to teach which responses. For example, if lever pressing and jumping are equally easy responses to learn, and if food and escape from shock are equally powerful reinforcers, it does not matter whether the lever pressing is reinforced with food and the jumping with escape from shock or vice versa; either will be learned equally well. This assumption makes it possible to state laws of learning in general terms, referring only to stimuli, responses, and reinforcers, without having to specify what particular ones are to be paired.

Species-Specific Behavior

Although the two assumptions above have been basic articles of faith for many if not most learning theorists, evidence has increasingly been accumulating over the last 20 years or so that they are not altogether valid. Perhaps the first widely noticed sign that all was not well with the assumptions was an article by Keller and Marian Breland. This husband-wife team had been leaders in the use of Skinnerian techniques of animal training, preparing animals to perform on television, at fairs, and in many kinds of exhibits. As such, they were dedicated believers in the power of reinforcement. To their surprise, however, they found their animals sometimes behaving in ways that seemed quite un-Skinnerian. For example, a raccoon that was supposed to put two coins in a slot machine in exchange for food would instead keep rubbing the coins together—as in the raccoon's familiar "food-washing" pattern. A pig in a similar situation would drop the coins and root them in the ground in typical pig fashion. The common problem was that the food-related consummatory responses characteristic of a species often interfered with the response that the experimenter was trying to shape with food reinforcement. Spence might have said that the fractional anticipatory goal responses were not fractional enough—they were full-scale responses that interfered with the reinforced response. What the Brelands said, parodying Skinner's book, *The Behavior of Organisms* (1938), was that they were observing the "misbehavior of organisms" (Breland & Breland 1961).

The "misbehavior" that the Brelands observed consisted of the responses that animals typically make in the presence of food. They are not learned food-getting responses, but innate responses that tend to occur when food is present or is anticipated. Since they vary from species to species, but are relatively fixed and stereotyped for the members of any given species, they are known as *species-specific responses.* Though there are many kinds of species-specific responses, those connected with food are among the most conspicuous to psychologists, since psychologists so often use food as a reinforcer. Since the psychologist arbitrarily selects some response to reinforce, there is always the chance that species-specific responses relevant to the reinforcer will interfere with the animal's making that response.

Species-specific responses do not always interfere with learning, however. In some cases they may make learning easier. Consider, for example, that Skinnerian favorite, a pigeon reinforced with food for pecking a lighted key on the wall of its cage. To Skinner it is obvious that the pigeon pecks because it is reinforced for pecking. However, we can show that things are not always as obvious as they seem. Suppose we vary the experiment by leaving the key dark most of the time, but every now and then lighting it briefly, followed immediately by presenting food. Since the light is always followed by the food, we might expect some form of classical conditioning to occur but we would not expect any operant behavior to be learned, since the food comes regardless of what the pigeon does. Nevertheless, pigeons exposed to this series of events show an increasing tendency to peck the key whenever the light goes on. Skinner might call the pecking a superstition, since anything the pigeon does is followed by food, but the interesting thing is that what pigeons almost universally come to do is that one response —pecking. This process of acquisition, in which pigeons come to peck the lighted key even though there is no systematic connection between the pecking and the food, is called *autoshaping* (Brown & Jenkins 1968).

Once we know that autoshaping will occur, we see the traditional learning to peck a key in a new way. Why do pigeons learn so readily to peck a key when they are reinforced with food? Perhaps it is not so much because pecking is reinforced as because food and a conspicuously peckable target (the key) occur close together. This possibility is strengthened by the fact that autoshaping can occur even when pecking *prevents* the food from appearing on that trial. With that arrangement, pecking is never reinforced; in fact it is punished by loss of food. Nevertheless, most pigeons peck the key often enough under these conditions to lose a substantial proportion of the reinforcers they could have obtained by simply waiting without pecking (Williams & Williams 1969). Apparently, in the presence of food, pecking at the most conspicuous object in the vicinity is a species-specific behavior of pigeons—fortunately so, for this is exactly the behavior that the experimenter wants the pigeon to learn. So, whereas the Brelands kept finding that species-specific behaviors were interfering with what they wanted to teach their animals, here species-specific behavior makes the learning exceptionally easy.

Not all species-specific behaviors involve reward situations. There are also species-specific responses to danger—responses that an organism makes under conditions of pain or fear. In general, such responses to danger involve either fleeing, freezing, or in some cases fighting, but the detailed form they take varies considerably with the species. They are the responses that members of the species tend to make automatically, without the need for any special learning, when confronted with indications of danger.

Just as with species-specific responses to reward, those to danger can either facilitate or interfere with new learning. If an animal can escape or avoid shock by doing something that resembles its species-specific fleeing or freezing behavior, that response will be learned very quickly. If, on the other hand, it can escape or avoid the shock only by doing something very different from its innate reactions to danger, that response will be quite difficult to learn. Bolles (1970) has shown that a number of findings about the way rats learn to escape and to avoid shock, ranging from responses that are often learned in one trial to responses that are nearly impossible for a rat to learn as a way of dealing with shock, can be explained by noting how similar a given response is to the species-specific behavior in situations of danger.

A similar example of a species-specific response giving rise to rapid learning is seen in the experiment by Guthrie and Horton (1946) that was mentioned in Chapter 2. The cats in that study escaped from a puzzle box by bending a flexible pole in the middle of the box. A large proportion of the cats made this response in a stereotyped way, by rubbing their sides against it, rather than moving it in the many other ways that would have been possible. Guthrie saw this stereotyping as evidence that they continued to make the response in whatever way they had made it before. (To Skinner it might be an example of superstition.) It now appears, however, that the cats were actually making a species-specific "greeting" response. Normally cats will rub up against people in that way as a form of greeting. When in the box they cannot rub against people, so they rub against what is available—the pole. The response need not produce escape from the box, or food, or any other obvious reinforcer. However, if there are no humans in the room, the cats do not make the response. This combination of facts suggests that the rubbing was not acquired, as Guthrie believed, by being the last thing done in the situation, but is rather an innate species-specific social reaction (Moore & Stuttard 1979).

Preparedness

What we have seen so far of the misbehavior of organisms is to some extent only an extension of what was already known: that some responses are easier to learn than others, and that those which are easiest for one species may be quite different from those which are easiest for another species. It is, however, a considerable extension. Whether a given response is easy or hard for a given individual to learn depends not only on whether the individual is pigeon, pig, or person, but also on the relevant drives and reinforcers. It is not simply that pecking is an easy and natural response for a pigeon, but that it is particularly natural for a hungry pigeon in an environment where there is or has been food. We thus see foreshadowed a new kind of specificity—that certain responses may be easy to learn for one reinforcer but not for another. And indeed that suspicion is quite correct, for pigeons are almost as bad at learning to peck a key to avoid shock as they are good at learning to peck to get food.

Moreover, it turns out that the relationship between responses and reinforcers is only part of the issue. Not only are certain responses easy to learn for some reinforcers and hard for others, but certain stimuli are effective cues for some responses but not for others. One example is what happens when sounds are used as discriminative stimuli for dogs. If the discrimination to be learned is whether to turn right or left for reinforcement, it works well to have a tone coming from above the dog as the cue to turn right and a tone from below the dog as the cue to turn left. If the tones come from the same place, with a high-pitched tone signaling that the food is on the right and a low-pitched tone signaling that it is on the left, learning is much more difficult. Suppose instead the discrimination is whether to go to get the food or to stay put. In that case just the opposite relationship applies. It is easy for the dog to learn that a high-pitched tone means "go" and a low-pitched tone means "stay," but hard to learn that a tone coming from above means "go" and one coming from below means "stay." In short, location of the tone is a good cue for location of the food, and pitch of the tone is a good cue as to whether going for the food will be reinforced, but not vice versa (Lawicka 1964).

So far we have seen that the specific pairing is important both for stimuli with responses and for responses with reinforcers. How about the pairing of stimuli with reinforcers? This too turns out to be important, particularly with negative reinforcers. Suppose you want to teach a rat not to drink a certain liquid by following the drinking with some unpleasant consequence. You might (like many psychologists) use electric shock as the unpleasant consequence. Or you might instead make the rat sick, which can be done by (among other ways) subjecting it to a heavy dose of X-radiation. Garcia and Koelling (1966) compared these two methods, but they also varied the characteristics of the liquid. In one case what made it distinctive was its sweet taste, in the other case the fact that it was accompanied by a light and a noise. By now the reader may be able to guess the outcome, even though it came as a surprise to a great many psychologists. If drinking was followed by shock, the rats learned to avoid lighted and noisy liquid, but not to avoid sweet liquid. If drinking was followed by illness, they learned to avoid sweet liquid but not liquid accompanied by light and noise. In this case, therefore, whether or not a negative reinforcer would lead the rat to avoid a stimulus depended not merely on what stimulus and what negative reinforcer, but on which pairing of the two.

Seligman (1970) has concluded from findings such as these that any given organism may be *prepared, unprepared,* or *contraprepared* to learn any particular response to any particular stimulus for any particular reinforcer. Prepared responses are especially easy to learn because they reflect species-specific tendencies; pigeons pecking a lighted key for food are an example. Contraprepared responses are exceptionally difficult to learn because they run counter to species-specific tendencies, as with dogs using the pitch of a tone as the cue for a left-right discrimination. Unprepared responses are those that are neither prepared nor contraprepared, those that can be learned with moderate effort, such as lever-pressing for food by a rat. Learning theorists have tended to think of all responses as unprepared, as neutral with regard to stimuli and reinforcers, capable of being learned but with no special advantage. It is this assumption that Seligman rejects.

We implied above that preparedness is a characteristic of the species—that learning a particular combination of stimulus, response, and reinforcer may have different degrees of preparedness for different species. There is not yet very much evidence for this claim, but there is some. For example, we noted above that rats did not learn to avoid a liquid on the basis of its appearance if drinking the liquid was followed by illness, even though they did when drinking was followed by electric shock. Quail, however, for which vision is more important in seeking food, *will* learn to avoid the appearance of a liquid that has been followed by illness (Wilcoxon, Dragoin, & Kral 1971). Thus belongingness involves not only species-specific behavior but also species-specific patterns of learning.

Do humans, like rats, pigs, and pigeons, have species-specific tendencies? Humans sometimes seem to be so adaptable, capable of such varied learning, that we might suspect they lack such tendencies. One striking piece of evidence to the contrary is the existence of language. Although many species communicate with sound, and chimps have been taught to carry on conversations in sign language (Gardner & Gardner 1969, 1980; Linden 1974), no species except *Homo sapiens* (at least so far as we know, the dolphin code not yet having been broken!) uses vocal sound as the basis of a complex, grammatical language. Most humans, by the age of three and usually without any deliberate training, have learned to speak in sentences, with an extensive vocabulary, and make reasonably correct use of a complexity of grammatical rules that they would be quite unable to explain. In fact, children under the age of 3 often use the rules more consistently than do adults. For example, they may follow the general rule for plurals by saying "two mans" or the general rule for past tenses by saying "bunny runned away," rather than using the correct irregular forms "men" and "ran." The use of vocal language thus appears to be an example of human species-specific behavior, and the learning of regular grammatical rules a form of prepared behavior.

Implications for Learning Theory

At first glance, the notions of species-specific behavior and preparedness seem rather disconcerting for learning theory. The great beauty of learning theory has seemed to be that it offered some hope of reducing all the complexities of learning (and possibly motivation, thinking, or perception as well) to a manageable list of general laws. These laws would not depend on the particular stimuli, responses, and reinforcers being learned or on the species being studied. Thus experiments on rats pressing levers would be relevant to the training of seeing-eye dogs, and experiments on pigeons pecking keys would be relevant to humans working on a production line. But if the laws of learning depend on what particular stimulus, response, and reinforcer are being paired, and for what species, can there be any such generality? Must the simplicity and generality of theory which psychologists of learning have sought be replaced by a bewildering complexity of highly specific laws?

Although the recent findings we have discussed are discouraging for the more optimistic hopes of learning theorists, they are by no means disastrous. For one thing, the degree of generality of any given law is a matter to be determined by research. It remains to be seen how many of the laws of learning are specific to the stimulus, response, reinforcer, and species, and how many have instead the degree of generality for which learning theorists hope.

For another thing, it has always been the role of theory to organize laws in some more general way. Perhaps the situation now seems confused only because we have no good way to predict what particular combinations of stimuli, responses, and reinforcers will be easily learned by which species. What is needed is a theory that can tell us under what conditions a response is prepared, unprepared, or contraprepared. Finding the right bases of classification for independent and dependent variables and finding intervening variables to link them meaningfully is what theories are all about. The task of learning theory may be even more challenging than had previously been realized, but that does not mean that theorists cannot rise to the challenge. If the world of variables and laws relevant to learning seems to be in a state of confusion, there is all the more need for theories to bring order out of that confusion.

Moreover, there is already a basis for starting to find that order. Species-specific behavior and preparedness are part of the biological heritage of a given species. This heritage, however, is by no means random. The characteristics of any species have come about through the process of evolution, according to the principle of natural selection. Presumably, therefore, the characteristics of any species are those which have helped that species to survive. If we want to find order in the patterns of learning, we need to ask what patterns are likely to have had survival value in the environment where the ancestors of a given species lived.

Let us consider the case of a rat learning what to avoid in its environment. (For the present purpose it does not matter whether we assume it is learning a habit of avoidance or a cognition about what is dangerous.) If it gets sick, it is

probably because of something it ate, and the best way of recognizing that food
again is by taste or smell. Whether the dangerous food was in a place that was
light or dark or noisy or quiet probably had nothing to do with whether the food
would make it sick. It would therefore be to the rat's advantage to learn to avoid
any food that tasted like what it ate before it became ill, but it would not be to
its advantage to avoid eating in places that looked or sounded like the place where
it ate the tainted food. Suppose, however, that it suffered an injury. In that case,
the taste or smell of anything it ate just before would probably be irrelevant, but
what the place looked or sounded like would be much more likely to serve as a
warning of traps or predators or other dangers. It would thus be to its advantage
to avoid places that looked or sounded like the place where it was hurt, but of
no advantage to avoid foods that tasted like what it ate before it was hurt. The
reader will note that this is exactly the learning pattern that Garcia and Koelling
(1966) found.

Organic evolution and learning have a good deal in common, at least if one
takes a reinforcement view of learning. In natural selection those behaviors (as
well as structures) that work for a species are passed on to subsequent generations.
In learning, those behaviors that work for an individual are continued by that
individual. In learning, the mechanism is reinforcement of some behaviors and
not of others. In evolution the mechanism is selective survival and procreation:
those organisms that tend to behave in certain ways because of their genes are
more likely to survive and pass those genes on to their offspring. In spite of their
differences, both evolution and learning are adaptive mechanisms that increase
the effectiveness of organisms in dealing with their environment.

Given that both processes are forms of adaptation to the environment, it
remains only to look at their connection. The capacity to learn in certain ways
is one of the characteristics that increases (or decreases) through evolution. Or,
to put it another way, evolution determines the ways in which learning will occur
for a given species. In trying to predict an organism's preparedness for given
patterns of stimuli, responses, and reinforcers, it therefore seems reasonable to
ask, "What pattern would be most likely to have survival value in the environment in which this species evolved?" What this means is that a theory of learning
is most likely to be complete and accurate if it is a theory of evolution as well
—or, most generally, a theory of overall adaptation to the environment.

chapter *12*

Learning Theory Present and Future

In any survey of an area of knowledge, such as that attempted in this book, there is a great danger that the reader will come away with a kaleidoscope of impressions—some, we may hope, interesting and enlightening—but with no overall picture of the field. To a cognitive theorist, at least, such an outcome would seem most regrettable. In hopes of avoiding this, let us consider what the various interpretations we have examined can contribute to our understanding of learning.

ISSUES ON WHICH LEARNING THEORIES DIVIDE

The theories we have considered in this book can be grouped according to the ways they answer certain basic questions, including questions about both the nature of learning and the process of theory building (Hillner 1978). The answers to these questions indicate not the details of the theory but in broad outline what it tries to do and how it tries to do it. Eight such questions (differing somewhat from Hillner's) are given below.

Eight Controversial Questions

The first question a learning theorist needs to answer is whether or not to use intervening variables. Tolman, who introduced the idea of intervening variables into psychology, and Hull, who developed the most elaborate system, are the two theorists who have given the most emphatically positive answers to this question. Skinner, with his rejection of theories of learning, has given the clearest negative answer. Most theorists have included elements in their theories that could reasonably be called intervening variables, but often without labeling them as such. The most common answer to this question might therefore be given as "yes, but . . ."

The second question is whether the intervening variables, or whatever else plays a similar role in the theory, should be connectionist or cognitive. This is the question that has caused more argument than any other in the history of learning theory, and around which more than any other this book has been organized. The majority of theories through most of the history of the field have been connectionist, though with various concessions to the cognitive position, as in Hull's r_G. Recently, however, cognitive approaches have become increasingly popular. That trend has not been particularly obvious in this book, since much of the trend involves topics that we have not considered here. However, we have seen some examples of it in the changing approaches to memory, in the views of Bolles and Bindra, in the respect accorded Piaget, and even in some of the newer approaches to Pavlovian conditioning.

The third question deals with reinforcement: Is reinforcement a basic and central principle of learning, or is it a sloppy way of talking about certain phenomena that could more appropriately be explained in other ways? Thorndike, Hull, and Skinner have been among the strongest supporters of the former answer, and Watson and Guthrie the strongest supporters of the latter, with other theorists taking weaker intermediate positions. However, it has become increasingly evident that this is not an either-or question, that there are a number of possible positions about the way in which the consequences of actions affect subsequent behavior.

The fourth question, not as strongly argued but nonetheless significant, is whether learning should be analyzed at a molar or a molecular level. All theorists work at least partly at the molar level, that is, at the level of everyday acts, but they differ as to whether these acts should be explained by analysis at a more molecular level. Though Tolman was most explicit about staying at the molar level, the majority of the theorists we have considered also took a predominantly molar position. Two striking exceptions were Guthrie and Estes, both of whom saw the learning of molar acts as resulting from a more basic kind of learning at the molecular level, a conditioning of tiny elements that combine to produce the molar acts. Hull's theory and Estes's stimulus-sampling model provide a sharp contrast in this respect, given their similarities in various other respects.

The fifth question is whether the theory should be presented formally or casually. The majority of systems have been closer to the casual end of the scale: even when there was the suggestion of a strong logical structure to the theory (as, e.g., with Guthrie), it was not worked out with the formal trappings of logic and philosophy of science. Hull and Estes represent theorists, in contrast, who did have those formal trappings, who presented the logical structure of their theories explicitly. Tolman was fairly formal at times, but had trouble sticking to any one particular structure. A number of mathematical model builders have been formal, but they have not achieved the position of major theorists.

The sixth question is one of breadth: How wide a range of topics should a theory try to deal with? There is some tendency for those theories that answer the fifth question in favor of formality to answer this one in favor of narrowness. Almost inevitably, the more formally a theory is stated, the more rigorous and precise it will have to be, which in turn makes it harder for it to deal effectively with a wide range of topics. A more casually stated theory, on the other hand, can deal with a wider range of topics with less danger of being caught in inconsistencies or ambiguities. Nevertheless, a theory that would combine formal precision with great breadth is such a desirable goal that its challenge has continued to lure theorists. Hull tried hard to achieve such a theory, and while part of his failure can be attributed to his invalidism and premature death, part of it also reflects the enormous difficulty of the challenge. While Estes also tried to combine formality with at least a substantial degree of breadth, few since Hull have been so bold.

The seventh question is how much emphasis to give to the innate aspects of behavior and to the biological constraints on learning. This has only recently become an issue and for most of the theories we have considered the answer has been, not much emphasis. American learning theory, from Watson and Thorndike on, has emphasized the acquired over the innate; while Watson's rejection of hereditary factors was extreme, it nevertheless set the tone for the field. Increasingly, however, theorists are considering this issue. Bolles has emphasized it, and the Skinnerians are increasingly making concessions to it. The question is how far those concessions should go. Are we now in a phase that overemphasizes the innate, as the earlier phase probably overestimated the acquired, or are we only beginning to discover the actual extent of biological constraints on learning and behavior? It is a question for which theorists are only starting to stand up and be counted.

Finally, there is the question of practicality. Is a theory of learning a creation of the laboratory and the armchair, an intellectual exercise in understanding the world, or is it a device for dealing with and perhaps changing that world? Though at times theorists have demanded the right to do pure science, undistracted by any pressures toward practical usefulness, that attitude has been distinctly the exception. The question is not so much whether or not theories of learning should be useful but rather who should do the applying. Some theorists, like Thorndike and Skinner, have jumped directly into applications. Others, like Miller and Tolman, have written about possible applications but played relatively little part in putting them into practice. Still others, like Hull, have been themselves pure scientists but had substantial influence on others of a more applied bent. Even these examples are debatable; the distinction is a hard one to maintain, given the generally applied nature of American learning theory.

Positions of the Right, Left, and Center

Although all of the above issues have to some extent divided learning theories, the two that dominated much of the history of the field were the second and third, as can be inferred from the table of contents of this book. If we look at the positions various theorists took on these two issues, we can see the history of

American learning theory through the greater part of the twentieth century as consisting of a mainstream that dominated the field, withstood challenges from different directions, incorporated some of those challenges within the mainstream, and continued on its way. This is the connectionist, reinforcement tradition that began with Thorndike, reached its greatest theoretical flowering in Hull, and has recently been dominated by Skinner. It may seem odd, given the sharp disagreements between Hull and Skinner about both theory construction and research technique, to group them together in this way, especially since Skinner is not a connectionist in the narrow sense of talking about habits or stimulus-response bonds as something inside the organism. Nevertheless, they stand together in contrast to two other traditions that have challenged the mainstream.

Perhaps it would be best at this point to change the metaphor to a political one and speak of the mainstream instead as a party of the center, whose basic principle is that what is learned is the tendency to make various responses, and that an essential feature in that learning is reinforcement. This party of the center has been challenged both from the right and from the left by smaller though vocal parties. The party of the right has agreed enthusiastically with the center that what was learned was responses, and has focused even more consistently than has the center on the stimulus-response bond as the unit of learning. It disagreed with the center, however, in rejecting the central role of reinforcement in favor of simple contiguity as the basic principle of learning. It is the most mechanistic of the approaches, and it focuses particularly on the importance of practice and of learning by doing. The outstanding figures in this party of the right were Watson and Guthrie. Its challenge to the center was thus most dominant in the earlier part of the century, though its influence continues to be felt.

The challenge from the left, in contrast, has to a considerable degree ignored the reinforcement issue and instead concentrated on rejecting the idea that responses are what is learned. Instead, they argue that we learn knowledge, beliefs, expectancies, understanding—in other words, cognitions. Among actual learning theorists, the outstanding early exponent of this position was Tolman. Although Tolman himself never succeeded in founding a school of psychology, his point of view remained influential. For a number of years, as we have seen, the dominant theme in learning theory was the attempt by the center to incorporate cognitive ideas like Tolman's into its theories while still maintaining a basically connectionist orientation. More recently, the cognitive approach has become increasingly strong, so that many would argue that it has now replaced connectionism in the center.

What is the present situation? Although the old right no longer represents a strong position, in a limited sense it made its point. Few theorists now regard reinforcement in the Thorndikian way, as stamping in stimulus-response bonds. Rather, the majority see learning as taking place by contiguity, as the right claimed, and reinforcement as affecting only the performance of what has already been learned. However, this learning by contiguity is seen as involving contiguity of stimuli with other stimuli rather than of stimuli with responses, so this view contains more of Tolman, Bolles, Bandura, and the later Mowrer than of Guthrie or Watson. Indeed, the main question is whether the left has now become the center, crowding the former center off to the right, or whether in spite of the expansion on the left, the situation remains basically the same as it has been through most of the twentieth century.

The argument focuses particularly on Skinner's place in the current scene. On the one hand, he more than anyone else represents learning theory to those outside the field. This is ironic, in view of his claim not to be a theorist, yet it is just as an exemplar of the traditional ideals of learning theory—straightforward, wide-ranging, practical—that Skinner stands. He does not represent the psychology of learning as a whole, which is now too cognitive for his taste, but the traditional connectionist-reinforcement mainstream of learning theory, a direct descendent of Thorndike. Does he represent the last flickering popularization of a dying tradition, one that is being replaced by a more solid, if more modest, analysis of learning, or does he represent those aspects of learning theory that will have lasting influence on psychology and on other fields when the present models of this or that learning phenomenon have been relegated to the dust bin of psychological history? Only time can tell.

CRITERIA FOR AN IDEAL THEORY

The arguments among theorists of learning are not as strident as they were in the "golden age" of learning theory, when Hull and Spence traded barbs with Guthrie on the right and Tolman on the left, while Skinner in effect said, "A plague on all your houses." More of the theorizing is in the form of models for predicting a narrower range of phenomena, with each theorist trying to see how far a given model can go in predicting data. An extreme example of this approach is seen in the title of an article by Frank Restle, (1966) "Run Structure and Probability Learning: Disproof of Restle's Model." Nevertheless, more general disagreements do remain, and we can reasonably ask to what extent the questions raised in the previous section can now be resolved. To put it another way, can we now see what the criteria for an ideal theory of learning would be?

The ideal kind of theory toward which the most ambitious theorists strive is much like the ideal that Hull set up but failed to realize: formal, precise, internally consistent, yet at the same time broad enough to cover the whole range of topics in learning and motivation. It would have postulates and theorems and would be so constructed that it could be changed to deal with new evidence as one or another theorem failed to be confirmed by experiments. Given this combination of breadth and precision, it inevitably would be useful in the solution of practical problems.

This ideal theory would undoubtedly include intervening variables, and being a formal theory it would be quite explicit about what they were. Whether they would be connectionist or cognitive is still not altogether clear. However, we can come closer to an answer now than we could without the computer to use as a model. It would have to deal with the acquisition, storage, and use of information, with beliefs and the evidence on which they are based, with both logical and illogical thinking and problem solving. It would thus have a very cognitive sound—not only more so than any of the connectionist theories we have considered, but perhaps even more so than some of the cognitive ones. However, there would be postulates linking the cognitions not only to behavior but also to the processes by which cognitions are acquired and changed, which would make it more behavioristic than such highly cognitive theories as Lewin's. So, while its format would be most like Hull's and also bear some resemblance to Estes's, its content would be most like Tolman's.

Such a cognitive theory would be less disturbing to connectionist theorists than would be the case if we were not familiar with computers. Since the computer, which is physically a connectionist device, can be programmed to behave in such cognitive ways, a connectionist theorist might argue that he was right all along, that this is really a connectionist theory which deals effectively with the behaviors, including internal ones, of reasoning, imagining, remembering, and planning. It could thus be considered either an updating of Tolman or an outstanding example of a connectionist move in cognitive directions.

Moreover, the theory would need to be somewhat connectionist in another sense. It would have to explain not only our knowledge and understanding but also the responses we make automatically without thinking and the skills we are able to perform without being able to explain just how we do them. Even Tolman (1949) conceded that there is noncognitive learning of "motor patterns." Again the computer analogy is helpful, since computers can just as easily be programmed to make certain specific responses under certain conditions as to behave in more cognitive ways. So, while the details of the theory will be very complex, there should be no problem for the theorist in having some of those details appear straightforwardly connectionist and others highly cognitive.

The complexity of the theory would be of a developmental sort. In other words, it would explain how humans and animals get programmed to function in the way they do. "Programmed," of course, reflects again the computer analogy. A computer system consists basically of certain "hardware," comparable to the physique, perceptual and learning capacities, and innate motivational tendencies of an organism. To be useful, it must also have "software," the programs to determine what it will do. Whereas computer programs are written by people, the programs of people and animals are developed through experience. Learning can thus be regarded as the process that corresponds to program writing. We might say either that a computer is like an animal that has been carefully trained, or that an animal (or person) is like a computer with a very open-ended program that in effect keeps rewriting itself on the basis of its experience.

The hardware, of course, corresponds to those species-specific characteristics that set constraints on behavior and learning. Some computers can do jobs that others cannot. Of two that can both do a job, one can often do it faster than the other or the procedure that is fastest for one computer to do it may be different from that which is fastest for the other. These are the same sorts of differences that are found among species of animals, and to a lesser extent among individuals within a species. They are the constraints within which learning has to work, but within which it can still produce enormous individual differences in behavior depending on differences in experience.

The results of this long-term programming would have a hierarchical structure, as suggested by Gagné and numerous other people. As indicated above, the hierarchy would include both knowledge that can be expressed in words or other symbols and skills that to a considerable degree cannot. These skills would very likely be analyzed in cybernetic terms, with each unit of skill in the hierarchy dependent on lower-level units that would serve to maintain the set point of the higher-level unit. The process by which all of these hierarchies would develop would be one of accommodation, as described by Piaget, in which the structure would gradually change in response to experiences that were inconsistent with it. However, in most cases these accommodations would not be simply changes but rather the incorporation of less adequate patterns of skill and understanding into higher-level patterns that would include their good points while at the same time improving on them. Though this process includes the possibility of mistaken or maladaptive learning, such as that discussed by Dollard and Miller, for the most part it would represent a continuing increase both in complexity and in effectiveness.

How would reinforcement and motivation be treated? This is probably the hardest question for which to provide even the rough outline of an answer. On the one hand, as we have noted, there is fairly wide support for the view that much learning depends only on contiguity, without the need for reinforcement. This includes not only learning by doing but also learning by observation, as emphasized particularly by Bandura. In this view we acquire knowledge and skills by a mixture of observation and practice. Among the things we learn are what activities toward what objects are rewarding or punishing. We then use our knowledge and skills to obtain access to the rewards and to avoid the punishments. When we speak of a motive what we mean is a certain class of rewards (such as food, or sex, or prestige) along with the knowledge and skills connected with obtaining those rewards.

On the other hand, there seem clearly to be some cases that do not fit this interpretation. When we gradually master a skill without being able to explain completely what we are now doing differently, the best explanation seems to be that the precise responses that work are being acquired and those that don't work are dropping out. Though Guthrie would say that "work" means "change the situation into something else," most people would insist that it means "change the situation into something *better.*" This latter meaning sounds like traditional Thorndikian reinforcement: stamping in the rewarded stimulus-response bonds. So, although the simple, old-fashioned notion of reinforcement is a good deal less popular than it used to be, it doesn't look as though we can entirely get rid of it.

Perhaps the ideas of cybernetics can help here. They suggest that all the stimuli which Skinner would call positive reinforcers are signals that a deviation is being corrected, that one is moving closer to a set point. With higher-level set points, we can describe accurately what is happening, and in those cases we may speak of the set point as an incentive toward which behavior is directed. With lower-level set points we are only hazily able to describe what is happening, making the term "incentive" seem inappropriate. However, what is actually going on is the same at all levels: a set point, deviations from it, behavior that serves to reduce the deviation, and "reinforcement" by getting closer to the set point. The principles are the same; only the degree of our conscious awareness is different. This is one direction from which a resolution of the question about reinforcement might eventually come. It would be ironic if cybernetics, which has very little to say directly about learning, should nevertheless provide the answer to such a persistent issue in learning theory as the nature and significance of reinforcement!

Two other aspects of learning need to be considered, though they were not referred to in the questions in the preceding section. One is the nature of memory. To the extent that we focus on knowledge and on learning by observation, it seems more consistent to treat memory as a matter of information stored and retrieved than as a matter of competing responses. On the other hand, for highly practiced skills, including verbal ones, interference theory seems more appropriate. To what extent these models lead to different predictions is not altogether clear. Moreover, no complete theory can afford to ignore the way that new experiences get assimilated into schemata. Though we considered this process as it is usually considered, in terms of information, it operates at the level of muscular coordinations as well. For example, a speaker of English assimilates foreign speech sounds to the sounds in English that they most nearly resemble, thus achieving an adequate approximation to the foreign language, but always with an English accent. Though such assimilation to schemata needs to be included in any complete theory of learning, it also needs to be developed in more precise detail than has so far been done.

The other aspect of learning that needs to be considered is perception. Most learning theorists have taken perception for granted, while the Gestaltists, who focused on perception, were only secondarily theorists of learning. However, learning can be no better than the perceptual input on which it is based, so that the topic cannot be ignored by any complete theory. Atkinson and Shiffrin's reference to the sensory register is one example of a perceptual concept in a theory of learning (or of memory). Theories dealing with how we interpret what we see and hear have become increasingly prominent in psychology, so much so, in fact, that to have included them in this book would have carried us too far afield. Nevertheless, they would represent an important part of any complete theory, if not of learning, at least of learned behavior.

Along with perception goes the related topic of attention. Though theorists differ as to whether it is possible to learn about something without paying any attention to it, we can at least say with confidence that one usually learns more about something to which one is paying attention than about something to which one is not. Such concepts as "observing response," "acquired distinctiveness of cues," and "blocking" all refer to the selectivity of attention, to our learning (not always correctly) which aspects of a situation are worth noticing and which are not. Though the selectivity of attention is itself receiving a lot more attention than in the "golden age" of learning theory, it is not yet fully integrated into most theories of learning. To what extent special principles are needed to deal with it remains to be seen.

THE PRESENT-DAY VALUE OF LEARNING THEORY

Whatever form the theory of the future may take, most of us have to make the best of the theories we have today. Granted that all of them fall short of the ideals we have set for a truly adequate theory, what use can we make of them? For the most part, whatever exact predictions they make are applicable only to carefully controlled laboratory conditions. They can rarely predict directly to the complex, uncontrolled conditions of everyday life. Even with the most precise of scientific theories, engineers are needed who can use their ingenuity and experience to apply the theory to practical ends. Since theories of learning are not among the most precise, this "psychological engineering" is perhaps even more challenging than in other areas of science. Such "engineering" enters into many jobs, from animal training to psychological warfare, but above all it is the province of the educator.

Hilgard (1964) has argued that a single category of behavioral engineers or applied psychologists, in contrast to pure research psychologists, is much too simple. He suggests that we can distinguish six steps along the scale from the "purest" of researchers on learning at one extreme to the "purest" of educational appliers at the other. The first three steps are all under the heading of "pure-science research," but vary in the extent to which the learners and the learned materials resemble those in ordinary educational practice. The remaining three steps, which he groups under "technological research and development," are of more specific interest here. These are: step 4—"research conducted in special laboratory classrooms, with selected teachers"; step 5—"a tryout of the results of prior research in a 'normal' classroom with a typical teacher"; step 6—"developmental steps related to advocacy and adoption" [1964, p. 409]. Here the research and development proceed from asking, "Will it work under the best of conditions?" in step 4, to "Will it work under typical conditions?" in step 5, to "Will it be generally adopted by educators?" in step 6.

The applied psychology of learning is important not only as a way of putting theories to practical use but also as a way of improving theories. Along with their other contributions, applied studies help to determine the boundary conditions of theories. If a theory based on laboratory data is used to make predictions to an applied situation, and the predictions are not confirmed, this event shows that the theory is not appropriate for that situation. It may still, however, be a perfectly good theory for predicting in other situations. In addition, applied studies reveal new laws that may then be used in the modification of old theories or the construction of new ones. For example, as we noted earlier, Gagné developed his ideas about the hierarchical organization of tasks largely as a result of an unsuccessful attempt to apply more traditional laws of learning to the problems of military training. The ideas about learning that emerged from that applied work served as the basis for new theoretical developments in the pure psychology of learning.

For most of us, the various learning theories have two chief values. One is in providing us with a vocabulary and a conceptual framework for interpreting the examples of learning that we observe. These are valuable for anyone who is alert to the world. The other, closely related, is in suggesting where to look for solutions to practical problems. The theories do not give us solutions, but they do direct our attention to those variables that are crucial in finding solutions.

Let us consider the ways in which various theoretical interpreters do these two things for us. Guthrie directs our attention to the importance of practicing the particular responses to be learned under the particular conditions in which they will be used, and also to the value of practicing them under varied conditions if they are to be firmly established. Skinner advises us always to find out what reinforces a given act, so that we can present that reinforcer if we want the act to occur or remove it if we want to extinguish the act. Miller and Dollard warn us to consider the secondary drives that may be learned in a situation and may then serve as the basis of new, often undesired, learning. Wertheimer and Köhler point out the importance of arranging learning situations so as to foster real, creative understanding rather than blind rote memorization. Lewin suggests that we try to reconstruct the learner's life space, with the tensions and goals and the paths and barriers that the learner perceives. Piaget and Gagné emphasize the extent to which present learning develops out of earlier learning. Tolman, Hull, and Estes offer many of these same suggestions in more technical form. All of these suggestions require ingenuity if they are to be put to practical use. Each, however, serves to emphasize some aspect of the learning process that we would be wise to consider. Thus each serves both to enrich our understanding of the learning situations we observe and to help us find solutions to the practical learning problems with which we have to deal. While many theorists aspire to make a greater contribution than this, and to some extent succeed in doing so, this contribution alone is enough to make these theories invaluable to the study of learning.

References

Allison, J. 1979. Demand economics and experimental psychology. *Behavioral Science* 24: 403–15.

Amsel, A. 1958. The role of frustrative nonreward in noncontinuous reward situations. *Psychological Bulletin* 55: 201–19.

———1962. Frustrative nonreward in partial reinforcement and discrimination learning: Some recent history and a theoretical extension. *Psychological Review* 69: 306–28.

———. 1967. Partial reinforcement effects on vigor and persistence. In *The psychology of learning and motivation,* eds. K. W. Spence and J. T. Spence, vol. 1. New York: Academic Press.

Atkinson, R. C. 1974. Teaching children to read using a computer. *American Psychologist* 29: 169–78.

Atkinson, R. C., & Shiffrin, R. M. 1968. Human memory: A proposed system and its control processes. In *The psychology of learning and motivation: Advances in research and theory,* eds. K. W. Spence & J. T. Spence, vol. 2. New York: Academic Press.

———. 1971. The control of short-term memory. *Scientific American* 224: 82–90.

Bandura, A., ed. 1971. *Psychological modeling: Conflicting theories.* Chicago: Aldine-Atherton.

———. 1973. *Aggression.* Englewood Cliffs: Prentice-Hall.

———. 1977. *Social learning theory.* Englewood Cliffs, N.J.: Prentice-Hall.

Bandura, A., Adams, N. E., & Beyer, J. 1977. Cognitive processes mediating behavioral change. *Journal of Personality and Social Psychology* 35: 125–39.

Bandura, A., & Walters, R. H. 1963. *Social learning and personality development.* New York: Holt, Rinehart and Winston.

Bartlett, F.C. 1932. *Remembering.* London: Cambridge University Press.

Benson, H., Shapiro, D., Tursky, B., & Schwartz, G. E. 1971. Decreased systolic blood pressure through operant conditioning techniques in patients with essential hypertension. *Science* 173: 740–42.

Berlyne, D. E. 1960. *Conflict, arousal, and curiosity.* New York: McGraw-Hill.

Berlyne, D. E., & Madsen, K. B., eds. 1973. *Pleasure, reward, preference: Their nature, determinants, and role in behavior.* New York: Academic Press.

Bindra, D. 1974. A motivational view of learning, performance, and behavior modification. *Psychological Review* 81: 199–213.

Bolles, R. C. 1970. Species-specific defense reactions and avoidance learning. *Psychological Review* 77: 32–48.

———. 1972. Reinforcement, expectancy, and learning. *Psychological Review* 79: 394–409.

Bolles, R. C., Holtz, R., Dunn, T., & Hill, W. 1980. Comparisons of stimulus learning and response learning in a punishment situation. *Learning and Motivation* 11: 78–96.

Boneau, C. A. 1974. Paradigm regained? Cognitive behaviorism restated. *American Psychologist* 29: 297–309.

Bootzin, R. R. 1975. *Behavior modification and therapy.* Cambridge, Mass.: Winthrop.

Bower, G. H. 1972. Mental imagery and associative learning. In *Cognition in learning and memory,* ed. L. G. Gregg. New York: Wiley.

Breland, K., & Breland, M. 1961. The misbehavior of organisms. *American Psychologist* 16: 681–84.

Brown, P. L., & Jenkins, H. M. 1968. Auto-shaping of the pigeon's key peck. *Journal of the Experimental Analysis of Behavior* 11: 1–8.

Budzynski, T. H., Stoyva, J. M., Adler, C. S., & Mullaney, D. J. 1973. EMG biofeedback and tension headache: A controlled outcome study. *Psychosomatic Medicine* 35: 484–96.

Buxton, C. E. 1940. Latent learning and the goal gradient hypothesis. *Contributions to Psychological Theory* 2: (6).

Campbell, D. T., & Krantz, D. L. "Tolman's failure as a tribal leader: An essay in the social psychology of science." Paper read at 82nd annual convention of the American Psychological Association, 1 September 1974, New Orleans. Mimeographed.

Cowan, P. A., Langer, J., Heavenrich, J., & Nathanson, M. 1969. Social learning and Piaget's cognitive theory of moral development. *Journal of Personality and Social Psychology* 11: 261–74.

Craik, F. I. M., & Lockhart, R. S. 1972. Levels of processing: A framework for memory research. *Journal of Verbal Learning and Verbal Behavior* 11: 671–84.

Daly, H. B. 1969. Learning of a hurdle-jump response to escape cues paired with reduced reward or frustrative nonreward. *Journal of Experimental Psychology* 79: 146–57.

Dollard, J. C., & Miller, N. E. 1950. *Personality and psychotherapy.* New York: McGraw-Hill.

Ebbinghaus, H. 1913. *Memory: A contribution to experimental psychology.* Trans. by H. A. Ruger & C. E. Bussenius. New York: Teachers College, Columbia Univ. Reprint. New York: Dover, 1964.

Elms, A. C. 1981. Skinner's dark year and *Walden Two. American Psychologist* 36: 470–79.

Epstein, S. 1967. Toward a unified theory of anxiety. In *Progress in experimental personality research,* ed. B. A. Maher, vol. 4. New York: Academic Press.

Ernst, G., & Newell, A. 1969. *GPS: A case study in generality and problem solving.* New York: Academic Press.

Estes, W. K. 1959. The statistical approach to learning theory. In *Psychology: A study of a science,* ed. S. Koch, vol. 2. New York: McGraw-Hill.

————. 1964. Probability learning. In *Categories of human learning,* ed. A. W. Melton. New York: Academic Press.

————. 1976. The cognitive side of probability learning. *Psychological Review* 83: 37–64.

Feigenbaum, E. A., & Feldman, J., eds. 1963. *Computers and thought.* New York: McGraw-Hill.

Ferster, C. B., & Skinner, B. F. 1957. *Schedules of reinforcement.* New York: Appleton-Century-Crofts.

Flavell, J. H. 1963. *The developmental psychology of Jean Piaget.* New York: Van Nostrand.

Fleming, R. A., Grant, D. A., North, J. A., & Levy, C. M. 1968. Arithmetic correctness as the discriminandum in classical and differential eyelid conditioning. *Journal of Experimental Psychology* 77: 286–94.

Frey, P. 1983. *Chess skill in man and machine.* 2nd ed. New York: Springer-Verlag.

Frey, P. W., & Sears, R. J. 1978. Model of conditioning incorporating the Rescorla-Wagner associative axiom, a dynamic attention process, and a catastrophe rule. *Psychological Review* 85: 321–40.

Gagné, R. M. 1962a. The acquisition of knowledge. *Psychological Review* 69: 355–65.

————. 1962b. Military training and principles of learning. *American Psychologist* 17, 83–91.

Garcia, J., & Koelling, R. 1966. Relation of cue to consequence in avoidance learning. *Psychonomic Science* 4: 123–24.

Gardner, B. T., & Gardner, R. A. 1980. Two comparative psychologists look at language acquisition. In *Children's language,* ed. K. E. Nelson, vol. 2. New York: Halsted.

Gardner, R. A., & Gardner, B. T. 1969. Teaching sign language to a chimpanzee. *Science*, 165: 664–672.

Glickman, S. E., & Schiff, B. B. 1967. A biological theory of reinforcement. *Psychological Review* 74: 81–109.

Goss, A. E., & Greenfeld, N. 1958. Transfer to a motor task as influenced by conditions and degree of prior discrimination training. *Journal of Experimental Psychology* 55: 258–69.

Greenspoon, J. 1955. The reinforcing effect of two spoken sounds on the frequency of two responses. *American Journal of Psychology* 68: 409–16.

Guthrie, E. R. 1960. *The psychology of learning.* Rev. ed. Gloucester, MA: Smith.

Guthrie, E. R., & Horton, G. P. 1946. *Cats in a puzzle box.* New York: Rinehart.

Haggbloom, S. J. 1981. Blocking in successive differential conditioning: Prior acquisition of control by internal cues blocks the acquisition of control by brightness. *Learning and Motivation* 12: 485–508.

Hanson, H. M. 1959. Effects of discrimination training on stimulus generalization. *Journal of Experimental Psychology* 58: 321–34.

Harlow, H. F. 1958. The nature of love. *American Psychologist* 18: 673–85.

————. 1959. Learning set and error factor theory. In *Psychology: A study of a science,* ed. S. Koch, vol. 2. New York: McGraw-Hill.

Hart, B. M., Allen, K. E., Buell, J. S., Harris, F. R., & Wolf, M. M. 1964. Effects of social reinforcement on operant crying. *Journal of Experimental Child Psychology* 1: 145–53.

Hebb, D. O. 1949. *The organization of behavior.* New York: Wiley.

Hilgard, E. R. 1964. A perspective on the relationship between learning theory and educational practices. In *Theories of learning and instruction. Sixty-third yearbook of the National Society for the Study of Education. Part I,* ed. E. R. Hilgard. Chicago: Univ. of Chicago Press.

Hilgard, E. R., & Marquis, D. G. 1940. *Conditioning and learning.* New York: Appleton-Century-Crofts.

Hill, W. F. 1956. Activity as an autonomous drive. *Journal of Comparative and Physiological Psychology* 49: 15–19.

———. 1968. Sources of evaluative reinforcement. *Psychological Bulletin* 69: 132–46.

———. 1978. Effects of mere exposure on preferences in nonhuman mammals. *Psychological Bulletin* 85: 1177–98.

Hillner, K. P. 1978. *Psychology of Learning: A conceptual analysis.* New York: Pergamon.

Hoffman, H. S., Eiserer, L. A., Ratner, A. M., & Pickering, V. L. 1974. Development of distress vocalization during withdrawal of an imprinting stimulus. *Journal of Comparative and Physiological Psychology* 86: 563–68.

Hull, C. L. 1943. *Principles of behavior.* New York: Appleton-Century-Crofts.

———. 1952. *A behavior system.* New Haven: Yale Univ. Press.

Huxley, A. L. 1932. *Brave new world.* London: Chatto & Windus.

Ingles, J., Campbell, D., & Donald, M. W. 1976. Electromyographic biofeedback and neuromuscular rehabilitation. *Canadian Journal of Behavioral Science* 8: 299–323.

Kagan, J., & Berkun, M. 1954. The reward value of running activity. *Journal of Comparative and Physiological Psychology* 47: 108.

Kamin, L. J. 1968. Attention-like processes in classical conditioning. In *Miami symposium on the prediction of behavior: Aversive stimulation,* ed. M. R. Jones. Miami: Univ. of Miami Press.

Katkin, E. S., & Murray, E. N. 1968. Instrumental conditioning of autonomically mediated behavior: Theoretical and methodological issues. *Psychological Bulletin* 70: 52–68.

Keppel, G., Postman, L., & Zavortink, B. 1968. Studies of learning to learn: 8. The influence of massive amounts of training upon the learning and retention of paired-associate lists. *Journal of Verbal Learning and Verbal Behavior* 7: 790–96.

Kimmel, H. D. 1967. Instrumental conditioning of autonomically mediated behavior. *Psychological Bulletin* 67: 337–45.

Kinkade, K. 1973. *A Walden Two experiment: The first 5 years of Twin Oaks Community.* New York: Morrow.

Koffka, K. 1925. *The growth of the mind.* Trans. by R. M. Ogden. New York: Harcourt Brace Jovanovich.

———. 1935. *Principles of gestalt psychology.* New York: Harcourt Brace Jovanovich.

Kohlberg, L. 1964. *The development of moral character and ideology.* In M. L. Hoffman & L. W. Hoffman (Eds.), Review of child developmental research. Vol. 1. New York: Russell Sage.

Köhler, W. 1925. *The mentality of apes.* Trans. from 2nd rev. ed. by Ella Winter. New York: Harcourt Brace Jovanovich.

Lawicka, W. 1964. The role of stimuli modality in successive discrimination and differentiation learning. *Bulletin of the Polish Academy of Sciences* 12: 35–38.

Lawrence, D. H., 1949. Acquired distinctiveness of cues: I. Transfer between discriminations on the basis of familiarity with the stimulus. *Journal of Experimental Psychology* 39: 770–84.

———. 1950. Acquired distinctiveness of cues. II. Selective association in a constant stimulus situation. *Journal of Experimental Psychology* 40: 175–88.

Lewin, K. 1935. Dynamic theory of personality. Trans. by D. K. Adams and K. E. Zener. New York: McGraw-Hill.

———. 1936. Principles of topological psychology. Trans. by F. Heider and G. M. Heider. New York: McGraw-Hill.

Linden, E. *Apes, men, and language.* 1974. New York: Saturday Review Press, E. P. Dutton.

Loftus, E. F. 1975. Leading questions and the eyewitness report. *Cognitive Psychology* 7: 560–72.

Loftus, E. F., Miller, D. G., & Burns, H. J. 1978. Semantic integration of verbal information into a visual memory. *Journal of Experimental Psychology: Human Learning and Memory* 4: 19–31.

Lorenz, K. Z. 1952. *King Solomon's ring.* New York: Crowell.

Lovaas, O. I., Koegel, R., Simmons, J. Q., & Long, J. S. 1973. Some generalization and follow-up measures on autistic children in behavior therapy. *Journal of Applied Behavior Analysis* 6: 131–66.

Mandler, J. M. 1978. A code in the node: The use of a story schema in retrieval. *Discourse processes* 1: 14–35.

Miller, G. A. 1956. The magical number seven, plus or minus two: Some limits on our capacity for processing information. *Psychological Review* 63: 81–97.

Miller, N. E. 1963. Some reflections on the law of effect produce a new alternative to drive reduction. In *Nebraska symposium on motivation,* ed. M. R. Jones, vol. 11. Lincoln: Univ. of Nebraska Press.

Miller, N. E., & Dollard, J. C. 1941. *Social learning and imitation.* New Haven: Yale Univ. Press.

Moore, B. R., & Stuttard, S. 1979. Dr. Guthrie and *Felis domesticus* On: Tripping over the cat. *Science* 205: 1031–33.

Mowrer, O. H. 1947. On the dual nature of learning: A re-interpretation of "conditioning" and "problem-solving." *Harvard Educational Review* 17: 102–48.

———. 1960. *Learning theory and behavior.* New York: Wiley.

Orwell, G. 1949. *1984.* New York: Harcourt Brace Jovanovich.

Osgood, C. E., Suci, G. J., & Tannenbaum, P. H. 1957. *The measurement of meaning.* Urbana: Univ. of Illinois Press.

Paivio, A. 1971. *Imagery and verbal processes.* New York: Holt, Rinehart & Winston.

Paskewitz, D. A., & Orne, M. T. 1973. Visual effects on alpha feedback training. *Science* 181: 360–63.

Pavlov, I. P. 1960. *Conditioned reflexes.* Trans. & ed. by G. V. Anrep. New York: Dover. (orig. trans. Oxford Univ. Press, 1927).

Phillips, J. L., Jr. 1969. *The origins of intellect: Piaget's theory.* San Francisco: Freeman.

Piaget, J. 1926. *The language and thought of the child.* Trans. by M. Worden. New York: Harcourt Brace Jovanovich.

———. 1932. *The moral development of the child.* New York: Harcourt, Brace.

Powers, W. T. 1973. *Behavior: The control of perception.* Chicago: Aldine.

Premack, D. 1959. Toward empirical behavior laws: I. Positive reinforcement. *Psychological Review* 66: 219–33.

———. 1962. Reversibility of the reinforcement relation. *Science* 136: 255–57.

Razran, G. 1961. The observable unconscious and the inferable conscious in current Soviet psychophysiology: Interoceptive conditioning, semantic conditioning, and the orienting reflex. *Psychological Review* 68: 81–147.

Rescorla, R. A., & Wagner, A. R. 1972. A theory of Pavlovian conditioning: variations in the effectiveness of reinforcement and nonreinforcement. In *Classical conditioning II,* eds. A. Black & W. F. Prokasy New York: Appleton-Century-Crofts.

Restle, F. 1966. Run structure and probability learning: Disproof of Restle's model. *Journal of Experimental Psychology,* 72, 382–389.

Rosenfeld, H. M., & Baer, D. M. 1969. Unnoticed verbal conditioning of an aware experimenter by a more aware subject: The double-agent effect. *Psychological Review* 76: 425–32.

Schank, R. C., & Abelson, R., 1977. *Scripts, plans, goals, and understanding.* Hillsdale, N.J.: Erlbaum.

Schank, R. C., & Colby, K. M., eds. 1973. *Computer models of thought and language.* San Francisco: Freeman.

Seligman, M. E. P. 1970. On the generality of the laws of learning. *Psychological Review* 77: 406–18.

Seligman, M. E. P., & Johnston, J. C. 1973. A cognitive theory of avoidance learning. In *Contemporary approaches to conditioning and learning,* eds. F. J. McGuigan & D. B. Lumsden. Washington, D.C.: V. H. Winston.

Seward, J. P. 1942. An experimental study of Guthrie's theory of reinforcement. *Journal of Experimental Psychology* 30: 247–56.

Sheffield, F. D., & Roby, T. B. 1950. Reward value of a non-nutritive sweet taste. *Journal of Comparative and Physiological Psychology* 43: 471–81.

Shiffrin, R. M., & Atkinson, R. C. 1969. Storage and retrieval processes in long-term memory. *Psychological Review* 76: 179–93.

Skinner, B. F. 1938. *The behavior of organisms: An experimental analysis.* New York: Appleton-Century-Crofts.

———. 1948. *Walden Two.* New York: Macmillan.

———. 1953. *Science and human behavior.* New York: Macmillan.

———. 1957a. The experimental analysis of behavior. *American Scientist* 45: 343–71. (a)

———. 1957b. *Verbal behavior.* New York: Appleton-Century-Crofts.

———. 1958. Reinforcement today. *American Psychologist* 13: 94–99.

———. 1968. *The technology of teaching.* New York: Appleton-Century-Crofts.

———. 1971. *Beyond freedom and dignity.* New York: Knopf.

———. 1979. *The shaping of a behaviorist: Part two of an autobiography.* New York: Knopf.

Smith, K. U., & Smith, M. F. 1966. *Cybernetic principles of learning and educational design.* New York: Holt, Rinehart & Winston.

Smith, M. L., & Glass, G. V. 1977. Meta-analysis of psychotherapy outcome studies. *American Psychologist* 32: 752–60.

Solomon, R. L. 1980. The opponent-process theory of acquired motivation: The costs of pleasure and the benefits of pain. *American Psychologist* 35: 691–712.

Solomon, R. L., & Corbit, J. D. 1974. An opponent-process theory of motivation: I. Temporal dynamics of affect. *Psychological Review* 81: 119–45.

Spence, K. W. 1956. *Behavior theory and conditioning.* New Haven: Yale Univ. Press.

Sperling, G. 1960. The information available in high visual presentations. *Psychological Monographs* 74, no. 11.

Spielberger, C. D., & DeNike, L. D. 1966. Descriptive behaviorism versus cognitive theory in verbal operant conditioning. *Psychological Review* 73: 306–26.

Spiro, R. J. 1976. Remembering information from text: The "state of schema" approach. In *Schooling and the acquisition of knowledge,* eds. R. C. Anderson, R. J. Spiro, & W. F. Montague. Hillsdale, N.J.: Erlbaum.

Strayer, F., Scott, W. B., & Bakan, P. 1973. A re-examination of alpha feedback training: Operant conditioning or perceptual differentiation? *Canadian Journal of Psychology* 27: 247–53.

Sullivan, E. V. 1967. The acquisition of conservation of substance through film-mediated models. In *Recent research on the acquisition of conservation of substance,* eds. D.

W. Brison & E. V. Sullivan. Education Monograph. Toronto: Ontario Institute for Studies in Education.

Terrace, H. S. 1963. Discrimination learning with and without "errors." *Journal of the Experimental Analysis of Behavior* 6: 1–27.

———. 1971. Escape from S—. *Learning and Motivation* 2: 148–63.

Thorndike, E. L. 1898. Animal intelligence: An experimental study of the associative processes in animals. *Psychological Review Monograph Supplements* 2, no. 8.

———. *The psychology of learning.* 1913. New York: Teachers College.

Timberlake, W., & Allison, J. 1974. Response deprivation: An empirical approach to instrumental performance. *Psychological Review* 81: 146–64.

Tolman, E. C. 1932. *Purposive behavior in animals and men.* New York: Appleton-Century-Crofts.

———. 1938. The determinants of behavior at a choice point. *Psychological Review,* 45: 1–41.

———. 1942. *Drives toward war.* New York: Appleton-Century-Crofts.

———. 1959. Principles of purposive behavior. In *Psychology: A study of a science,* ed. S. Koch, vol. 2. New York: McGraw-Hill.

Tolman, E. C., Ritchie, B. F., & Kalish, D. 1946. Studies in spatial learning: I. Orientation and the short-cut. *Journal of Experimental Psychology* 36: 13–24.

Underwood, B. J. 1948. Retroactive and proactive inhibition after five and forty-eight hours. *Journal of Experimental Psychology* 38: 29–38.

———. 1957. Interference and forgetting. *Psychological Review* 64: 49–60.

Verplanck, W. S. 1955. The control of the content of conversation: Reinforcement of statements of opinion. *Journal of Abnormal and Social Psychology* 51: 668–76.

Wagner, A. R. 1963. Conditioned frustration as a learned drive. *Journal of Experimental Psychology* 66: 142–48.

Wagner, A. R., & Rescorla, R. A. 1972. Inhibition in Pavlovian conditioning: Application of a theory. In *Inhibition and learning,* eds. R. A. Boakes & M. S. Halliday. London: Academic Press.

Walter, W. G. 1953. *The living brain.* New York: Norton.

Watson, J. B. 1913. Psychology as the behaviorist views it. *Psychological Review* 20: 158–77.

———. 1930. *Behaviorism.* Rev. ed. Chicago: Univ. of Chicago Press. (6th printing, 1966.)

Welker, W. I. 1961. An analysis of exploratory and play behavior in animals. In *Functions of varied experience,* eds. D. W. Fiske and S. R. Maddi. Homewood, Ill.: Dorsey.

Wertheimer, M. 1945. *Productive thinking.* New York: Harper & Row.

Wiener, N. 1948. *Cybernetics.* New York: Wiley.

Wilcoxon, H. C., Dragoin, W. B., & Kral, P. A. 1971. Illness-induced aversions in rat and quail: Relative salience of visual and gustatory cues. *Science* 171: 826–28.

Williams, D. R., & Williams, H. 1969. Auto-maintenance in the pigeon: Sustained pecking despite contingent non-reinforcement. *Journal of the Experimental Analysis of Behavior* 12: 511–20.

Wulf, F. 1922. Uber die Veranderung von Vorstellungen (Gedachtnis und Gestalt). *Psychologische Forschung* 1: 333–73. [Translated and condensed by W. D. Ellis as "Tendencies in figural variation" in *A source book of gestalt psychology.* London: Kegan Paul, 1938.]

Wyckoff, L. B. 1952. The role of observing responses in discrimination learning. *Psychological Review,* 59: 431–42.

Yates, A. J. 1980. *Biofeedback and the modification of behavior.* New York: Plenum.

Suggestions for Further Readings

A. GENERAL READINGS

Readers wanting to study more thoroughly the topics covered in this book will find the following references helpful.

Bower, G. H., & Hilgard, E. R. 1981. *Theories of learning.* 5th ed. Englewood Cliffs: Prentice-Hall. The standard secondary reference on contemporary theories of learning, providing both authoritative descriptions and critical evaluations. The chapters vary in ease of reading; some are rather technical.

Koch, S., ed. 1959. *Psychology: A study of a science.* vol. 2. New York: McGraw-Hill. A collection of 12 readings on various modern learning theories, most of them written by the theorists themselves. The study, of which this volume forms a part, emphasizes certain topics in the philosophy of science, with the result that the distinctive styles of some of the authors are partly lost. However, this is the most complete source book available.

Hill, W. F. 1981. *Principles of learning: A handbook of applications.* Sherman Oaks, Calif.: Alfred. [Now distrib. by Mayfield, Palo Alto, Calif.] A fairly short, nontechnical treatment of learning and motivation, organized by topics, with heavy emphasis on both actual and speculative applications.

Mackintosh, N. J. 1974. *The psychology of animal learning.* New York: Academic Press. A large, moderately difficult book covering current data and theory on a number of topics relevant to learning theory. The arrangement is by types and aspects of learning rather than by theorists. The majority of readers are unlikely to read it from cover to cover, but it is an excellent reference source.

Schwartz, B. 1978. *Psychology of learning and behavior.* New York: Norton. Somewhat similar in coverage to Mackintosh, but shorter and less comprehensive. The research considered is largely in the Skinnerian tradition, with some reference to species-specific behavior.

Ellis, H. C., & Hunt, R. R. 1983. *Fundamentals of human memory and cognition.* 3rd ed. Dubuque: Wm. C. Brown. Among a number of books that deal with human learning and thinking as part of the current interest in cognitive processes, this one has the advantages of being fairly short and of having a balance among topics similar to that in the present book.

B. PARTICULAR THEORISTS

Among the primary sources mentioned in the text, the following are especially recommended for their readability and their concern with the applications of learning theory.

Dollard, J. C. & Miller, N. E. 1950. *Personality and psychotherapy.* New York: McGraw-Hill. An outline of Miller's learning theory, followed by its application to the development of personality and the learning and unlearning of neuroses.

Guthrie, E. R. 1960. *The psychology of learning.* Rev. ed. New York: Harper & Row. The author's interpretation of a number of learning situations and his comments on several other theorists.

Skinner, B. F. 1953. *Science and human behavior.* New York: Macmillan. A popular summary of the chief variables in learning as studied by the author, followed by the interpretation of organized social behavior in terms of reinforced learning.

Wertheimer, M. 1945. *Productive thinking.* New York: Harper & Row. A consideration of education, problem solving, and creativity from the gestalt point of view.

C. A FICTIONAL COMMENTARY

McConnell, J. 1962. Learning theory. In *Great science fiction by scientists,* ed. G. Conklin. New York: Macmillan. A cynical view of learning theory in the form of a science-fiction short story. Though the discerning reader will see evidence that the story anticipates recent interest in species-specific behavior, it can be read simply as a general-purpose spoof on learning theory and research.

Summary Table of Theorists

Most of the theorists discussed in the book are listed here in the order in which they were considered in the text. With each theorist are one or more key terms or summary comments to serve as mnemonic devices.

Ivan P. Pavlov (1849–1936) — Classical conditioning, excitation and inhibition

John B. Watson (1878–1958) — Founder of behaviorism, laws of frequency and recency

Edwin R. Guthrie (1886–1959) — Single principle of learning by contiguity of a stimulus and a movement, maintaining stimuli, movement-produced stimuli, three methods of changing habits

Edward L. Thorndike (1874–1949) — Law of effect, satisfiers and annoyers, cats in a puzzle box

Neal E. Miller (b. 1909) — Drive, cue, response, reward, imitation, personality, and psychotherapy

Clark L. Hull (1884–1952) — Postulates and theorems, $_sE_R = {_sH_R} X D X K - I_R - {_sI_R}$, oscillations, r_G

B. F. Skinner (b. 1904) — Rejection of intervening variables, emphasis on reinforcement, respondent and operant behavior, shaping, behavior modification and other applications

Max Wertheimer (1880–1943) — Founder of gestalt psychology, emphasis on insight, laws of proximity and closure

Kurt Lewin (1890–1947)	Topological psychology, life space, valences, vectors
Jean Piaget (1896–1980)	Development of schemata, accommodation and assimilation, four stages of development, conservation
Edward C. Tolman (1886–1959)	Purposive behaviorism, originator of intervening variables, sign-gestalt expectations, cognitive maps, latent learning
Robert C. Bolles (b. 1928)	S-S* expectancies and R-S* expectancies
Dalbir Bindra (1922–1980)	Central motive state, view that all learning is about stimuli
Robert M. Gagné (b. 1916)	Development of hierarchical organization
Kenneth W. Spence (1907–1967)	Boundary conditions of theories, $D = H(D + K) - I$, $K = r_G$
Abram Amsel (b. 1922)	Frustration, r_R and r_F, explanation of partial reinforcement effect
O. Hobart Mowrer (1907–1982)	Sign and solution learning, learning of hope, fear, relief, and disappointment
Harry F. Harlow (1905–1981)	Learning sets, manipulation drive, contact hunger
Charles E. Osgood (b. 1916)	Semantic differential
Albert Bandura (b. 1925)	Imitation, modeling
William K. Estes (b. 1919)	Stimulus sampling model, all-or-none model, probability matching
Allan R. Wagner (b. 1934) & Robert A. Rescorla (b. 1940)	Mathematical conditioning theory for compound stimuli
David Premack (b. 1925)	Response interpretation of reinforcement, reversibility of reinforcement relationship
Norbert Wiener (1894–1964)	Cybernetics, negative feedback
Richard L. Solomon (b. 1918)	Opponent-process theory of motivation
Benton J. Underwood (b. 1915)	Forgetting through proactive and retroactive inhibition
Richard C. Atkinson (b. 1929) & Richard M. Shiffrin (b. 1942)	Three memory stores
Martin E. P. Seligman (b. 1942)	Biological constraints on learning, species-specific behavior, preparedness

Glossary

A1 and A2 (*Estes*)   The two possible response classes to which a stimulus element may be conditioned.

a **process** (*Solomon*)   The hedonic effect produced immediately by a stimulus and lasting as long as the stimulus lasts.

accommodation (*Piaget*)   A change in a schema to incorporate new experience.

assimilation (*Piaget*)   Interpretation of new experiences in terms of an existing schema.

asymptote   The limit that a curve approaches and can never go beyond.

b **process** (*Solomon*)   The hedonic opponent process that lags behind and serves to counteract an *a* process.

behavior modification (or **behavior mod**) (*Skinner*)   The process of changing behavior in practical situations, such as education or psychotherapy, by appropriately changing the contingencies of reinforcement.

behavioral contrast (*Skinner*)   Higher rate of responding on a given schedule of reinforcement if it alternates with another schedule that provides fewer reinforcers.

behaviorism   Any learning theory that focuses on observable behaviors and the stimuli that control them.

biofeedback   Presentation to an individual of information about one's own bodily processes in a form that helps one learn to control them.

boundary conditions (*Spence*)   Those conditions that must apply in order for a theory to be valid in a given situation.

central motive state (*Bindra*)   A predisposition to act toward various positive or negative incentives or reinforcers with appropriate instrumental, consummatory, and regulatory responses.

cognitive   Explaining behavior and learning in terms of cognitions.

cognitive map (*Tolman*)   A cognition about where various things are located.

compound   Two or more stimuli presented simultaneously.

conditioned inhibition (*Hull*)   Learned tendency not to make a given response, resulting from reactive inhibition.   (*Pavlov*, and *Rescorla & Wagner*)   The inhibitory effect that a stimulus acquires if it is presented always in compound with another stimulus and not reinforced, whereas the other stimulus is reinforced when it is presented alone.

conditioned stimulus   See *conditioning, classical.*

conditioning, classical   A form of learning in which two stimuli are presented together and the response originally elicited by one of them, the unconditioned stimulus, comes to be elicited also by the other, the conditioned stimulus.

conservation (*Piaget*)   A person's understanding that certain characteristics of things, such as their length or number, remain the same when other characteristics are changed.

consummatory response   A response by which one takes in or uses a reward.

contiguity   The occurrence of two or more events together.

contingencies of reinforcement (*Skinner*)   Specific relationships of reinforcers to the responses and stimuli that precede them; determinants of when reinforcement occurs.

contraprepared (*Seligman*)   Especially difficult to learn; applied to a response in relation to particular stimuli or reinforces with which that response is hard to learn.

controlled quantity (*cybernetics*)   A variable maintained at a set point by the operation of negative feedback.

critical delay duration (*Solomon*)   The longest delay between successive presentations of a stimulus that will still permit the *b* process to increase with repetition.

cue   A stimulus that serves to guide behavior.

cybernetics (*Wiener*)   The study of control mechanisms.

D   Abbreviation for *drive.*

demand (*Tolman*)   Motive or desire for a given goal object.

discrimination   Learning to make different responses to similar stimuli.

disinhibition   Removal of inhibition.

drive   An aroused state which motivates action in an organism, and the reduction of which often functions as a reinforcer.

E (*Spence*)   Abbreviation for excitatory potential.

encode   To convert (information) into a specific form, especially for entering into memory.

error factor (*Harlow*)   Systematic wrong way of responding in a problem situation.

excitation (*Pavlov*, and *others*)   Activation of a response tendency, distinguished from inhibition.

excitatory potential (*Hull* and *Spence*)   The strength of the tendency for a given response to occur.

extinction   Weakening of the tendency to make a response when the response is not followed by a reinforcer.

feedback (*cybernetics*)   Process by which the effects of a response control that response.

     negative   The form of feedback that compensates for deviations so as to maintain a steady state.

positive   The form of feedback that enhances deviations so as to produce larger and larger changes.

fixed interval schedule (*Skinner*)   Arrangement in which reinforcement follows the first response after a fixed period of time since the previous reinforcement.

fixed-ratio schedule (*Skinner*)   Arrangement in which reinforcement follows a given number of responses since the previous reinforcement.

fractional anticipatory frustration response (*Amsel*)   Some part of the response of frustration, when it occurs in anticipation of possible nonreward.

fractional anticipatory goal response (*Hull* and *Spence*)   Some part of the response normally made when reaching a goal, when made before reaching the goal in anticipation of reward.

frustration   The drive produced by not receiving an anticipated reward.

generalization   Tendency for a response to a new stimulus to occur that is similar to one that was present during original learning.

gestalt   A form or pattern perceived as a whole.

H (*Spence*)   Abbreviation for habit strength.

habit   Learned tendency for a certain stimulus to elicit a certain response.

habit strength (*Hull* and *Spence*)   The strength of the bond connecting a stimulus with a response.

hedonic   Pertaining to pleasure and displeasure.

homeostasis   The process by which various physiological processes are regulated automatically at set points.

hypothesizing   Assuming for theoretical purposes that something is true although it has not been shown to be definitely true.

I (*Spence*)   Inhibition resulting from competing responses.

imprinting   The formation of attachments early in life, especially attachments of young birds to their parents.

incentive motivation (*Hull* and *Spence*)   The strength of the tendency to approach a given goal object.

induction (*Pavlov*)   Greater response to a positive stimulus just after presentation of a negative stimulus (positive induction), or less response to a negative stimulus just after presentation of a positive one (negative induction).

inhibition   Suppression of a response by any active process within the organism (cf., various kinds of inhibition).

insight   A sudden understanding of the solution to a problem.

I$_R$ (*Hull*)   Abbreviation for reactive inhibition.

K (*Hull* and *Spence*)   Abbreviation for incentive motivation.

key   A disk that when pressed closes an electrical circuit to activate a recording and/or reinforcing device, especially one designed to be pecked by pigeons.

law, scientific   A statement about the conditions under which certain events occur.

learning curve   A graph showing how much has been learned at each stage of practice.

learning set (*Harlow*)   Systematic improvement in solving a series of different discrimination problems that have a principle in common.

life space (*Lewin*)   The world as it affects a person's behavior, distinguished from the objective world.

long-term store (or memory) (*Atkinson & Shiffrin*, and *others*)   The place or process in which material is stored permanently in memory.

maintaining stimuli (*Guthrie*)   Strong stimuli that keep an organism active; their removal contributes to learning.

mand (*Skinner*)   An utterance that instructs someone to do something.

mediating responses   Responses whose main function is the stimulation they produce, so that they serve as intermediate steps in a sequence running from an initial stimulus to a final response.

mnemonic device   Any technique helpful in memorizing specific items.

modeling (*Bandura*)   Trying to make oneself more like someone else (the model), either in specific behavior (equaling imitation) or in more general characteristics.

movement-produced stimuli (*Guthrie*)   Stimuli produced by one's own responses, which serve to direct further behavior.

observing response   A response whose main function is to provide information.

operant (*Skinner*)   A unit of behavior emitted by the organism without being elicited by a specific stimulus, contrasted with respondent.

orienting reflex   An aroused reaction to a novel stimulus.

oscillation (*Hull*)   Momentary random fluctuations in excitatory potential.

partial reinforcement effect   Greater resistance to extinction of a response that has been reinforced only some of the time than of a response that has been reinforced all the time.

postulates (*Hull*)   The basic statements in a theory assumed to be true without proof and then used to deduce theorems.

prepared (*Seligman*)   Especially easy to learn; applied to a response in relation to particular stimuli or reinforcers that go well with it for rapid learning.

proactive interference (*Underwood*)   Forgetting resulting from interference by something else previously learned.

program   A series of instructions, as for a computer or for a student using a teaching machine.

psychotics   People who are mentally ill.

reactive inhibition (*Hull*)   Tendency not to repeat a response immediately after it has been made.

reinforcement   The strengthening of the tendency to make a response that occurs when the response is followed by a reinforcer.

reinforcer   One of a class of events that, when they follow a response, increase the tendency for that response to occur.

    conditioned   One that is effective because of previous pairing with a primary reinforcer.

    negative   One whose removal strengthens the tendency for the response to occur.

    positive (Understood when neither positive nor negative is specified.)   One whose presentation strengthens the tendency for the response to occur.

    primary   One which is effective without prior learning.

respondent (*Skinner*)   A response elicited by a specific stimulus, distinguished from operant.

response   Any item of behavior (usually analyzed in relation to a stimulus).

consummatory One that takes in or uses a reward.

instrumental One that leads toward a goal.

retroactive interference (*Underwood*) Forgetting resulting from interference by something else learned more recently.

r_F (*Amsel*) Abbreviation for fractional anticipatory frustration response.

r_G (*Hull* and *Spence*) Abbreviation for fractional anticipatory goal response.

r_R (*Amsel*) Abbreviation for fractional anticipatory reward response, equivalent to fractional anticipatory goal response.

R-S* expectancy (*Bolles*) Cognition that a certain response will lead to a certain biologically important stimulus.

S (*Estes*) The set of all stimulus elements available for sampling on a given occasion.

S′ (Estes) The set of all stimulus elements not available for sampling on a given occasion but potentially available on another occasion.

scalloping (*Skinner*) A pattern of responding in which the rate is lowest immediately after reinforcement and then gradually increases.

schedule of reinforcement (*Skinner*) Relationship of responses emitted to reinforcers received; the systematic pattern according to which reinforcers are delivered.

schema (*Piaget*, and *others*) A fairly generalized cognition; an element of cognitive structure.

semantic differential (*Osgood*) A technique for expressing the meaning of words in terms of how those words are rated on a series of scales.

sensory register (*Atkinson & Shiffrin*) The very brief recording of information as received by the senses before it either enters the short-term store or is lost.

$_sE_R$ (*Hull*) Abbreviation for excitatory potential.

set point (*cybernetics*) The particular level at which a controlled quantity is maintained by negative feedback.

S_G (*Hull* and *Spence*) Stimuli produced by fractional anticipatory goal responses.

shaping (*Skinner*) Teaching a novel response by reinforcing closer and closer approximations to that behavior.

short-term store (or **memory**) (*Atkinson & Shiffrin*, and *others*) The place or process in which information is stored temporarily in memory after being transferred there either from the sensory register (new information) or from the long-term store (old information).

$_sH_R$ (*Hull*) Abbreviation for habit strength.

sign-gestalt-expectation (*Tolman*) A cognition about how the world is organized and what things lead to others.

sign learning (*Mowrer*) Classical conditioning of stimuli to emotional responses, so that those stimuli become signals for coming events.

$_sI_R$ (*Hull*) Abbreviation for conditioned inhibition.

solution learning (*Mowrer*) Learning of responses that reduce drives.

species-specific behavior Behavior particularly characteristic of a given species of animal that will tend to appear in that species under a wide variety of conditions and without any special training.

spontaneous recovery The tendency for a response that has been extinguished to recover in strength with the passage of time without further training.

S-S* expectancy (*Bolles*) A cognition that a certain stimulus will be followed by another, biologically important, stimulus.

stimulus Any input of energy to the organism that tends to affect behavior.

subject A person or animal studied in an experiment.

tact (*Skinner*)   An utterance that conveys information; distinguished from mand.

theorem   A statement deduced logically from a set of postulates.

theory   A systematic way of describing and analyzing regularities in the way events occur, organizing scientific laws in a broader framework.

θ (theta) (*Estes*)   The proportion of elements in S (see above) sampled on a given trial.

threshold   The weakest stimulus that will elicit a response.

token economy (*Skinner*)   A form of behavior modification in which the desired behavior is reinforced with some form of symbolic reward (functioning as a conditioned reinforcer) which can be traded for primary reinforcers.

topology (*Lewin*)   The form of geometry that deals only with boundaries, not with distances or specific directions.

trigram   A sequence of three letters, usually not spelling a word, used as a stimulus or response in studies of verbal learning.

V (*Rescorla & Wagner*)   The strength of the tendency to respond to a given conditioned stimulus, which is usually identified by a subscript.

$\overline{V}$ The combined value of V for all the stimuli in a compound.

valence (*Lewin*)   The positive or negative value of a given place or situation for a given person.

variable   A characteristic that can vary from one situation to another.

  dependent   One that changes in response to changes in other (independent) variables.

  independent   One whose changes produce or predict changes in other (dependent) variables.

  intervening   Concepts hypothesized by a theorist to explain the connection between independent and dependent variables.

variable-interval schedule (*Skinner*)   Arrangement in which reinforcement follows the first response after a predetermined time since the previous reinforcement, a time which varies randomly with a specified average.

variable-ratio schedule (*Skinner*)   Arrangement in which reinforcement follows a predetermined number of responses since the previous reinforcement, a number which varies randomly with a specified average.

vector (*Lewin*)   A line representing the strength of the tendency to move in a given direction in the life space.

  identification performance (*Tolman*)   Vector referring to a tendency to observe something.

  pragmatic performance (*Tolman*)   Vector referring to a tendency to go somewhere or otherwise act on the environment.

working memory   A synonym for short-term memory (or store).

Index